myrtleville

A Canadian Farm and Family,
1837–1967

BETH GOOD LATZER

Library of Congress Cataloging in Publication Data

Latzer, Beth Good
  Myrtleville : a Canadian farm and family, 1837–
1967.

  Includes index.
  1. Good family.   I. Title.
CS90.G66   1976   929'.2'0971   75-33742
ISBN 0-8093-0747-2

First published 1976 by Southern Illinois
  University Press, Carbondale
Canadian edition published by the author, 1980
Printed in Canada
Designed by Gary Gore

To

my children, descendants of Myrtleville, and their father,

a devoted Myrtlevillean by marriage

Contents

List of Illustrations

Preface

When I was a very small girl, at the time of the First World War, I lived in a new house on a farm called Myrtleville, near Brantford, Ontario. Across the lawn was a big old house built by my great-grandfather. I had been born in its north wing, but I did not remember living there. I knew, however, that the people living in the south part of the house, the front, had been there for a long time. They were "Aunt Annie" and my grandmother, whom we called "Gramoozie." Usually one or more of my father's sisters lived there, too, depending on who was not yet married, and who taught school nearby.

Aunt Annie was my father's aunt, and she was much older than his mother. She walked with a crutch, because she had broken a hip, and in those days doctors did not repair hips as successfully as they do now. She spent a great deal of time sitting in a big chair by a window, but she was not idle. She knitted useful and pretty things; she braided strips of woolen rags and sewed them into small rugs to lay on the cold floors beside our beds. She had been fond of drawing and painting when she was young, but I do not think she went back to that hobby in her old age. Perhaps she would have felt that it was wasting time.

Aunt Annie had never married. Although she had no children of her own, most of her nieces and nephews felt that they really belonged to her. Those who lived in southern Ontario and Buffalo, New York, came to see her quite often. We children on the farm knew them. Occasionally a stranger would appear. "That's Cousin Allen Laird from Chicago," we might be told. "He came to see Aunt Annie." Or, "That's Cousin Winefred Good from New York. She came to see Aunt Annie."

My brothers and I belonged to Aunt Annie in a special way. We were the fourth generation of Goods to live with her at Myrtleville. We knew that she really enjoyed having us with her, and sometimes my oldest brother and I listened, fascinated, while she told us stories of her childhood. She had come from Ireland when she was a little girl. She remembered a long voyage on a sailing ship, a long wintry trip by sleigh. She remembered seeing a bear with two cubs lumbering across a wheat field. There was something about Aunt Annie's speech that made her different from other people I knew. I was too young to analyze the difference, but I decided later that she had always kept something of Ireland in her tongue.

It seemed to us children that Aunt Annie left us quite suddenly. I was taken to see her lying motionless and silent in her coffin. There were spring flowers in the room, though it was early April and still wintry outdoors. I was not taken to the funeral, but I remember looking out a window, surprised at the number of horses and buggies, and even cars, up and down the lanes and under the bare trees around the yard. Where had all the people come from?

As I grew older I learned more about the history of Myrtleville, and about Aunt Annie's importance to her family and neighborhood. She was the oldest of my great-grandfather's children, the one who lived at Myrtleville the longest, more than eighty years, and, as my father said, "Aunt Annie took care of everybody." She and my grandparents also took care of many family papers and letters. My father's generation continued to keep them, in boxes in storerooms and attics. Those boxes held the history of a family and the world it knew. There were letters from relatives in Ireland, telling of famine and pestilence and political unrest. There were letters from a son who went to British Columbia during the Gold Rush of 1862, a long trip via New York, Panama, and San Francisco, and from a daughter who was a pioneer in Manitoba in the 1880s, and much later descriptions of life in the trenches of the First World War. Many letters reflected changes in farming over three generations, from the clearing of land in the

1830s to the "scientific" farming of the early twentieth century. All told of a society in which far more people lived on farms and in villages than in cities. I can remember their rural way of life in part; it was gone before the memory of my children.

Almost every summer I have spent a good deal of time at Myrtleville. During the last few years, with my children grown, I have organized and read old family documents, and browsed in history books and in the files of local newspapers. This book is the result.

                                              Beth Good Latzer
St. Louis, Missouri
April 1975

myrtleville

Genealogical Table

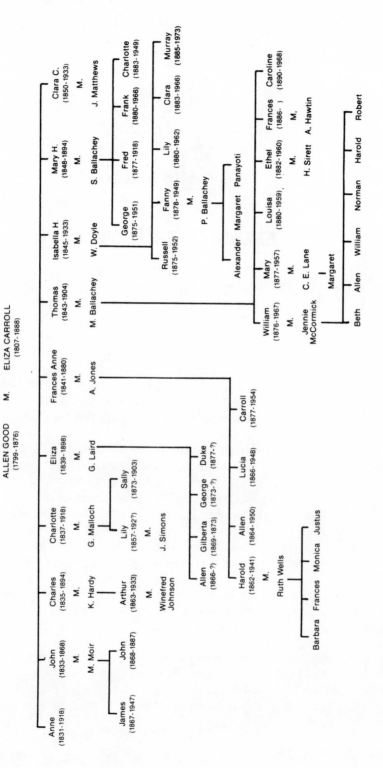

ALLEN GOOD   M.   ELIZA CARROLL
(1799-1876)   (1807-1888)

NOTE: Most fourth generation descendants are omitted here because they do not appear in this book, at least by name.

1

From Cork to Canada

Myrtleville Farm nowadays is on the northwestern edge of the city of Brantford. Its cluster of barns and its two houses, surrounded by tall old trees, can be seen from a recently paved street named Balmoral Drive. Until a few years ago, the people of Myrtleville called this street "the back lane." The remains of the "front lane," which served as chief entrance to the farm for more than a hundred and twenty-five years, can be glimpsed from a new highway, 403, which joins Highway 2, the historic Montreal to Detroit road, just past the location of Myrtleville's old gate.

Allen Good, a young Irish banker from Montreal, settled at Myrtleville in 1837. It was about three miles from the village of Brantford then, and was mostly virgin forest. Many of the trees were oaks, and one of them, massive-trunked and ancient even in 1837, still survives beside the old front lane. The primitive ancestor of Highway 2 meandered up and down gentle hills for about seven miles between Brantford and the next village, Paris. The road was said to be based on an Indian trail, but the white men who had been settling at Brantford in the previous twenty years had given it the dignified old-world name of Dumfries Street. Outside of town, however, it soon became known as "the Paris road," and this is the name of Highway 2 in that district today.

What kind of man was Allen Good, and how and why did he come to the wilderness in 1837? He was born in Cork, second largest city of Ireland, on November 14, 1799. That very week Napoleon Bonaparte became First Consul of France,

1

and Allen's elders were very worried about the threat of invasion. Three years before this, a French fleet of thirty-five ships, with twelve thousand troops aboard, had slipped past the British blockade and entered Bantry Bay, less than ninety miles west of Cork. As in the time of the Spanish Armada, Britain was saved by a storm; the French ships had to cut their cables and flee before the wind; ten of them were lost and with them four thousand men.

The year before Allen's birth, there were uprisings of the local populace here and there in Ireland, and the French took advantage of the turmoil to make another attempt at invasion. They landed about a thousand men in western Ireland and stirred up a good deal of trouble before they surrendered to forces under the command of the British viceroy. (This viceroy was Lord Cornwallis, who years before had surrendered British forces at Yorktown, Virginia, to rebels under George Washington.) A larger French expedition was soon intercepted by the British navy. Allen Good's relatives were grateful for the British navy, and Lord Cornwallis, and the storm which had scattered the French fleet.

The Goods belonged to a group against which much of the anger of Irish rebels was directed. It was a minority group, called by historians the Anglo-Irish Protestant Ascendancy, and it had dominated the political and economic life of Ireland for generations. Because it had been in Ireland for generations, it was considered Irish by itself and by the English of England, but it remained "English" to the majority of the Irish.

Allen Good's ancestors probably came to Ireland from England early in the seventeenth century. Some of them certainly did, the Aldworth family of Berkshire, one of whom was knighted by James I in 1613. This Sir Richard was provost marshal of Munster, the old province which included the counties of Cork, Limerick, Kerry, Tipperary, Waterford, and Clare, and he founded the town of Newmarket in County Cork. About 130 years later, Elizabeth Aldworth of Newmarket married William Allen of Cork City, who was for some years a partner in Ireland's oldest brewery, the Cork Porter Brewery, later known as Beamish and Crawford's, and now owned by Canadian Breweries Limited.

There had been Allens in Cork for generations; two earlier Allens had been mayors, and a son of William and Elizabeth was mayor in 1800. Their oldest daughter married another Allen, Aylmer, who was high sheriff of County Cork in 1780. The sheriff ("shire-reeve," that is, reeve of the county) in England and Ireland was the executive authority of a county. Most of the seventeenth- and eighteenth-century mayors and sheriffs of Cork bore English names, because, until the Emancipation Act of 1829, no Roman Catholic could hold public office in Ireland. A surprising number of these mayors and sheriffs were Allens or men whose wives or mothers were Allens. After Emancipation, of course, men in Irish offices tended to be of Celtic families.

Charlotte, youngest daughter of William and Elizabeth Allen, married John Good in the early 1780s. We know nothing of the Goods before John, except that they are said to have come to Ireland from Sussex in the seventeenth century. They were not prominent in local government as were the Allens and Aldworths, but seem to have been prosperous farmers and merchants. John probably grew up a few miles south of Cork, at Ballinvorosig, a farm near the village of Carrigaline. Ballinvorosig still has a handsome, eighteenth-century-style house with a squarish center, and a long wing on each side.

As a young man, John Good was a member of the county unit of the True Blue Legion of Cork. It was one of the famous Irish Volunteer companies formed in the few years before and after 1780 when the British troops which guarded Ireland were withdrawn for service in the American Revolutionary War. Most of the Volunteers were Protestant (they called themselves "the armed property of the nation"), but they also considered themselves thoroughly Irish, and they resented their political and economic subjection to England. They became strong enough to put pressure on the British government, which responded by granting Ireland free trade with the Colonies and admitting that the people of Ireland should be bound only by their own laws and their own courts. A relief bill also allowed Catholics to purchase land freely and to have their own schools.

The Irish economy blossomed after 1782, but for less than

twenty years. During the period of prosperity, John Good became a grain and wine merchant in Cork. He probably felt the decline of business after 1800, but the combination of his efforts and his and his wife's inheritances enabled him to support his large family in comfort. Of his twelve children, nine grew to be adults, a healthy score in those days of high infant mortality.

John Good's children were educated well by the standards of the time. There are a few old school books at Myrtleville which were used by Allen and his brothers—history, geography, Latin, and so forth. There is also a leather-bound copy of *Robinson Crusoe* which someone gave Allen when he was fourteen. He learned to admire Shakespeare's plays and later brought a handsome set of Shakespeare's works to Canada with him. Cork had no university until the middle of the nineteenth century, but it seems to have had an active intellectual life. The English author, W. M. Thackeray, wrote in his *Irish Sketch Book* of 1842 that he had found in Cork "an extraordinary degree of literary taste and talent," and a great love of music. He was also impressed with the wit and vivacity of the ladies and gentlemen of Cork.

When Allen Good was about fourteen he left school and was apprenticed for seven years to a merchant firm of Cork, Morgan and Reeves. They prepared, packed, and exported beef, pork, flour, butter, and ship's biscuits. They had their own mill and a cooperage where they made their "well-seasoned, iron-bound casks." For about two years Allen worked in Morgan and Reeves' Counting House (we would say office), copying letters and documents and keeping accounts. Then he became a cashier, dealing in money from various countries, later a salesman to grocers of the produce which came from places to which Morgan and Reeves sent produce—Lisbon, the West Indies, Newfoundland, and other parts of the Americas.

Toward the end of Allen's apprenticeship, he went to the West Indies and had the misfortune to contract yellow fever in Jamaica. He blamed this illness for his early baldness; his hair never came in thickly after he lost it from the fever. He was lucky to recover with nothing worse than loss of hair. Allen seems to have visited Newfoundland also during his apprenticeship and was unfavorably impressed. Years later, he refused a chance to take his family there.

John Good died in 1826, when his son Allen was about twenty-seven. For some years Allen was in business for himself as "Bacon Manufacturer and Provision Merchant, Rutland Street, Cork." By 1836, he was employed by the Agricultural Bank of Ireland in Cork.

In the spring of 1830, when Allen was thirty years old, he married Eliza, daughter of the late Charles Carroll of Cork. Eliza, seven years younger than Allen, had been motherless since she was a child. Her mother had been Allen's first cousin, Anne, daughter of the high sheriff Aylmer Allen. Consequently, Eliza's mother-in-law was also her great-aunt; in fact, she spoke of her as "Aunt Good." Complicated relationships were not unusual among the Goods' relatives and friends; there was a great deal of intermarriage within Cork's Protestant and English-descended group. Eliza's father's name, Carroll, is strange in this setting; the Carrolls, or O'Carrolls, are a very ancient Celtic tribe, who are described as having been "for ages a thorn in the side of the Englishry, for their territories lay on the verge of the Pale" (that is, the only part of Ireland under English law until the time of Elizabeth I). Charles Carroll, however, was a devout member of the "English" church.

Mr. Carroll was an apothecary, combining the functions of doctor and druggist. His wooden apothecary's case is still at Myrtleville; it contains a few instruments and a number of labeled bottles for drugs. His senior partner, to whom he had once been apprenticed, was a Mr. Thomas Daunt, who had a country house called Myrtleville, close to a bay on the Atlantic about fourteen miles southeast of Cork. No doubt it got its name, like Sir Walter Ralegh's old house, "Myrtle Grove," farther east, from the glossy green myrtle shrubs which grow so well in that part of the world.

The Daunts were an old Anglo-Irish family, and Mr. Thomas Daunt was an executor of the will of Anne Allen's father, who was a close friend. It was probably through Mr. Daunt that Charles Carroll met the girl who became his wife. At any rate, the Daunts' Myrtleville was a second home to Mrs. Carroll, who had lost both her parents early, and she visited

Myrtleville House, County Cork, Ireland. (Porch no doubt a Victorian addition)

there with Eliza when she was ill, probably with her last illness. There is a short, undated letter from her to her husband.

> My Heart's Darling
>   I write though I have nothing particular to say, as we are all here Ditto. I think if there is any change in Mr. Daunt it is for the better, as his spirits and appetite seem tolerably good. For my own part, I cannot boast, as I do not feel myself one bit better, if as well, as the day I came here, therefore, am very anxious to be at home. But, as I said I would stay another week, I intend to do so. Eliza . . . is as good as possible; she is writing to you herself. Give my darling Fan [her younger daughter] a thousand kisses for me. Best love to all friends,
>   Believe me, your own, own
>
>   A. Carroll

After Anne Carroll died, her daughters attended boarding school, first in Cork and then in Dublin, but they often spent holidays at Myrtleville House and loved it dearly. When Eliza and Allen Good built their house in Canada, they named it Myrtleville and used the Georgian style of the old place in Ireland, though it was somewhat out of fashion even in the backwoods of Upper Canada, as Ontario was then called.

Some of Eliza's early school reports survive. When she was ten years old, she was studying history of the Bible, E. Mann's Catechism, English grammar, geography, ancient history, French, arithmetic and music. She was a good student; the headmistress usually reported that Miss Carroll had done "very well" or "remarkably" in her courses; once, however, the lady felt bound to call attention to "a little degree of violence in temper, but only very seldom, and a thorough conviction of its being wrong. . . . She shews every desire to conquer what is so unamiable." Eliza must have learned to control herself; she is described in family tradition as "a strong-minded woman," while her husband is spoken of as a jovial old gentleman who occasionally lost his temper in quite spectacular fashion.

When Eliza was about sixteen, she left school and returned to Cork to keep house for her father. She seems to have learned some of his skills; years later she was famous around the Canadian Myrtleville for the medications she could concoct. Perhaps her father also trained her in simple bookkeeping; certainly she learned to keep detailed household accounts. Her musical education stayed with her; throughout her long and busy adult life she enjoyed playing the piano.

No early portraits of Allen and Eliza survive at Myrtleville, although there are miniatures of Aylmer Allen and Charles Carroll, and a rather primitive pastel sketch of Aylmer's daughter, later Charles's wife, as a very small, blue-eyed strawberry blonde, dressed in white with a wide blue sash. A silhouette of Eliza in her youth, and incidental descriptions left by people who knew her, depict her as an attractive slender girl with fair skin, blue eyes, a straight nose, rather full lips, and red gold hair done in a loose knot on top of her head. Allen was a tall, lean, prematurely balding young man with coloring much like his wife's, except that what hair he had was probably a good deal darker than hers. He had well-cut features

Allen Good (1799–1876), probably taken in early 1870s

with a large aquiline nose, and was, of course, clean-shaven, as had been the fashion most of the time for the past century and a half.

The first of the Allen Goods' ten redheaded children was born on July 14, 1831, and given the name of her mother's mother, and her father's sister, Anne. On Allen's and Eliza's third wedding anniversary, May 8, 1833, their first son was born. He seems to have been the first grandson in the male line, and was named John for his paternal grandfather. A

Mrs. Allen Good née Eliza Carroll (1807–88), probably taken in late 1870s

silver cake basket, still in the family, is said to have been given to Eliza by her husband in celebration of that proud event.

Less than two years later Charles Carroll Good arrived, and was named for the other grandfather, the apothecary. By the time he was learning to walk, his father was thinking of leaving the Agricultural Bank of Ireland in Cork, and practicing banking in the Colonies. A native of Cork, James J. Cummins, was a director of a new bank being established in London, the Bank of British North America. He talked to Allen Good about it when he visited Cork in the spring of 1836, and wrote in July, offering the position of manager of a branch to be opened in St. Johns, Newfoundland. Allen declined, writing, "I would prefer being placed in Canada, . . . as presenting a better climate and holding out more cheering prospects for the application of industry to the young members of my family. . . . This Colony is rising fast into importance." (Until 1867 "Canada" referred only to what are now the provinces of Ontario and Quebec.) On October 9, 1836, Mr. Cummins wrote again. "I ought to have advised you sooner that we are about to appoint managers for Canada, one of the first you will be, and I strongly recommend your paying a visit to London without delay."

Allen Good's trip to London precipitated great changes in the life of his family. He was appointed manager of the branch bank to be established in Montreal, at a salary of four hundred pounds per annum, with a house provided. This was roughly equivalent to 1970s ten thousand dollars plus housing, and since there was no income tax, it was a very good salary. The family sold all their furniture, and packed up their clothing and linens, their fine sterling silver pieces made in Cork, their handsome Sheffield plate candelabra, their ivory-handled knives and forks, their leather-bound sets of seventeenth- and eighteenth-century classics, and a number of battered old school books. Books were always important to the Goods. Eliza left no record of what she thought about all this. She was pregnant with her fourth child; it was probably the kind of situation in which she both drew on and developed her "strong-mindedness." She was a woman of very considerable physical and moral stamina.

The Goods set out on November 22, 1836. They were ac-

companied by a young lady, identified only as Miss C., whose
fare they paid in return for her assistance in caring for the
children. They drove to the Cove of Cork, the seaport on
magnificent, sheltered Cork Harbour. From here, they probably made the next part of their journey by steamship to Liverpool where they waited in lodgings for twenty-three days until
wind and weather allowed them to sail.

The crossing took more than five weeks on the packet *Hibernia*, 551 tons, bound for New York. It was a very small ocean-
going ship by our standards (twentieth-century liners are as
much as 80,000 tons) and it was bounced around unmercifully
by the rough Atlantic. Eliza was desperately seasick, and
Miss C. even more sick, if possible. Fortunately, Allen was not
disabled and he took care of the children. They did not mind
stormy weather; in fact, Anne always remembered the fun she
and her brothers had, sitting on the deck and sliding back and
forth as the ship tossed.

The *Hibernia* reached New York late in January of 1837.
The Goods were astonished at the amount of snow and ice,
for it seldom snows in Cork. New York was growing fast and
was the largest city on the continent with over two hundred
thousand people, more than twice as many as Cork. It already
had a number of handsome public buildings, for instance, the
fine classical-style city hall it still boasts. But it would not have
been a very impressive city in the 1830s to people who knew
Dublin and London.

Allen Good stayed more than two weeks in New York, making various banking arrangements; the Wall Street district was
already the financial center of the continent. His family lived
in a boarding house at 282 Pearl Street, in what we now call
Lower Manhattan, and Eliza spoke warmly of the "kind and
attentive" landlady. Weak and tired as she must have been,
she would have appreciated the comfort of her lodgings more
than the sights of New York.

Finally they all set out for Montreal. The four hundred
miles took twelve days. They went by public conveyance at
first. Eliza noted where they stayed overnight, Somers Town
(in the northern part of Westchester County), Poughkeepsie,
Albany. The stage took them forty to fifty miles each of the
first two days; about seventy-five the third. It was hard on

three little children and a mother almost eight months pregnant. They hired an open sleigh and went on more slowly. Pittstown, Tuesday; Castleton, Vermont, Wednesday; Ferrisburg, Thursday and Friday (Anne remembered being "snowed in" one day); Burlington, Saturday; St. Albans, Sunday; Highgate (Vermont), Monday; St. Johns (on the Richelieu River in Canada), Tuesday; Montreal, Wednesday.

Eliza was not too miserable to notice the beauty of the landscape as they drove up the Hudson Valley and along Lake Champlain, nor to appreciate the quality of their lodgings. She wrote, "The accommodation at the Inns in the small places is quite comfortable, very superior to anything of the kind at home, and a look of plenty and comfort, far beyond anything in Ireland among the middle or lower order." No doubt she saw many of the sturdy and well-designed farm and village houses which still adorn New York State and Vermont.

The Goods crossed the Richelieu River at St. Johns, and there they spent the last night of the trip. On the twelfth day of their journey from New York, they reached the mile-wide St. Lawrence. Across it was their new home, Montreal, by far the biggest city they had seen since Albany, the capital of New York State.

There was no bridge yet across the wide river, but the St. Lawrence at Montreal freezes over for months every winter. The Goods simply drove across the thick, rough ice. Eliza wrote her sister: "I never was really frightened until then, but thank God we got no upsets, nor any worse than good poundings. . . . The travelling is worse than you can form the most distant idea of. . . . Imagine us in a thing on a frame like a large Piano Box, dragged over holes of snow by two Horses, where every minute you fell up and down." Anne always remembered vividly that river-crossing. She said that she and her brothers enjoyed the bumpy ride, but that her father held her mother and said, "Now, Bessy, me heart, we must expect the ups and downs of life." And her mother answered, "Yes, what can't be cured must be endured!"

Allen's and Eliza's first reaction on arriving in Montreal was relief that the river was safely crossed; their second reaction was disappointment that their new house was not ready, and not an article of furniture bought for it. They had to go to a hotel for ten days, then move into the upstairs of the new bank building. At last, after two weeks in Montreal, Eliza wrote a long letter to her sister. She had hoped to be settled before writing, but had been told she would have to move again soon, into the house next door, and decided to wait no longer to send news. She was cheerful again: "The House we are going into is just the same as this, but we will have the rooms downstairs which are the Bank in this House. The two Houses are alike very large and handsome, the one we are to live in all nicely painted . . . for us, and when furnished will be very comfortable. . . . The furniture we have bought is very nice, but Mahogany things so much dearer than at home. . . . We will have a Splendid view of a Mountain from the Back of the House, which will be quite delightful, like the country."

Eliza told her sister that she had not been troubled much by the intense cold, but she did complain about the overheated houses in North America. People from the British Isles still make this complaint. In the twentieth century, we attribute it to efficient central heating, which was certainly not available in the Montreal of 1837.

Eliza was already speaking of "dollars and cents" although British money was official. She wrote that she had hired a cook for "5 dollars or 25 shillings" per month, a "child's maid for 3 or 15 shillings." Allowing for the great change in the value of money, these are still very modest wages, at most $30 and $18 per month. Of course, the servants would also get room and board. Whether or not Eliza was "settled," nineteen days after she wrote Fanny Carroll, her fourth child and second daughter was born. The Goods named her Charlotte, for her grandmother back in Ireland.

Meantime, Allen was busy setting up the bank. The *Montreal Gazette* of March 23, 1837, carried a notice.

BANK OF BRITISH NORTH AMERICA

This Establishment has commenced business at its Office in Great St. James Street. Days of Discount—Wednesday and Saturday. Notes offered for discount to be left with the Manager the previous day.

Allen Good, Manager.

The bank was on the river side of St. James Street, close to the Place d'Armes and only a few doors from the three-story cut-stone building of the Bank of Montreal, Canada's oldest bank. A photograph of the B.B.N.A. building, which stood for seventy-five years, shows part of one side, apparently brick, and the front, which was either stone or plaster simulating stone. It was considerably more pretentious than the eighteen-year-old building which housed the Bank of Montreal and was, as Eliza said, large and handsome for a city the size of Montreal, population about thirty thousand at that time.

Since their new house was unfurnished, Eliza and Allen had to do a good deal of shopping. They found plenty of good furniture available, though mahogany was very expensive, as Eliza noted. They bought twelve chairs and a sofa of that precious wood, upholstered in black horsehair, and most of these are still at Myrtleville. A massive four-poster bed and several "low-post" beds also probably came from Montreal to Myrtleville. According to Eliza's account book, they spent £106 on furniture, perhaps $2500 in our money. They did not get a piano for Eliza in Montreal; Allen asked his brother John in Cork to buy and send an English piano.

Besides furniture, they bought playthings for the children. Allen ordered a dollhouse for Anne. It is at Myrtleville now, a neat, two-story Georgian house painted in a sandy color. A rocking horse bought for John, at the time of his fourth birthday, wore out many years ago.

Eliza made arrangements to put Anne in school. The little girl had learned to read as a five-year-old, back in Ireland, and Eliza wrote her sister after reaching Montreal, "Anne has not forgot her reading though she has been so neglected." In May a payment of two pounds was made for school, and three shillings and six-pence for school books.

Allen Good was interested in the possibilities of Upper Canada (Ontario) to which many immigrants had been going since loyalists started settling there following the American Revolution. Soon after he arrived in Montreal he received a letter from a friend in Peterborough, almost 250 miles west of Montreal, and 30 miles north of Lake Ontario. There was quite a group of Irish settlers at Peterborough. and Allen's friend urged him to buy land there as an investment. But Mr. Good made other plans; the land he did buy in the spring of 1837 was a hundred acres, then eight more, from William Ewing, who had a farm several miles northwest of the village of Brantford. This was a good deal farther away than Peterborough; it was about 400 miles southwest of Montreal, and 25 miles north of Lake Érie. Some of the land purchased from Ewing may have been cleared; most of it was still virgin forest.

There is a family tradition that Allen bought land near Brantford on the advice of an English banker acquaintance, Thomas Coleman, who had settled several years earlier just outside of the village of Paris, a few miles northwest. No documentary evidence of this remains, but the tradition is interesting because Allen Good's grandson who farmed Myrtleville married a girl who grew up at Coleman Place on the Governor's Road, now Ontario Highway 5.

Allen Good met many of the bankers and businessmen of Montreal that spring of 1837. There were at least three banks besides the new one, and by far the most prestigious was the twenty-year-old pioneer, the Bank of Montreal. Its president was the Honorable Peter McGill, Scottish-born, but not of the same family as the James McGill who left much of his fortune to found McGill University. Peter was not only president of Canada's oldest bank; he was also head of Canada's first railway, the tiny St. Lawrence and Champlain line. He was, moreover, a merchant prince and a member of the province's legislative council, appointed by the Crown. It was the council which wielded political power; the elected assembly was mainly advisory (and dissatisfied with its role). At any rate, Peter McGill was a man of immense influence in Canada.

May of 1837 was an anxious month for the businessmen and bankers of Montreal. There was a financial panic in the United States and on May 10 New York banks suspended specie payments. Bankers and merchants in Lower Canada argued that continuing cash payments would drain metals to the United States and cause Canadian banks to fail. About a week after the suspension of payments in New York, Allen Good was invited to a private meeting of bankers and merchants at the Bank of Montreal. In the chair was the Honorable Peter McGill, who urged Mr. Good to join in a notice of suspension to be made public the following day. Allen said

that his bank was not yet chartered, that the specie he had was
only deposited for safekeeping at no interest, and that he
would have to consult his local directors. He said later that this
answer "annoyed" Mr. McGill, who was doubtless taken aback
that the young newcomer did not immediately agree to his
proposal.

The next morning, Mr. Good and his directors resolved to
continue returning specie to their depositors. This decision
was, of course, reported promptly to Peter McGill. Mr. McGill
called on Mr. Good and remonstrated with him. Mr. Good was
adamant, and reported later that, "Mr. McGill became perfectly rude and left . . . stating that he would use all the influence which he had . . . to prevent my remaining as manager
of the Bank and to prevent my succeeding in any business in
which I might be engaged." It must have been a profound em-
barrassment to be in the bad graces of Peter McGill, but Allen
Good carried on his business as best he could.

It took two and a half months to get a prompt answer from
England to a letter from Canada. On July 31 word came from
the directors in London that Mr. Good was dismissed with a
year's salary. Allen was given no explanation other than the
statement that the directors "were very reluctantly forced into
a conviction, that altho' a zealous and upright officer, he did
not possess that calmness of temper, cool discretion and
judgement absolutely needful for the post he occupied."

To the end of his life, Allen Good maintained that he was
really dismissed because he had opposed Peter McGill and the
Bank of Montreal. Probably that and the statement of the
directors are both true; there was, no doubt, quite a clash between a hot-tempered Irishman and a hot-tempered Scotsman. Also minutes of the B.B.N.A. Court of Directors in London show that they had been negotiating with the Bank of
Montreal for some kind of union. Allen Good's antagonizing
of Peter McGill would have disrupted their plans. Ironically,
the B.B.N.A. minutes are now in the Archives of the Bank of
Montreal, which absorbed the Bank of British North America
in 1918—long after Allen Good was in his grave.

In their shock and dismay, Allen and Eliza paid little attention to the public proclamation on August 1, the day after the
fateful letter from London, of Victoria as queen of British

North America. There was a good deal of discussion about the family's next move. There were the 108 acres near Brantford; Eliza loved the country. She urged Allen to get away from the turmoil of the business world and be "independent."

The only document surviving which describes the Goods' trip from Montreal to Brantford is a note by Eliza: "Montreal to Kingston, Thursday to Saturday; Kingston to Hamilton Sunday to Tuesday; Hamilton to Brantford Wednesday, where I hope to remain for a home for the rest of my days." She also recorded travel expenses. It cost the family over nineteen pounds for their transportation, and thirty-three pounds for "furniture carriage." The total would be well over a thousand dollars in our money. Travel was expensive as well as difficult in Upper Canada.

They made the four-hundred-mile journey in seven days, much less time than the twelve days for an equal distance in winter with Eliza "in a delicate condition." Probably they went by stage to Kingston, along the road which later became Highway 2. It saved a good deal of time to use that road, bad as it was, because most of the St. Lawrence canals had not yet been built and the two-hundred-mile trip upstream would have been interrupted by fearsome rapids and long portages.

Less than fifty miles out of Montreal, the Goods left French Canada behind. The French heritage of Upper Canada was slight, indeed. There were a few towns built on the sites of French forts and trading posts, for example Kingston and Toronto where Forts Frontenac and Rouillé had been. There were also a number of French place-names, especially in the neighborhood of old Fort Detroit, on the "narrows" (*étroit*) between Lake St. Clair and Lake Erie.

The Goods traveled on, by Prescott, famous for smuggling to and from the United States across the river, and Brockville, described as the prettiest town in Upper Canada. Between Prescott and Brockville, on the shore close to the village of Maitland, the family passed a pleasant stone house in the Georgian manner. It was "Homewood," about forty years old, one of the first substantial buildings in that district, and it was to play a prominent part in the Good family history because one of Allen's daughters became mistress of it when she married.

Above Brockville came the Thousand Islands, and at the upper end of the St. Lawrence, Lake Ontario and the most important settlement the Goods had seen since leaving Montreal. This was the gray limestone town of Kingston, guarded by Fort Henry, which overlooked it from a high hill to the east of the harbor. Here the family would take a boat for Hamilton at the other end of the lake, a stubby, shallow-draft steamer with large paddle-wheels on each side. They would make stops at some of the ports which were flourishing at that time—Cobourg or Port Hope, and Toronto.

Hamilton, where the Goods disembarked, was much smaller and younger than Toronto. Just outside it, on a hill overlooking the bay, stood the imposing mansion of Allan MacNab, leading citizen of the town. He called his great house Dundurn Castle after a MacNab castle in Scotland. Beautifully restored for Canada's centennial in 1967, it is still one of the most impressive buildings in southern Ontario. The sight of it would have been comforting to Allen and Eliza; civilization was still with them. The Goods' journey from Hamilton to Brantford paralleled the trip made a few weeks earlier by a literary Englishwoman, Anna Jameson, who found the country "rich, and beautiful, fertile beyond description." She wrote: "Before sunset I arrived at Brandtford, [sic] and took a walk about the town and its environs. The situation of this place is most beautiful—on a hill above . . . the Grand River. And as I stood and traced this noble stream, winding through richly-wooded flats, with green meadows and cultivated fields, I was involuntarily reminded of the Thames near Richmond; the scenery has the same character of tranquil and luxuriant beauty."

Brantford, a village with a population of about a thousand, was in Gore District, which embraced the future counties of Wentworth and Halton and most of what was to become Brant County. Local government was simple—and unrepresentative—Courts of Quarter Sessions presided over by appointed justices of the peace.

The country around Brantford in 1837 was far from settled, though there were many fields and pastures and a few good houses. The village, however, was a place where one could live in civilized comfort, though not in elegance. There were several streets of modest frame houses, and one large house, also frame, belonging to John A. Wilkes, whose family owned a general store, a grist mill, and a distillery. It was the only building in its block, set well back from the main street, and furnished with a semicircular driveway. One of Mr. Wilkes's political opponents called it a "Baronial Hall." There were also in the village a flour mill, sawmill, tanner, shoemaker, saddler, blacksmith, tailor, chairmaker, wagon-maker, painter, carpenters, and several general stores.

For the care of body and soul there were a barber, at least one doctor (Digby), and a resident clergyman, the Reverend James C. Usher of Grace Episcopal Church. His parishioners worshiped in a five-year-old white frame church on Albion Street. It had a tower surmounted with two balls of wood connected by an iron bar, and midway between these a sheet-iron figure of an angel with a trumpet. Other denominations were meeting in various buildings and without regular clergy.

Brantford had a small weekly newspaper, the *Sentinel* (soon to become the *Courier*) and a school housed in a Market Square building which also served as civic hall, courtroom, and place for entertainments. There was plenty of conviviality in town; Brantford shared in Upper Canada's reputation for heavy drinking. There were a number of taverns and inns, a brewery, and a second distillery besides the Wilkes's. Common Canadian whiskey sold for half a York shilling, that is, twelve and one-half cents a gallon, perhaps seventy-five cents in our money.

The Goods lived for some months in a rented house close to the junction of Colborne, Brantford's main street, and Dumfries Street, which headed toward Paris, running roughly parallel to the river. Their quarters were near the present location of the Armory at the end of Lorne Bridge. Letters from Ireland followed the family from Montreal to Brantford. These were on large sheets of paper folded with a blank space outside for the address. They were sealed with a dab of wax and bore no postage stamps, merely the notation, "paid at Cork," and a postmark. Above the address was written "via Liverpool and New York," presumably the fastest route.

On June 29, 1837, Allen's mother, Charlotte, and his brother, John Daunt Good, joined in writing him. Charlotte was happy to hear that her son's family were so comfortably settled in Montreal. Her oldest daughter, Eliza, had been feeling bad for some time after "influenze," but was finally "so much better that she hopes to pay you a visit." Her daughter Mary, Mrs. John Ottley, had come to town to see the ceremonial proclamation of Queen Victoria. "It was a grand sight." Unlike the "spidery," flowing script of her daughters and daughters-in-law, Charlotte's writing curves in an older fashion, resembling that of Abigail Adams, wife of the second president of the United States, who was, like Charlotte, a product of the mid-eighteenth century.

John wrote that he had sent 500 pounds to London to be placed to Allen's credit in the Bank of British North America. (John was in charge of Allen's business affairs in Cork. This money seems to have been proceeds of sale of Allen's property there.) He had not yet bought the piano Allen had asked for, but would soon send one on a vessel for Quebec. Letters came for little Anne. Her Aunt Fanny Carroll wrote in loving and exceedingly pious terms on July 17.

"You have still a fond Aunt Fanny who dearly loves you, and prays to God night and day to make you his own dear child. I hope you do not forget me, nor forget the psalms and verses I often taught you. Do you pray for yourself and for me. I hope I may be with you, and see you again, for I am very lonesome without you. How I should like to see your dear little sister, Charlotte! You will, I hope, love her very much, and be able to do a great deal to assist kind Mamma in taking care of her. How very kind and good God was to carry you all safe such a long and dangerous journey, and part of it over the ice that you never saw before. Papa told me of the nice baby house he got for you, and I must send you some furniture to put in it. [A hundred years later there were still pieces of furniture in Anne's dollhouse, among them dainty parlor chairs and a settee upholstered in red.] Do you love your brothers very dearly and never fight with them. Always remember, 'thou, God, seest me'—learn off these words and when you are going to do anything wrong remember that God is looking at you and would be angry; and this will, I hope, keep you from sin. I suppose you read very nicely now, and will soon be able to write to me. As soon as you can, do."

Anne had a letter from her Aunt Eliza, too. Perhaps she was not as well as her mother had thought several weeks earlier, because she did not mention a voyage to Canada.

Cork, July 21, 1837

My own darling Annie,
I am very happy to hear such good accounts from you all, that you are so well and comfortable in your nice new house. I don't forget (when you were going to the western land) that you said you would watch for me at the window, open the door wide for me, and pick the nicest flowers in the garden and give them to me, and you may be very sure if you come here again I shall open my arms and door very wide to receive you. I am now writing on a desk [there is a little writing-case at Myrtleville with "Anne" in mother-of-pearl on its lid] which I hope you get safe, and accept it from me as a trifling token of the affection I have for you, and that I shall before many years have the pleasure of receiving a letter from you written on it. I often think of you, my darling Child, and of John and Charles. Give my love to little Charlotte but I don't think she will have sense to understand you. Uncle John is sending out the Piano, I think it is a very good one, and hope Mamma and you will have much pleasure in playing on it. When you write let me know if you sing as much as when you were here, and whether the sheep in Canada "carry their tails behind them." Grandmamma sends you and all her affectionate love and blessing, and all your uncles and Aunt Anne, with Charlotte and Tom Evans [Anne's cousins, children of Mary Ottley] unite with me in love to your Father, Mamma, yourself, Johnny, Charles and baby. May God almighty bless you all is the constant prayer of your
affectionate Aunt

Elizabeth Good

The piano, said to be the first piano in the neighborhood, finally arrived. It was made by Collard and Collard of London, and still stands in the drawing room at Myrtleville. For generations, there were well-worn blankets at Myrtleville described as the instrument's travel wrappings. This story is borne out by an entry in Eliza's account book, "Piano and Blankets, £46," well over a thousand dollars in our money. At that time "old country" blankets were considered much superior to North American ones.

While the Goods were living in Brantford, the Rebellion of 1837 broke out. For years there had been rumblings of discontent, especially among farmers and small shopkeepers who felt that most of their hard-earned tax money was being spent on building expensive canals to encourage commerce which enriched urban merchants rather than the general populace. They knew that their elected assemblymen had little control over government; real power lay in the hands of a governor sent from England and his appointed councillors, men like Peter McGill. Allen Good, new to Canada and a member of the merchant class, had little sympathy with the rebels. He joined the loyalist volunteers. There is a family tradition that he took his turn patrolling the bridge with a gun. It was probably the same structure that Anne described nine years later as "a long wooden bridge with a roof to it." Allen's wife and children were in a house a stone's throw from it.

Before the rebellion broke out, a contract had been drawn up for the building of the Goods' farmhouse "in Dumfries Street," that is, in the midst of the woods along the Paris Road. Allen's land had many oaks, elms, and maples on it, a good sign, for experienced settlers noticed that the presence of hardwoods indicated fertile soil. Anne remembered that her mother chose the exact location of the house by pointing to a large oak tree as its center. Another big old oak stood east of the house until about 1910, and a cross-section of it is still at Myrtleville.

The contract and the specifications for a two-story, nine-room house survive. The builder agreed to finish it "in a plain good workmanlike manner and find all materials to the turn of the key, for the sum of four hundred and sixty-seven pounds, five shillings and nine pence halfpenny [sic]." The original exterior was stucco, like Myrtleville in Ireland, but it was clapboarded before the memory of anyone now living.

The cost of the house would be about twelve thousand dollars in 1970 money, but no one nowadays could build such a large handsome house for that amount. The crucial difference is that labor was cheap and the old place was simple to construct, having no plumbing, wiring, or heating ducts.

GROUND FLOOR PLAN

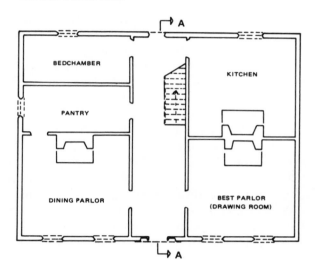

SECOND FLOOR PLAN

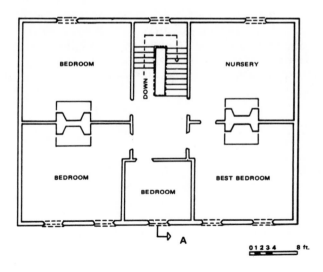

01234   8 ft.

Floor plan of original Myrtleville House, Brantford, Ontario, Canada

Myrtleville faces south, looking down a pleasant slope, and is typically Georgian, with a wide center hall and most of the rooms about sixteen feet square with ten-foot ceilings. There had been three stoves in the house above the bank in Montreal, but Myrtleville was built with fireplaces only (seven of them), as in "the old country." There was plenty of fuel from the forest, but every winter it took weeks to cut down, chop, and bring home a year's supply of firewood.

There was no basement; Eliza said she hated cellars, "nasty, damp places." She did not realize that a cellar in Cork, whose very name comes from a Gaelic word for "marsh," was very different from one on a sandy hill in Canada, and that a cellar might have helped to keep her family warm. They were often very cold in winter; tradition says that the first generation of children at Myrtleville used to change sides of the dining-room table at the end of the main course, so that all could be close to the fire at some time during the meal.

There was some delay in the building of the house because of workmen leaving for military service. A friend wrote Allen in January of 1838: "It afforded me much pleasure to learn that you were progressing satisfactorily in your movements notwithstanding the distracted state of the country, but I should have been better satisfied had the carpenters you wot of first put the finishing strokes to your abode ere they exchanged the weapons of their art for those of a less peaceful calling." The family did not move from Brantford to the farm until almost spring.

2

A Farm and Ten Children

In his first years on the farm, Allen Good directed most of his energy toward clearing the land and farming it. Soon after reaching Brantford he bought another 100 acres of land adjoining the 108 he had bought from William Ewing. It was Crown land, completely uncultivated, and available at small expense. Allen said that he spent the winter of 1837–38 "chopping, and trying to make a home out of a wilderness." In the spring he took on another 100 adjoining acres of Crown land. He did not know much about farming, but he was intelligent and industrious and learned fast. In the library at Myrtleville there is a book on farming, published about this time. It was probably his text. No doubt he also learned much from the Irish laborers he employed.

Allen needed many "hands" to carry on a sizable farm operation, because the machine age, which had already transformed factories, had barely touched the farm. Grain was still sown by hand-scattering, reaped with a fingered scythelike implement called a cradle, and threshed by beating with a flail or trampling with oxen or horses.

Allen was concerned about protecting his buildings and crops. He joined the Gore District Mutual Fire Insurance Company when it was organized, and at its first meeting in May 1839 was elected one of the directors.

Settlers kept pouring into the Brantford area. By the beginning of 1842, the village had a population of fifteen hundred, and white farmers had put so much pressure on the Indians that they had surrendered all lands except those actu-

Myrtleville House, Brantford, showing east side. Main building constructed in 1837, north wing in 1858 (greatly altered in 1905)

ally farmed by them and twenty thousand acres of "Reserve." On February 21, 1842, Allen Good was a member of a committee in charge of a meeting of citizens at Doyle's Inn, corner of Colborne and King streets in Brantford. This meeting prepared an address to the governor-general on the "interest and advancement of the town and township of Brantford." It petitioned against a proposal that the twenty-thousand-acre Reserve should be near Brantford, as was the Mohawk village.

The petition was effective; the Reserve was set up some miles from Brantford, in Tuscarora township and part of Onondaga. Grand River Indians now controlled only about 55,000 acres of the 675,000 granted after the American Revolution. Within two years the Mohawk village was largely abandoned. The Indian School, later known as the Mohawk Institute, was turned into a boarding school because its pupils' parents had moved away. The historic Mohawk Chapel, the first Protestant church built in Upper Canada, henceforth was attended by few of the people for whom it was built. Indians were much more rarely seen in Brantford, though they used to emerge from the Reserve to do day labor at harvesttime.

Eliza Good was very busy with house and children; it was always hard to get domestic help in this new country. She let the children play as far from the house as a big stone in the middle of the front field. She could see them there. The landmark was known in the family as the Bear Stone, because they had once seen a bear that close to the house.

Mrs. Good had to do many things which had been done for her by servants in Cork and Montreal, although she never had to be as self-sufficient as pioneer women in more isolated areas. Her account book shows that she continued to buy candles, sugar, soap, and butter for a time, though she soon took to making butter, part of which she sold. Later Anne made candles for the household.

Eliza tried native products. The first spring she was at Myrtleville, she bought maple sugar and "maple molasses." The Goods liked maple sugar for variety; they did not *have* to use it for sweetening, as many pioneers did. A traveling Briton, John Howison, some years earlier had been forced to use it, and found its flavor "very unpleasant."

In the early years at Myrtleville, all cooking was done in the big kitchen fireplace. The crane on which the pots were hung is still there, and Anne remembered bread being baked in a round iron pot which sat in the fireplace and had coals heaped upon its lid. There is a tradition that at one time an outside bake-oven was built north of the house, but there is no trace of it. Probably there was such an oven, because there were many people to cook for, and an oven could produce much larger batches of bread than an iron pot. A row of buildings grew up behind the house, a workshop, a smokehouse, an icehouse, a woodshed, and a necessity known by the genteel name of "privy." The workshop has been expanded but the other buildings have gone.

Allen and Eliza never knew the loneliness of many pioneers. Allen had men who worked with him; Eliza had at least one house-servant much of the time. They had good neighbors, the Ewings on the south, the Smiths on the north, the Moyles up the road toward Paris. They were only about three miles from Brantford, and they were active members of Grace Epis-

Old Kitchen, Myrtleville House, showing Anne Good's dollhouse made in 1837

copal Church. Its first rector, James Usher, was there for thirty-five years after Allen and Eliza came, and his family and several other families in the parish became close friends.

In the busy days of settling at Myrtleville, Allen and Eliza did not forget Ireland. It is very unlikely that Allen's oldest sister, Elizabeth, ever made her hoped-for visit to Canada; there is no record of it, and the first spring the Goods were at Myrtleville a letter came from Allen's brother, Jonathan, telling of Elizabeth's death at the age of fifty-three. The same letter also referred to the recovery of their youngest brother, John, from a serious illness. There are frequent references to sickness in the old letters, but little evidence of the nature of the illnesses. Often doctors were completely baffled; without diagnostic tests and X-rays, they could only treat symptoms, and hope for recovery.

On May 22, 1838, Allen's brother, Jonathan, married Kate Cripps in Cork. Charlotte wrote her son in Canada about the wedding and the parties given the following week. Jonathan and Kate spent a few days in the country; then their mothers each entertained in their honor. Charlotte also wrote: "Thank God my John is a great deal mended in his health. I got a great fright about him . . . to tell the truth, I am extremely nervous and lonesome since Jonathan left us, altho' he calls in two or three times in the day."

Poor Charlotte did not have much time to recover her spirits after her Eliza's death and Jonathan's leaving home. John died soon, in his thirties. Fortunately, she had her daughter, Anne, and her grown-up granddaughter, Charlotte Evans, still with her. The following summer she had the pleasure of greeting another namesake, Jonathan's baby daughter, and a few months later Allen and Eliza had a third daughter, named Eliza (Elizabeth in full), after her mother and her aunt. A good description of the Canadian Myrtleville and its five little redheads went to Ireland in a long letter Mrs. Allen Good wrote her sister when little Eliza was about ten months old. The family had now been on the farm for three harvest seasons.

"As I now have an opportunity by hand of a Mr. Murphy going home who has promised me to call and see you and tell you how he saw us today, I write to some of my dear old friends. I send you a little drawing of the House & Barn which will give you some idea of it. It was done by our neighbour, Wm. Smith, indeed they are a kind family and so are Mr. Ewing's family next us. We are three close neighbours and all on the best terms which is very pleasant, as bad neighbours on a farm are most disagreeable. After being about six weeks without any one to help me I have now got a family of man, wife, and child just out from the county Tipperary, the child a great pest but must be borne, indeed I am so used to unpleasant things now that it is all much alike. Allen went to Hamilton yesterday . . . I past an uneasy night by having had the pleasure of a visit from three Bears in our field in the afternoon. Our men hunted them into a swamp and there has been a chase after them today. The old father was shot last week & the mother & 2 cubs are about the country. There have been numbers of Black Squirrels this year, & the people say the Bears always follow them. Thank God we and our cattle have as yet been preserved, but we must be on the watch for sheep, pigs, & poultry. This summer we had 4 Rattle Snakes killed inside our fences, but no one was hurt.

"I send you a little bit of each of the children's hair. I wish you could see them. I must now give you a particular account of them all. Anne [age nine] is small, thin, and plain, very like her Uncle John, but a smart, sensible, well-principled child. A lady who was with me in the spring for a few days taught her the notes on the piano and brought her on to play 2 lessons, but I never have had time to go on for I am so overloaded with needlework & housework that I have hardly time to keep them clean & whole. John [age seven] is as tall as Anne, an affectionate but very bold troublesome Boy. He is beginning to read a little and I trust that this winter the 2 Boys will learn something. Charlotte is a pretty child but cross [and] troublesome, Eliza is a very nice Baby, very fair and pretty, very smart and sensible like them all, Charles still the flower of the flock, very like Henry Hardy [a cousin], but as well as the rest, has his faults of temper & passion. My dear Fanny I have a hard task to rear them and attend to them properly, but I pray for them night and morning and talk to them and try to teach them what is right, and must only trust in the Lord to change their hearts for man cannot do that. I have reason to thank the Lord for sparing me my health and giving me strength to do what I am often obliged to do; no servant I ever had at home or here ever went through the work I have to do when I am without one . . .

"Allen has . . . got in about 60 acres of wheat for next year. We have now a large clearance and the place looking very pretty. Mr. Murphy will tell you about it. When the governor-general [Lord Sydenham] was up about the country the place attracted his notice and he enquired in town who Allen was. The next day Allen waited on him with the Gentlemen and Address [a formal speech] of Brantford and told him how he was used by the Bank people."

The last letter from Allen Good's mother in the Myrtleville collection was written on October 22, 1840. Jonathan's little girl was "stout and strong," and he and Kate expected another child about Christmas. Kate was very well, but Charlotte felt weak and nervous and did not go out at all. Her daughter

Anne took good care of her and, she wrote, "All my friends come very often to see me." She was in her late seventies; it was a grief but not a great shock when she died rather suddenly early in 1841.

By the end of that year, the Canadian Myrtleville welcomed another member of the family, Frances Anne Good, born on December 8. Hard work and motherhood agreed with Eliza; when the baby was less than three weeks old, her husband wrote his sister-in-law, Fanny Carroll, "I don't think I ever saw Bessy so well. She is completely restored to her accustomed good health." He also sent advice on how best to get from Ireland to Canada. One should sail for Quebec in late spring "to avoid bad weather on the coast of America." At Quebec one could transfer to steamer for Montreal, a twenty-hour trip. Another four days would bring one to Hamilton. Allen did not recommend the way he had made the journey to Montreal, by sleigh, in winter.

There was no school conveniently close to Myrtleville and the older children were taught at this time by their parents. Anne remembered that her father, whom they called "Dada," used to "set them a copy" in writing. They had to make rows of "pothooks," and then pothooks upside down, and try to get the same slant on them all. As the children grew older, Allen read Shakespeare to them.

In the summer of 1842, Frances Anne Carroll came to Canada. She spent the rest of her life at Myrtleville, and helped a great deal with the care and teaching of the children. She left her mark on the landscaping of Myrtleville, too. Tradition says that she brought willow twigs with her from Cork, carefully keeping them moist en route. She planted a willow tree on each side of the gate on the Paris Road, and a row of locust trees in front of the house. Several knobby old giants are still there, and the family still tends to call them "acacias" after the British custom. The botanical name of the trees is *Robinia pseudoacacia,* and they have been popular in the British Isles for a long time. At an early date a grove of ornamental trees was also planted between the house and the barn. There were a double row of "acacias" and one row of willows in this grove.

Allen had two hundred acres in wheat that summer of 1842, compared with sixty the year before. It was a time when Canada West (as Upper Canada was now called) was primarily a wheat-growing region, and the Corn Laws of Britain gave preferential treatment to colonial wheat. In England, the Anti-Corn Law League was campaigning vigorously for free trade, and Allen Good was uneasy about the future of Canadian farming. He wrote a series of letters published in the *Brantford Courier*. In one, he pointed out that agriculture was the business of most Canadians, but that of eighty-four members of the House of Assembly only eight were farmers. He urged farmers to elect many of their number; then the assembly could speak clearly to the home government on the necessity of Canada's wheat being admitted to Britain in such a way that it would not have to compete with American and European produce.

Allen's sister-in-law, Mrs. Jonathan Good, died early, tradition says of "consumption," that is, tuberculosis of the lungs. When Jonathan wrote Allen in the autumn of 1842, his motherless children were three years old and almost two. He was still working for Beamish and Crawford, the brewery in which his grandfather Allen had been a partner, but he was afraid, because of "the great slackage in Business," that he would be leaving in a few months. Allen had been urging him to come to the Canadian Myrtleville; Mrs. Cripps, however, having lost her daughter to death, was much upset about the prospect of losing her grandchildren to distance, and Jonathan was staying in Cork, at least for the present.

The family in Canada kept growing. On August 28, 1843, Allen's and Eliza's seventh child and third son was born. They named him Thomas, after Allen's brother who had been a lieutenant in the Royal Navy "and died young on the coast of Africa." Twelve-year-old Anne, a capable and responsible girl, was an expert nursemaid by now. When there was a new baby she took almost complete charge of the next-to-youngest child.

After Allen's mother died and Eliza's sister came to Canada, most of the Irish letters to Myrtleville came from Jonathan. There were only four of John and Charlotte Good's nine children left in Ireland now. Anne, who had never married, kept house for the widower, Jonathan. Mary Ottley visited in Cork frequently. Charles, a bachelor, who had been a lieutenant in the Cork Militia, now lived on the old family farm, Ballinvorosig, near Carrigaline, a few miles south of Cork. In November of 1844, Jonathan wrote that Charles was in town being treated for a sore back which had abscesses on it. He had been confined to his room for six weeks. Allen kept writing Jonathan that everyone seemed much healthier in Canada than in Ireland!

Allen himself was full of energy and ambition. In 1845 he bought another hundred acres of land, giving him over four hundred acres of farm land, though rather briefly, because the following year he sold sixty acres across the Paris Road to a retired army officer, Colonel Charles Dixon. In 1845 Allen also ran in the election for district councillor. He was not elected, and Jonathan, commenting on the new acreage, went on to say, "Perhaps it is well that you were not returned District Councillor, as it would take up so much of your time attending the Duties of it, and I suppose without any emolument arising from it, except Honor."

Jonathan was now working at the Cork Savings Bank, his place of employment for the rest of his life. Charles had recovered from his mysterious illness and was out at his farm again, but Anne had been sick for a fortnight with liver trouble: "She is quite as yellow as Saffron, but the Doctor says that in a short time it will wear off her again." Obviously, she had the jaundice form of hepatitis.

In the fall of 1845, Allen sent his oldest son, twelve-year-old John, to Caradoc Academy, at Delaware, a village near London, almost sixty miles from home. Small boarding schools proliferated in Canada at this time. An educated man, with small funds but a capable and accommodating wife, often passed on his store of classical knowledge in his own home. Shortly after the birth of his new sister, Isabella Harriet, John wrote a very formal letter from school.

Nov. 17th, 1845

My dear Anne,

I was delighted to be handed your welcome little note yesterday informing me of the welfare of all my dear friends at home.

I felt very anxious about our dear Mother which has been the only drawback upon my happiness since I left home. Mr. Gilkison was here on Friday and anticipated your news about our infant sister—How pleased I shall be to embrace and kiss the little dear when I return.

I was much obliged to Father for his parental and affectionate advice to me and beg to assure him that I will endeavor to comply with his requests by being very attentive to my studies and the directions of my kind preceptor.

I am overjoyed to think we may have the pleasure of seeing some of you before long—Mr. & Mrs. Livingston desire their respects and request me to say it will afford them much pleasure to have the honour of a call from dear Mother or Aunt. Mr. L. you will perceive has had a hand in the composition of this but I hope to be able before long to pen a letter which will at least possess the merit of originality.

Till then, with best love to all at home
Believe me to remain
Your most affectionate brother,

John Good

That same fall of 1845, Allen's brother Jonathan sent bad news. A strange blight had ruined the potato crop in parts of Ireland. The Irish peasants (about four million people, Jonathan said), depended on the potato for their basic food, and there was a good deal of anxiety. "In some places about Cork," Jonathan wrote, "whole fields have been entirely lost, not even being fit for Pigs to eat."

By the spring of 1846, there was famine in Ireland, followed by typhus. For generations there had been a stream of emigrants fleeing hard times in Ireland; now the stream became a torrent. There is a tradition that at one time Myrtleville sheltered seventeen refugees from Ireland. It is likely that some of these were among the farm laborers listed by the Goods a few years later: Quinlan, O'Donnel, Cloughnessy, Casey, Fitzgerald, Ryan.

It would be hard to exaggerate the miseries endured by most of the Irish emigrants. Many of them did not survive the long voyages, jammed into the crowded "steerage," or the epidemics that swept the sheds they were housed in on arrival. Then many carried epidemics as they moved inland. Wagon after wagon came into Brantford laden with sufferers of cholera and "ship's fever." Temporary hospitals were set up for them, but one can still see long low mounds, the traces of their unmarked graves, in the back of Greenwood cemetery in Brantford.

Many of them survived, however. It is estimated that a few years after the famine, there were more Irish in Canada West than the combined number of English and Scottish. Far more went to the United States than to Canada, and it is a symptom of the connection between politics and religion in Ireland, that the majority of the Irish who came to Canada in the nineteenth century were Protestant. Most Irish Roman Catholics chose to go to the country which had thrown off the yoke of the English, thus giving Boston and New York large Irish Catholic settlements.

Famine in Ireland, combined with poor harvests in England, brought to a head the clamor for repeal of the Corn Laws, and in the summer of 1846 the British government, under Sir Robert Peel, officially adopted Free Trade. The prospect alarmed many farmers and businessmen in Canada, who were used to preferred treatment of their goods in Britain. However, with the tremendous growth of industrial population in both Britain and the eastern United States, Canadian produce still was needed. Repeal of the Corn Laws certainly did not cure the Irish problem, though it may have alleviated it.

The potato blight struck for the second successive year. The Goods were among the fortunate who could afford to buy bread. Jonathan wrote on September 16, 1846: "For the last month, we have not had a potato in the house, it is Bread we use entirely for Dinner. I am afraid that prices will run high if we do not get a supply from your side. I understand that large orders are out for Indian Corn, which the people are beginning to like very well here now. . . . We are, I think, in the beginning of a very disturbed winter. As to ask for Rent, it is quite useless, as the farmers say they will not pay them (& starve)—which is a very bad prospect for the country gentlemen."

Charles Good, Allen's farmer brother, was ill as well as worried about economic conditions. He was trying to sell his farm and go to Cork to live, but the few offers he had were so low that he felt he could not afford to sell. Allen continued to prosper in Canada. In the fall of 1846, he brought John home from boarding school and employed a tutor, Mr. Wright, to live at Myrtleville and teach the five oldest children: Anne, fifteen; John, thirteen; Charles, eleven; Charlotte, nine; Eliza, seven. A number of their weekly reports survive. They list quite a variety of subjects: Scripture, recitation, composition, reading, history, geography, writing, spelling, grammar, arithmetic. They also usually record "black marks," most of which were accumulated by John. Six years earlier his mother had described him as "bold and troublesome"; the passage of time and his experience at boarding school had not reformed him. The children all did well in their studies; Anne and Charles were excellent students; John was weak in spelling. Mr. Wright does not seem to have taught them any ancient or modern language. The boys learned Latin at other schools; perhaps the girls learned a little French, which was considered so important in a lady's education, from their mother and aunt.

Allen Good was anxious about the education of his own children, but he was not greatly concerned about the local struggle to set up the "Common School" prescribed by the 1840 Act of Union. In 1846, his friend, Henry Moyle, wrote him a letter upbraiding him for his lack of cooperation in the school matter. No doubt he lacked the democratic New World concept of universal free education. He had been brought up in a rigid society which expected the lower classes to be almost illiterate. There was, indeed, widespread illiteracy in Canada in the 1840s, but the laborer from the old country, who now farmed his own land, was determined that his children should learn to read and write.

It was at this time that Allen Good became deeply involved in the business world again. In April 1847, he became secretary of the Gore District Mutual Fire Insurance Company. For more than fifteen years he spent much time at an office in Brantford, or traveling on company business, by whatever conveyance was most convenient, often a riding horse.

Among the Myrtleville documents is a diary that Anne started at the beginning of 1847. The early part of it is filled with reports of comings and goings, comments on the weather, and on the troubles and pleasures of a houseful of children. On January 16, little Tommy broke a pane of glass in the parlor window. On January 18, Eliza fell and sprained her wrist. On January 22, Anne wrote "We are so much engaged in our studies we have scarcely any time for other reading. The house has been in a great hub-bub today, the effects of various bad tempers. The pump was frozen all morning." On January 25, "This morning the ground is all a sheet of ice, it having rained and frozen in the night. The boys are able to skate about the house outside." February 16, "This is Shrove Tuesday . . . I made a number of pancakes in the evening." March 30, "Fanny has the measles." April 5, "We have all of us had the measles." April 18, "We are all together in the parlor, it being the first day that the boys have got up since the measles." June 24, "We are preparing for our long talked of journey to the Blue Lake." June 25, "Aunt Fanny stayed home with the three young children. Mamma went." The journey to Blue Lake provided Anne with a composition.

THE 25TH OF JUNE
We left home in company with Mr. Ewing [neighbor on farm to south] and family about 9½ o'clock in the morning. . . . We went the side line by Mr. Baker's. The road here was very rough. We went out of our way about two miles by mistaking our road, so that we did not reach the Lake till about 12 o'clock. As soon as we arrived there, after feeding and taking off the horses; we sat down under the shade of some trees and took our dinner. The Ewings provided part, and we the other part. After dinner we all went down to the Lake. It is rather scattered with a large island in it which is so close to one side that a plank connects it with the main land; the largest part of the lake is on the west side, where it is said a short distance from the shore the bottom cannot be found. It is surrounded on each side by very high hills which are covered with trees except at each end where there are low marshes so that you cannot go all round it easily. The boys were catching a few fish, and we were walking about trying to see what we could. In the course of the afternoon Mr. Ewing and Mr. Wright went on the island from which they got into the lake. Mr. Ewing swam out a long way and found no bottom in his depth. As he staid in some time we were rather un-

easy at seeing him in so deep a place. Mr. Wright did not go out very far. We found a little shanty made of boughs of trees where Miss McIlwain and Mamma spent the day. We commenced our journey home about three o'clock by a road much better than the ones by which we went and got home in two hours. I drove our wagon home. The Ewings staid here for tea, and went home about eight o'clock. Thus ended our eventful day.

The excursion was a bit too much for twelve-year-old Charles. Anne's diary recorded on the following day. "Charles's stomach has been a great deal disordered by all the good things and the ride yesterday." In a couple of weeks Charles was in even more trouble. Anne wrote, "We got a dreadful fright this morning. . . . About 5 . . . Charles was seized with a fit. [Probably a convulsion.] We did everything we could for his recovery and sent for the Doctor, who bled him. He had not entirely recovered his senses till then. He is pretty well this evening." The old and dangerous practice of bloodletting is mentioned several times in the Myrtleville documents of this period. John wrote that a servant was ill, and Dr. Marter came and "bled her largely." Fortunately both Charles and the maid recovered in spite of the loss of blood.

On her sixteenth birthday, July 14, 1847, Anne noted solemnly, "I have much to do in the improvement of my temper and mind and do, I hope, sincerely desire to be more conformed to the image of my Lord." A few days after her birthday, Anne and John drove to Hamilton, twenty-five miles east. This journey produced a composition, too.

The sun had just risen above the horizon with the color of blood as an indication of the extreme heat of the commencing day, when John and I set off for Hamilton to bring up Mr. Wright who had been staying there for a week. The sun had not shed forth its greatest heat till we arrived near Mr. Duff's tavern, about ten miles from our destination, where we rested for about half an hour and gave the horses water. The country all along the road looked very pretty, especially near Ancaster and Hamilton, where the bright red of the numerous cherry trees contrasted beautifully with the ripening corn [that is, wheat], some of which was now beginning to be cut. We arrived at the "Burlington Academy" about ten o'clock, and after eating our dinner at the table filled with about sixty young ladies we went down to the Lake and saw all through the steamboat. We also went through a great part of the school, which is ornamented with numerous handsome paintings and other specimens of handiwork. I remained till about four o'clock with Miss Wright when we started for home where we arrived in safety in the evening with the object of our jaunt. [It is not clear what relation Miss Wright was to Mr. Wright, who presumably had been visiting her for a week.]

Anne's diary has several references to bad news from Ireland. She wrote on February 4, 1847, "Numbers are dying in Ireland for want of food." The family were affected more personally by news of a death not caused by famine. Jonathan sent her father, Anne said, an account of the passing of "the dear, amiable and beloved Charlotte Evans" (daughter of Mary Ottley).

Jonathan's next letter had a vivid description of the Irish troubles: "Times . . . have been awful in almost all parts, Starvation & Death, more especially in our county & the next—Kerry. In the district around Skibbereen, Dunmanway, Clonakilty, etc., it is estimated that for the 4 or 5 past months there has been close to if not more than ten thousand deaths from actual Starvation, or Fever brought on by want of food. . . . Indian Corn Meal, which was, during last Summer, selling at 12 to 13 £ per Ton now readily brings £ 20 & difficult to get at same. In our city only for the steps taken by having Soup Houses established in different parts, the people would die in the Streets—in every direction you turn, you see nothing but men, women & children begging." Things were, if possible, worse in April. Jonathan wrote: "Our Country is in a wretched state with want of Employment for the people & starvation & deaths in all directions around us. A good number of our respectable citizens have been cut off by Fever [typhus] which has now reached to the higher class."

In August, Jonathan wrote more cheerfully, that crops were good, including most of the potatoes. But family disaster came a second time in the year. Jonathan wrote on September 15,

1847: "I am sorry to have so soon again to mention the death of another member of our family, Mary Ottley, who died on the 9th Instant in Cork where she was stopping with Anne & me for about a fortnight before. She came to town to assist Tom Evans [her son] in clearing out the House at Sunday's Well which he has let, & took the Complaint which is now very bad in this place, the Dysentery, which notwithstanding all that could be done for her, took her off in a fortnight. She was buried yesterday in St. Finn Barr's [the old Protestant Cathedral, not the big Gothic one built after 1864]. She has left a great blank now in our family as she was very often in town with us, & always if any of us should be ill, was sure to be ready to come."

Meantime, school went on at Myrtleville. Anne wrote a composition describing the daily schedule. It sounds like a full day.

The schoolroom door is opened every morning at six o'clock when the preceptor rings a bell for the purpose of summoning the scholars to study their lessons. At seven they are generally called to breakfast and [an] interval [between] that and nine is allotted to them for recreation and any business which in a farm and farmhouse may then be necessary. At nine precisely the bell calling on the students to recite is rung. The first task which is recited is Scripture, the next poetry, or correcting compositions or composition exercises. The next is the juvenile grammar class which is succeeded by the senior one. These studies occupy an hour and the preceptor allows the pupils to retire for five minutes. He also keeps a memorandum of the manner in which each task is recited. Arithmetic including both classes occupies the following hour, at the termination of which the same indulgence is granted. Writing and spelling is over at twelve when a recess of two hours is granted for dinner, recreation, etc. A lesson on common objects in which the properties and powers of various things are explained is followed by both classes in geography which concludes another hour, while Natural Philosophy and English history finish the second one. Two hours in the remainder of the day are devoted to study. Punishments when necessary are usually administered by giving black marks, which are regarded as signs of very bad conduct, and sometimes by hurting the actual feelings when a pupil is too hardened to allow his natural feelings to influence him. The pupils are in many cases very refractory and noisy and greatly try the patience of their preceptor.

Whether Mr. Wright's patience gave out, or he found more attractive employment, or he disagreed with his employer, whatever the cause he departed on October 22, 1847, with very little notice, at least as far as the children knew. That was the end of Myrtleville School, and of Anne's formal education. She went on "improving her mind" with reading, however, until the end of her long life. People lent her books, and sometimes the family bought books from peddlers. Anne was glad to get rid of arithmetic. Many years later she quoted to her nieces that

> Multiplication is my vexation.
> Subtraction is as bad.
> The rule of three, it troubles me,
> And practice drives me mad.

She was a well-organized young girl. On November 27, 1847, she wrote, "I have arranged my time in the following order, namely: Get up between 6 and 7 and get breakfast; after breakfast make the beds with Mamma; ½8 attend Aunt Fanny's reading; then make candles. ¼ to 10 hear the children spelling. 10 read Rollin's Ancient History. 11 to 12 music. The rest of the day to be spent in needlework, writing, or any business about the house which may be necessary. The afternoons of Tuesday and Friday to be devoted to drawing."

John and Charles also kept diaries for a few years after this. In the spring of 1848, the two boys were attending a school which had been opened in Brantford. There were thirteen pupils, and on Saturday they went to school only in the morning. After one term there, John, not yet sixteen, became a farmer. Charles continued to study in town; some of the younger children attended a school opened by Colonel Dixon on his farm between Myrtleville and the Grand River. Tradition says that Allen Good's three sons went to boarding schools, but there is no surviving record of Charles's schooling other than at Brantford. He may have been away about 1850, when he was fifteen. The diaries petered out at that time.

The year 1847, in which Allen Good took over the insurance office in Brantford, was the year of Brantford's incorporation as a town. It now had three thousand people, almost three times as many as when the Goods first knew it ten years earlier. Anne wrote a description of Brantford at the time of its incorporation: "The town is built on an eminence a little above the river. About three-fourths of the town is on the north side, while the other quarter is on the south side. These two parts are united by a long wooden bridge with a roof to it. . . . There are seven churches in it, one Church of England, two Methodist, one Roman Catholic, one Baptist, one Congregationalist, and one Scotch Church [Presbyterian]. It has one large bell [on the Market Square] which rings on all occasions of fire, etc. They have also an insurance company, and a fire engine. [Brantford had volunteer fire companies from 1836 to 1889.] It also contains three banks, the British North American, Gore and Montreal Bank. It has a few mills and distilleries, etc. There is a canal which is being made, which will come up to the bridge. There are a number of very fine stores in it, which are increasing daily."

The following year, the Grand River Navigation Company finally opened its canals and locks at Brantford. This was the consummation of a project talked of since the completion, almost twenty years earlier, of the Welland Canal. (The Welland by-passed Niagara Falls and was Canada's answer to New York State's famous Erie Canal completed in 1825.) On November 7, 1848, there was a great parade in Brantford to the landing at the end of Wharfe Street (down the hill on the river side of the main street). Fifteen-year-old John Good wrote in his diary, "I went to town to see the steam boats, and I went in the boat about three miles down the canal and had to pay two shillings."

Produce could now be shipped from Brantford via the Grand River and Lake Erie to St. Catharines in the Niagara Peninsula and to Buffalo, N.Y. Wagonloads of wheat came to the canal at Brantford from almost as far away as London, that is, about fifty miles. Cargoes from Brantford went on steamers and horse-drawn barges, and about forty passengers

could take a paddle-wheeler which left for Buffalo twice a
week. Industry as well as commerce boomed at midcentury. In
the 1840s Brantford acquired a stove factory, an "engine
works," and "the only stone-ware manufactory in Canada
West" (it imported its clay from New Jersey). By 1850 the new
town hall was erected in the center of the Market Square, a
sizable brick building with a cupola on top sheltering a fire bell
larger and louder than the one bought by public subscription
thirteen years earlier. All but very young Brantfordites remember the 1850 hall; it stood on the Market Square until
1965. Now the market has moved to the filled-in canal basin,
and where it and the city hall stood, there is a large parking
lot.

Allen Good was a Brantford businessman now, but he continued to do well with his farming. Young John wrote his
uncle Jonathan in 1849: "The Farm is getting on pretty well.
We had very fine crops this year. . . . Papa has three hundred
and forty acres of land, and there is another farm between
our two, which I think Papa will have yet. . . . We have ten
working horses and seven colts." Mechanization was beginning
to affect Canadian farming. John's diary mentions some of the
threshing being done with a "separator." Grain was still sowed
by hand, with teams of horses pulling harrows behind the
sowers, but on September 25, 1848, John wrote, "Mr. Bennett
came up with a sowing machine to try it. Some of the neighbours came to see it in operation, and approved of it."

Harvesting was still a laborious operation. 1847 was the
year that Cyrus McCormick began large-scale manufacturing
of his reaper, but no doubt the wonderful machine was only a
dream at Myrtleville as yet. Anne wrote on July 31, 1847,
"The wheat is all cut except about enough for a day's work for
a man. We have had an immense number of men, 36, for two
days, 22 of them Indians." Presumably, Eliza had to provide
food for these men.

There were few laborsaving devices for the housewife,
though some processes had been turned over to industry. The
Goods were able to take grease and ashes to a factory and
exchange them for soap. John's diary mentions getting four
and a half pounds of soap for nine pounds of grease. Allen
Good always kept sheep, but his busy wife did not learn to

spin. A neighbor instructed the older girls in spinning. There is no record of any weaving at Myrtleville.

Anne poured a daily batch of tallow candles in the molds which are still in the old house. At intervals she made tallow by carefully straining off the liquid from heated pieces of mutton, beef, or lamb fat. For candle-making this tallow was melted again and poured into the molds, which were strung with wicks. As much as one part of lard (hog fat) could be mixed with three parts of tallow; more would make the candles too soft. The refuse left from tallow-making went for soap grease.

In these midcentury years, Fanny Carroll exerted great influence on her oldest niece. Before she was sixteen, Anne was helping her aunt teach at a nearby Sunday School. Later Miss Carroll had the Paris Road Sunday School built, a small frame structure beside the eastern willow tree at the gate to Myrtleville. That tree and the schoolhouse vanished long ago, but the western tree remained as a landmark until the whole entrance was obliterated by Highway 403 in 1964.

If Fanny Carroll had been a Roman Catholic (an idea which would have horrified her), she would probably have become a teaching nun, and Anne might well have followed her into a cloistered life. Anne's attitudes at sixteen, as reflected in her diary and compositions, were much closer to her aunt's than to her parents'. For instance, there is her composition on "Dancing," which most of the Goods loved: "Dancing is a foolish and frivolous way of spending time. . . . The mere act of dancing brings nothing bad with it except that the time engaged in it might be more profitably employed. But when used as it is by the world it creates many other sins. When persons are engaged in dancing in a ballroom many proud and foolish thoughts arise and the heart is puffed up with pride and vanity, or they are envious because some one else is better dressed, has greater beauty, or is paid more attention to. Thus the time is not only idly wasted but sinfully employed for all the evil, sensual, and worldly tempers are indulged and God never thought of, for the god of this world too often blinds the eye of those who indulge in much worldly enjoyment which is but a shadow not to be compared with the glorious joy and peace of the children of God."

Anne also wrote a composition "On the Evils of Novel Reading." She said that much reading of such books "unfits the mind for more serious thought and reflection . . . gives false ideas and accounts of many things." She took her First Communion on Christmas Day of 1847, and wrote in her diary: "I experienced the blessed privilege of taking my seat at the table of the Lord. I trust it may never turn to my condemnation but to my everlasting salvation. Indeed, the more I see of my own heart and the world around me, the more I have to bless the Lord for his great and particular love to me. . . . I have now by my act this day bound myself in presence of God's Church to renounce the world with all its pomp and vanities, and to lead a new life from this day forth."

At this period, Anne's reading turned to devotional and theological books, and her diary became increasingly a record of sermons heard and prayers prayed. There were still a few notes of family news. In January 1848, John was very ill with scarlet fever. On February 12, another "sweet little sister" was born. Her parents gave her the name of her late "Aunt Ottley," Mary. (On Anne's eighteenth birthday, July 14, 1849, she wrote at some length about all that God had done for her, and she formulated a covenant devoting herself to His service. A year later, she appended a note: "I find myself guilty of breaking this my covenant in many points. I have not had the Lord constantly in my thoughts, neither have I lived in such peace with those around me as I would wish.")

The early winter of 1848 was one of sickness for the Goods on both sides of the Atlantic. Jonathan wrote on December 22: "I was very ill indeed, for nearly a month confined to Bed, having ruptured a Blood Vessel on the Lungs, but am now, Thank God, much better and am able to go out. . . . I perceive by a letter which I received from you last week, dated the 14th November, that all your children were in the Hooping Cough. . . . Charles still lives at Ballinvorosig. He is not very well at present. Our Country is in a very bad way & I fear will be much worse. No Rents paying, the farmers turning away from their ground & selling off what stock they have to go to America. . . . Numbers of our Landlords, who were always considered men of property . . . are reduced almost to a state of Beggary, having encumbrances on their ground, the

Interest of which, in consequence of them not receiving Rent, they are unable to pay, & . . . mortgages will be foreclosed."

A year later, at the end of 1849, Charles Good was still at Ballinvorosig but in deteriorating health. Jonathan wrote: "He [Charles] has a very careful man to look after him. I am sorry . . . to say that he is not improving from the fits which he generally has every month & prevents his being able to act in the management of the place; indeed, I have taken on me for the last 12 months almost the entire charge of it."

Ironically, as Ireland's economy suffered, Canada's prospered, and fortunately Allen Good shared in this prosperity; he certainly had a large family to provide for. On September 9, 1850, his tenth and youngest child was born, Clara Caroline. She was the only one of the ten who did not bear one of the old family names. With seven daughters, the Allen Goods were running short of hereditary names.

Late in the following summer, a woman who had nursed Jonathan's Charlotte brought a letter of introduction to Myrtleville. She reported that in mid-July, Allen Good's brother, Charles, had seemed very weak. (He had been living at Jonathan's since the preceding September.) At the beginning of the new year, 1852, Jonathan wrote his brother in Canada that on December 30, Charles had been "released from all the pains of this life." He had managed to get to the table for Christmas dinner, but did not leave his bed again. There is no hint as to the medical reasons for his death; probably no one knew. Jonathan wrote: "Our family now are reduced very low. . . . I should much like to be able to pay you all a visit . . . but how to manage for so long a time with the Savings Bank. . . . It would take me, I may say, the whole summer, & in these times when we have so many looking for places in Cork, I should be afraid that our Committee may vote me out altogether if I did such a thing."

The following spring Jonathan's children had measles, and in August he wrote that Charlotte had been "rather delicate since she had the meazles," and that she had been in the country for some time. The "change of air" did not cure the child. By midwinter she was really ill, and on March 25, 1853, Jonathan wrote Allen about the death of his only and beloved daughter. "Perhaps I placed too much of my thoughts on her.

She has left a sad blank to me in this world. . . . She died young, 13 years & 7 months old. My poor little John I am sorry to say is not very strong, indeed at times I feared that the seeds of the same disease [tuberculosis] were in him. Doctor Hobart says there are no symptoms that we need fear about him."

3

The Tide of Prosperity

By 1850 Brantford was an incorporated town with a fine town hall. It was time for Brant County to organize itself. The government of Canada, in 1851, substituted groups of counties for the old districts, with the provision that "so soon as a Court House and Gaol in any of the said counties shall have been erected at the county town of such County," then the governor in council should have the power to issue a proclamation dissolving the union between such county and its associated counties.

On April 15, 1852, representatives of the municipalities of the new county of Brant met in the town hall of Brantford and constituted themselves a provisional county council. They soon awarded a contract to Messrs. Turner and Sinon for the building of a courthouse and jail, and in November petitioned for separation from Wentworth and Halton counties. The first "warden," head official of the duly constituted county, was Eliakim Malcolm of Oakland Township, who had been a rebel in 1837. Most "Reformers" were thoroughly respectable by now.

Communications improved rapidly at midcentury. We often speak of the way distance has shrunk in our century with the development of radio, television, and airplanes; the nineteenth-century's steamship, train, telegraph, and telephone made as impressive a change in communications. Steamships regularly crossed the Atlantic in the 1840s. The telegraph, first successfully demonstrated by Samuel Morse between Baltimore and Washington in 1844, reached Canada West within

48

a few years. News came to Brantford newspapers by telegraph, and businessmen like Allen Good used the wires for
urgent messages.

The first regularly scheduled train in Canada West steamed
out of Toronto toward Georgian Bay on May 16, 1853. By
December of the same year trains from Hamilton were coming into Paris. Brantford's heavily subsidized line to Buffalo
opened the next month. There had been severe financial difficulties; at one point, construction gangs, short of pay and
provisions, marched angrily into town. One councillor suggested calling out the militia, but Mayor Matthews had a better
idea: "We'll shoot those men with barrels of flour." Food was
indeed the ammunition that worked.

On January 13, 1854, in spite of miserable, snowy, slushy
weather, an estimated twelve thousand people turned out at
Brantford to see the first trains. A parade, headed by the
Philharmonic Band, marched to the station, and three train-
loads of people from Buffalo, about five hundred in all, were
greeted with cheers and cannon salutes. Speeches were made,
of course, by the mayors of both towns, and banquets enjoyed
by many citizens. Then there were eight o'clock fireworks in
front of the courthouse, and a grand ball in the second story
of the new machine shops.

There was a new hotel for the new age, the Kerby House,
the largest hostelry in Canada, with room for five hundred
guests. Though reduced in size, it still operates on the main
street of Brantford. Improved lighting became available that
year of 1854 for the Kerby House and others. A gas company
was formed, and a local newspaper proclaimed, "Brantford
will soon repudiate tallow, sperm oil, and all the multifarious
and dangerous burning fluids now in use, illuminate her
streets, and light up her shops and private dwellings with gas."
No such amenities were in the cards for most farm homes, of
course.

The Buffalo and Brantford Railway was soon extended to
Lake Huron. On the way from Brantford to Paris, it went
through the southern part of Allen Good's farm, and angled
across Colonel Dixon's place. He now sold the railroad somewhat over six acres of the sixty he had bought from Allen, and
sold the rest back to Mr. Good. It took a long time for work-

men with primitive earthmoving equipment to build an em-
bankment across the valley of Myrtleville's creek, and little
houses were put up along the Paris road for the use of the laborers. Children of the railway builders were among the
pupils at Miss Carroll's Sunday School.

Within a few years, a network of railroads brought the well-
settled parts of the country into close touch with one another,
and opened up many markets. For instance, trains ran daily
from Brantford to Buffalo in four hours. At best, the run by
steamer was twenty-four hours via the Grand River Navigation Company's system. Railroads transformed the whole Canadian economy and doomed canals, except for those of the
great St. Lawrence system. After only five years of operation
as far upstream as Brantford, the Grand River Company rapidly lost its business, and by 1861 it was bankrupt. For more
than a century the old canal ran between the business district
of Brantford and the river; about 1950 it was filled in.

In 1854, the year the railroad came to Brantford, the
governor-general (Lord Elgin, Durham's son-in-law, who had
already guided Canada into the full functioning of "responsible government") skillfully negotiated a reciprocity treaty with
the United States. Most natural products, such as grain, fish,
timber, and coal were now admitted free by both countries
and a great deal of North American trade grew up. Also, in
spite of Canada's anxiety about free trade in Britain, the
mother country absorbed more and more Canadian produce,
especially during her war with Russia from 1854 to 1856.

Soon after the introduction of reciprocal trade with the
United States, everyone in Canada had to learn to live with
American-style money instead of pounds, shillings, and pence.
The shilling was worth about twenty-five cents then, and it was
years before people got out of the habit of saying "a shilling's
worth" when they meant "a quarter's."

During the prosperous early 1850s, Allen Good enlarged
his farm to about six hundred acres and invested in land elsewhere in the province. He suffered some loss in 1853. Jonathan wrote his brother anxiously on October 15: "I received a
paper some time back which I suppose came from you &
which contained an account of the burning of your Stables & a
quantity of Hay. It states that you were partly Insured. My

Dear Allen, I hope that you have not suffered much loss. It was fortunate that it was removed some distance from your Dwelling House, or it might have been worse." The modernization of Myrtleville House began at this period. One by one the fireplaces, except in the drawing room, were blocked up, and stoves were installed. In winter there seemed to be stoves and stovepipes all over the first floor.

Allen Good's children were growing up. In 1853, Charles, aged eighteen, left Myrtleville to enter the business world via a hardware store in Paris. There was a sense of finality about this; Charles was leaving, not to go visiting, or to school, but to earn his living. He was the first child to leave the nest. The same year, Anne spent nine weeks visiting family friends in Buffalo. It was probably the first time since the building of Myrtleville that she had left it for an extended period. There are letters surviving which she received from her parents and from her Aunt Fanny. The latter wrote, "I am not surprised at the account you give of the state of religion. From what I saw last year I fear it is nearly the same all over the country. Perhaps there is no more difficult character to convince of the truth of the Bible than the educated and enlightened Unitarian."

Whatever Anne's dealings with Unitarians, she came home in a glow of good intentions, but soon was confiding to her diary: "I received many lessons when absent from home, and which I hoped to improve by when I returned, but alas I am a creature of circumstances and always longing for sympathy, which I find very little of at home, where the finer feelings of the heart are in question. I must walk alone with my God . . . but I am constantly forgetting my Creator, and setting my thoughts on other objects. . . . I especially desire to be filled with a more meek and quiet spirit and more government over my tongue."

The closeness between aunt and niece had broken down. In June of 1852, Anne had written, "My special trial now is my conduct to my Aunt. I fear I am not doing my duty to her, and know not what to do." We can only guess at the trouble. Fanny Carroll truly "went about doing good." She cared for and taught her sister's children; she attended the sick, neighbors as well as relatives. Did she do it with a "holier-than-thou"

attitude and a martyred air? Was Anne torn between irritation
and guilt that she should become annoyed at her saintly aunt?
Or did Fanny Carroll become peevish with poor health, and
try the family's patience? At least one of Anne's friends tan-
gled with her. She wrote to Anne in July, 1852. "How is your
Aunt? Do you know, it gives me pain often when I think I
have lost her favour—I wish I heard she made herself and you
all more happy—but forgive me for mentioning so painful a
subject. I had written half of this sentence when I remembered the difference between writing and speaking."

Fanny Carroll was not with the family at Myrtleville much
longer. She died August 31, 1854, at the age of forty-five, attended by Anne in her last illness. No record has been found
of the cause of her death, but there is a paper filed away with
her will: "F.A.C. wished . . . that Anne Good should have the
school house. . . . Miss C. also desired that her watch should
be given to Tommy. Miss C. also gave to Anne Good her gold
pencil case. . . . I think the above is, as nearly as I can recol-
lect, the substance of several conversations which I had with
my Aunt Fanny, within the last two weeks of her sickness.
Brantford, 1 Sept. 1854. [signed] Anne Good." Fanny Carroll's will offended her brother-in-law. Years after her death,
he sent a copy to Jonathan, whom he had asked for assistance
in tracing Carroll assets still in Ireland. He wrote, "Fanny Carroll made a most extraordinary will. I don't believe it possible
for anyone to be more kind to her than Bessy and I were, but
we were not saints, she, I suppose, was, at least she thought so.
She is gone, I shall say no more about her."

Miss Carroll's natural heirs were her sister's children, and
about five years before her death she had made a will, leaving
all her money to three of the girls: four hundred pounds to
her devoted assistant, Anne; six hundred to her namesake,
Frances Anne; and one hundred to little Isabella. Her books
and plate were to be divided equally among Anne, John,
Frances Anne, Isabella, and Thomas. Her jewelry, clothing,
and other personal possessions went to the three girls named
above. At the time she made the will, Charles was fourteen,
Charlotte twelve, Eliza almost ten, and baby Mary a year and a
half. Not one of them is even mentioned.

Anne wrote about her aunt's death to various friends of
Fanny Carroll's in Ireland. Some of them carried on corre-

spondence with her for years. They shared her aunt's evangelical interests, and felt that she had succeeded to Fanny Carroll's mission. Anne was quite a letter writer; she had been writing with some regularity to her Aunt Anne and her young cousins in Cork. Postal services were getting faster and cheaper, helped by steamships, trains, and the use of prepaid postage stamps. With cheaper postage, people used envelopes instead of the "single sheet" folded several times, though many saved space by writing crossways over the original writing on a page.

A good description of Myrtleville, no doubt romanticized by distance, in the last summer that Fanny Carroll was there, comes from a letter written by Mr. Wright, the ex-tutor, who had recently paid the Goods a visit. He wrote on July 3, 1854, from Rochester, New York: "How I should like to be at Myrtleville today (hot as it is). I just fancy I should find Mrs. Good and Annie doing up the house-work, just as they know how to do it, in the very best style—Mr. Good and Tommy in town, the one in the Insurance Office and the other at school—Aunt Fanny diligently moulding the minds of the little ones, upstairs, just as I used to do—John and Charles out in the fields taking care of those noble 600 acres—Charlotte and Eliza, the former discoursing sweet music at the Piano (I must say I have not heard as sweet since I left Canada) and the latter with her sun-bonnet on, weeding a flower bed, or trimming a plant, so as to make the garden and the yard look beautiful—and last, not least, some friend, who is always sure to find a hearty welcome at Myrtleville."

Anne was twenty-three when her Aunt Fanny died, the age at which her mother had married. Did any young men come courting her? Did she deliberately choose "single-blessedness"? Did she scare off young men with her piety? None of the available documents answers these questions. It is clear that she was a pleasant, sociable girl, but she was not impressed with her own attractions. Years later, when a little niece remarked that Aunt Annie looked like a picture of her mother, Mrs. Allen Good, Anne said, "Oh, she was a much taller and handsomer woman than I am." It is true that Anne was a small and rather plain member of a tall, good-looking family.

Several of Anne's brothers and sisters were adults in 1854.

Anne Good (1831–1918) in her eighties

Eliza Good had described her oldest son at seven as "an affectionate but very bold troublesome boy." John remained affectionate; he wrote long homesick letters when separated from
his family, and he attracted a group of loyal friends. There is

no evidence that he was "bold and troublesome" as an adult, but he was impulsive, perhaps even erratic. Certainly he was restless at twenty-one; he was toying with the idea of going to the new goldfields of Australia, where some of the Irish Goods had gone in the early 1850s. This was normal enough; the other boys dreamed of adventure too, but somehow John lacked a quality both his brothers exhibited, which relatives referred to as "steadiness." He was, however, endowed with charm and good looks. His training for life, beyond the influence of high moral and cultural standards, was the basic classical education of a gentleman, and the practice of farming.

Charles, whom his mother had called "the flower of the flock," had grown into a strikingly handsome man, tall and slender, with finely cut features and large blue eyes. More important in the long run, people found him "a pleasant and sensible young man." He was more studious than John, and was trained as a businessman. He worked in at least two stores and several offices, becoming an expert bookkeeper. His personal letters now seem rather pompous and high-flown, but that was the style of much business correspondence in his time.

Charlotte, whom her mother had described as a pretty, but cross and troublesome three-year-old, became a tall young woman who was handsome, rather than pretty, and definitely strong-willed. Many years later, her nieces referred to her (behind her back) as "Queen Charlotte." Besides being "bossy," she was kind and generous.

The younger Eliza, a fair and pretty baby, "smart and sensible," according to her mother's letter in 1840, was growing into another handsome young woman. Intelligent she may well have been; sensible, in the modern meaning of the word, she was not. Her judgments of people often were faulty. She yearned for romance, as young girls usually do, and she craved it in dramatic form, adoring the novels that Anne regarded with disapproval. Her letters were effusive, in Victorian terms, "gushing." The other five redheaded children were still children in 1854.

In 1855 Allen Good was elected reeve (chief executive officer) of Brantford township, and became warden of Brant County, that is, chairman of the county council. His period in office was marked by a great deal of argument about paying overcharges on the building of the courthouse and jail. There was unhappiness on all sides; there were delays in completion of wells, cistern, and the like, and in the end the contractors, Turner and Sinon, lost heavily.

Allen Good made an eloquent address to the county council on June 18, 1855, on the subject of prison reform. He was particularly upset about the number of youthful first offenders who were incarcerated with hardened criminals, and given no educational or useful work. He hoped that several counties might cooperate in setting up a training institute, a self-paying establishment. "Surely a good day's work is worth three times the cost of support." The council instructed him to communicate with other counties on the question. There were no immediate results, but in a few years the province did set up separate institutions for offenders under the age of sixteen. Unfortunately, more than a century later, penologists are still complaining that reformatories are designed more for punishment than reformation.

One of the pleasanter duties of Allen Good, as warden of the county, was to read a welcoming address when Lord Elgin's successor, Sir Edmund Head, visited Brantford on October 19, 1855. Mr. Good was always a man who enjoyed the use of language. In fact, a Brantford newspaper hinted that the printed address to voters distributed by a contender for a Conservative nomination was really written by Allen Good. "Ghostwriting" of political documents was frowned upon in those more leisurely days. At any rate, the speech which Mr. Good delivered, immediately after the mayor's, from a platform in front of the new courthouse, was longer and more elaborate than Mayor Matthews's (also an Irishman).

To His Excellency Sir Edmund Walker Head, Bart., Governor-General of British North America, etc., etc.

May It Please Your Excellency: I have the honour to appear before you as Warden of the County of Brant, and to tender to your Excellency, on behalf of the county, a hearty welcome within its precincts. The short notice which we have had of Your Excellency's arrival, and the limited time which you can spare from your other duties to remain amongst us, have prevented me from calling the Council together—residing as the members do in different parts of the county—to meet you in the manner I should have wished.

I have no hesitation, however, in stating to your Excellency that the inhabitants of this county yield to no portion of this valuable appendage of the British Crown in loyalty to our Most Gracious Queen, and in devoted attachment to the free constitution under which we live. The untiring industry of the inhabitants, and the efforts made by them to promote their own and the county's prosperity, have under Providence made the county what it now is; and I cannot entertain a doubt that when the national advantages as to soil, water-power and other privileges shall have been fully developed and worked out, the County of Brant will be behind none in the Province in everything which can make it one of the richest and most respectable in the land.

The great facilities afforded by the railways for the conveyance of produce to the markets of the United States, with the free admission of our agricultural productions into that country, have very materially assisted to promote this state of things, by affording to the farmers of the county all the advantages of a large and increasing demand. The inhabitants fondly cherish the hope that nothing may prevent the reciprocal feeling on all matters of trade which now exists between the two countries from being more fully carried out and acted upon, fully impressed as they are that the more intimate the connection in all matters of business, the more rapidly and the more fully will the resources of Canada be developed. The inhabitants of this county have viewed with anxiety, and have watched with solicitude, the various phases and movements of the struggle now pending between Her Majesty and her august ally the Emperor of France, against the despotic power of Russia. Never in the history of the country has a war been more generally supported in the length and breadth of the land. It may indeed be called a struggle between liberty and despotism, between free institutions and unmitigated thraldom. That the efforts of the allied troops may be crowned with success is, I may venture to assure Your Excellency, the prayer of every inhabitant of the County of Brant.

Signed on behalf of the county,

Allen Good, Warden

After the welcoming ceremony, the procession moved on to the town hall, where about sixty prominent citizens lunched with His Excellency. Meantime, Lady Head was entertained at Dr. Digby's handsome house, which stood almost across Market Street from the courthouse, where the Bell Telephone building now stands.

Earlier that same year, Allen Good sent his youngest son to boarding school. Perhaps John's old school, Caradoc Academy, near London, had gone out of existence; perhaps Allen and Eliza for their own reasons chose to send Tommy elsewhere. Late in January, 1855, a letter had come from Ingersoll, a town about thirty-five miles west of Brantford.

> At the request of Mr. Hughes I beg to inclose my prospectus, a printed copy of my testimonials, and a small treatise, which embraces the leading features that form the basis of my present school; it is in fact a "Home Institute," for both Mrs. King and I endeavor by kind and assiduous care to atone for the unavoidable absence of the endearments of home, and to make our home a happy one, the pupils are our household. . . . Their moral training and gentlemanlike deportment are also particularly attended to. I can send you the address of the parents whose sons are at present under my care (as references) if you require them. If you could visit my Educational Establishment, you will then be better able to judge of its leading features. I have only three vacancies.
>
> respectfully yrs.
>
> John King

Shortly thereafter, Tommy, then eleven and a half, was at Mr. King's school. Thirteen-year-old Fanny wrote him on February 10.

> I promised to write to you soon after you went away. . . .
> How are you getting on up there, you know you must tell me all about the place you are in when you write. Charlotte is a good deal better . . . Charley goes to Brantford every day with Papa to write in the office. Isabella and me go to school every day and Mary began to go yesterday. . . .
> your ever affectionate sister
>
> Frances Anne Good

On February 23, Charles wrote his little brother. He explained that he was taking the place of an office worker who had imbibed too freely. "Mr. Young got slightly corned the day after you went to Ingersoll, and I have been in the office ever since." There was a smallpox scare. Charles asked Tommy, "Have you been vaccinated yet? We have all been and have a pretty sore lot of arms at present."

There is an undated letter from seven-year-old Mary, dictated to someone.

My dear Tommy,
This is the first time I wrote to you. I hope you like school very much. Two servants came to hire, but they never came back. . . . The pedler of Books came & we bought some nice books. Charlotte was in Church yesterday & she was not there for some weeks before. Little Clara is asleep on the sofa. The snow is going away & I hope summer will soon come. I hope to see you at Easter which will soon come.
Your affectionate sister,

Mary Henrietta Good
I am getting on to write very well. I hope to write a History before long.

On March 2, there was another letter from little Mary. "You may come home at Easter. . . . I want to see you very badly as I suppose you are a finished gentleman by this time. . . . Write to me soon." (The demand for education in gentility was not satisfied by a few private schools. Brantford's papers at this period advertised evening classes in "dancing and deportment.")

Allen Good had a worried letter from Tommy. He answered promptly on March 5.

My dear little boy,
I got your letter of the 3rd. . . . I am glad to find that you are so well engaged in your lessons. Try to get all the information you can as it will be of use to you in after life. . . . There is not much of small pock in Brantford—2 or 3 cases is the amount of it. You must not believe all you hear about it. . . . I will try to

see you before a week goes by. I send you a note from Fanny
and one from Eliza.
Believe me
Your own dada

Allen Good

Tommy stayed at Mr. King's school for at least a year and a
half. During that time, the school moved about sixty miles
eastward from Ingersoll to Dundas. At Myrtleville is a book,
A Lady's Second Journey Round the World, by Ida Pfeiffer, which
is inscribed, "Thomas Allen Good received this Book for a
Prize at Mr. King's School, Dundas, Canada West, June 27th,
1856."

During the busy year of 1855 George Malloch called
frequently at Myrtleville. He was the son of Judge Malloch of
Brockville, on the St. Lawrence, and he was practicing law in
Brantford. On February 21, 1856, he married Charlotte
Good. It is said that the drawing room at Myrtleville was repa-
pered for the occasion, with a pattern of grape leaves and
large bunches of grapes, one of the early manifestations of
Victorian fashion in the decoration of the house. Charlotte
was not quite nineteen when she married, and she was not yet
twenty when Charlotte Elizabeth, called Lilly (or as she later
spelled it, Lily), was born the following January. Family tradition says that the long embroidered dress, every stitch done by
hand, of course, which some descendants wore at their chris-
tenings in the 1940s, was made by Eliza Good for her first
grandchild. Mrs. Allen Good was an accomplished needlewoman as well as pianist. Another tradition is that she made a
long embroidered dress for each of her ten babies. At any rate
two of the little garments are still in existence.

None of Jonathan Good's 1855 letters have survived, and
none of his letters in 1856 or later mention his son, John. He
had written in October of 1854 that "John is improved a good
deal in his health which was not at all well for this some time
past." There is a much later reference to Jonathan's two children by Catherine Cripps dying young of "consumption." It is
likely that John died in 1855 at the age of fourteen. Poor
Jonathan was besieged by premature deaths in his family.

Allen's oldest brother, Henry, mysteriously estranged from

Mrs. George Malloch née Charlotte Good (1837–1918), "Charlotte, Queen of Paisley." Photograph by Notman and Fraser, Toronto

the family years before, is finally mentioned in an 1856 letter from Jonathan, but he becomes only more mysterious. Jonathan and his sister, Anne, were trying to sell some inherited land at Changetown and send Allen his one-third share of the proceeds. They were offered £340 for it (about $8,500 in our money) but were having trouble with the papers for the sale. Jonathan wrote Allen on Christmas Eve, 1856: "I suppose you are aware that everything was at one time settled on my brother, Henry—and where to get his signature now I am sure I could not say as we have not for the last ten years heard anything about him." He wrote a few months later: "Henry . . . is now the only person who can give a legal title to any purchaser. We have made enquiries to different parties to ascertain whether he may be alive or not, but can get no information respecting him. It is now, I think, over ten years since we heard any account of him & he was then on his way to California. I still have some hopes that we may be able to manage in some way without his signature [presumably by court order]."

Two and a half years after his first letter on the subject, Jonathan wrote, "The sale of Changetown has not as yet been carried through the Courts." A year and a half after that, it was finally known that Henry was dead, though how this was ascertained is not clear. The land was sold, and Jonathan sent Allen one hundred pounds for his share. None of the available documents gives any further details, and the intriguing question remains: Why did Henry, the oldest son of a large, close family, cut himself off?

On New Year's Day, 1857, Anne wrote a meditation, feeling lonely in the midst of her big busy family. "Dada is all excitement about elections, as well as most of the men in town. John & Charles out all day, last night spent at a ball. O that my dear relations would come to Jesus, but all His mercies seem in vain. There is not one of brothers or sisters who can in the least sympathise with me, & I must try to run the heavenly race alone so far as they are concerned."

Anne's family were all faithful members of Grace Church, but they were, in her mind, preoccupied with worldly interests. Yet she herself enjoyed society and travel. In July 1857, she accompanied the three Mallochs on a trip to Brockville to visit George's family. They went by boat from Hamilton to Gananoque on the St. Lawrence (Anne spelled it "Ganynockwe"). She wrote her mother: "We left Hamilton at nine o'clock on Thursday morning, and as the lake was very rough had but little comfort till we came to Toronto where the Boat remained three hours during which time we had dinner and a short walk in the City. It seems to be increasing rapidly, some splendid buildings. [The population was over forty-two thousand.] We passed a very good night on board & got up at four in the morning, saw all the entrance to Kingston, remained for a time to take on Passengers, etc. The morning was most delightful, the water as smooth as glass, and we had a full view of the Thousand Islands which are beautiful. . . . Mrs. Robertson says she saw the comet last night about 1 o'clock A.M. If the children wish to look out for it, it might be seen."

While Anne was visiting in Brockville, her father was engaged in preparations for the twelfth annual exhibition of the Provincial Agricultural Association. Allen Good, president of the Brant County Agricultural Society, was chairman of the finance committee for the fair. Brantford hoped not to be outdone by Kingston's exhibition the year before. An 1883 history of Brant County describes the preparations.

"The ground chosen was an elevated piece of dry sandy land, immediately overlooking the Brantford station of the Buffalo and Brantford Railway, overlooking the town, and commanding an extensive and pleasant view of the surrounding country. [The fairgrounds were on Terrace Hill, built up as part of the city before the end of the century.] Temporary buildings, pens and fences were erected by the local committee. . . . Nearly opposite the entry gate, in the shape of a Greek cross, stood a large building, one hundred and fifty feet long by forty feet broad, with an octagon tower rising in the centre. This was the Floral Hall, devoted to floriculture, horticulture, the educational department, ladies' work and the fine arts. Behind it . . . was another building of the same shape, for the agricultural, dairy and other products. Between the fence and these buildings the space on the right hand was devoted to the exhibition of the horses. To the left on entering were placed the ploughs and other implements and machines and the refreshment booths. All around the inside of

the fence were pens for cattle, sheep and pigs. . . . For the
convenience of people having animals or heavy articles for
exhibition, the Railway Company made a temporary switch to
the lower corner of the grounds."

The exhibition had trouble with the railroad and the
weather. "Wednesday [September 30], the first day of admitting the public, was generally wet and cold, with occasional
sunshine. Owing to detention by the railway, articles which
should have been upon the grounds the previous day before
noon were arriving all day, and the judges consequently could
not get through with their duties so promptly as was desired."
The weather, however, was not bad enough to disrupt the
"trial of ploughs, mowing machines, and combined mowers
and reapers" on Mr. Good's farm. A Toronto newspaper reported: "A very nice piece of sod was selected for the ploughs,
which were set to work, and the judges then went to test the
reapers in an oat field adjoining. Some twenty-eight or thirty
ploughs were taken out for trial; many of them were remarkable specimens of nice workmanship both in iron and wood;
and there was presented every variety of shape and pattern,
some new, and others of old and approved make." The newspaper also stated that "An entire transept of the Floral Hall
was occupied with the various educational requisites which
may be obtained for public schools from the depositories in
connection with the Education Office." The school exhibit
showed many maps and charts and an "extensive collection of
philosophical instruments and apparatus." (People still called
science "natural philosophy.") There were operating models
of steam engines and "that greatest of wonders—the electric
telegraph." A Brantford reporter was particularly impressed
with the "immense electrical machine . . . kept in constant
requisition, shocking the multitudes as they pass, and throwing off sparks like a disdainful lady." (Brantford newspapers
warned fairgoers, "Beware of pickpockets.")

On Thursday afternoon (October 1), Sir William Eyre, the
Queen's representative in Canada West, "and other distinguished persons" arrived, and were greeted with the usual
formal speeches. They inspected the fair, whose grounds were
by this time in deplorable condition. "Rain fell heavily all day,

the air was cold and disagreeable, and the ground, although a sandy, porous soil, became, from the trampling of the crowd of visitors, deep mud." Among the distinguished visitors was William Lyon Mackenzie. Twenty years earlier he had been a rebel leader, fleeing for his life. Eight years before the Brantford exhibition he had returned to Canada under the Amnesty Act. For six years now he had been a member of the assembly again. Much later, his grandson would be prime minister of Canada for a long period.

It had been a very poor season for crops, and the grain exhibits showed this, but otherwise farmers' displays were impressive. "In the whole department of livestock," went a Toronto report, "the entries are much more numerous than formerly, and the quality of them very superior, a feature in the exhibition especially desirable, as a proof of the progress of the Canadian farmer, and the growing interest in the improvement of farming stock." In spite of the terrible weather, cash receipts from the fair set a record at forty thousand dollars.

From the excitement of the big fair, Brant County turned to the excitement of elections to the Legislative Assembly. Years later, M. J. Kelly, an educator who came to Brantford about this time, writing about men active in politics there in the late 1850s, said: "Among the prominent men in the neighborhood . . . who frequented Brantford, were the late Hon. David Christie, . . . [and] Mr. Allen Good who came out to Canada from the City of Cork. . . . He lived on a [large] farm . . . on the Paris road, took an active interest in politics, both municipal and provincial; he became Warden of the County and had parliamentary aspirations. He was an Irish gentleman of the old school, quick-tempered, but hospitable and a friend to his friends." David Christie made an excellent standard-bearer for the Liberals. He was a very successful farmer of South Dumfries Township, and had represented the combined counties of Wentworth and Brant from 1851 to 1854, and the new constituency of East Brant since 1855. Christie was an ardent "Reformer," campaigning for broadening of the franchise and the introduction of the secret ballot. He proclaimed that he was interested in men of "clear grit" as colleagues, thus

giving Liberals a nickname which stuck for at least two generations. (Well into the twentieth century, people spoke of "Grits
and Tories.")

The Conservative, or Tory, camp in East Brant had several
contenders for the nomination, chief among them George
Wilkes, recently builder of a dam and mills in the Holmedale
section of Brantford. Another possible candidate was Allen
Good. No midcentury files of Brantford's Conservative paper,
the *Courier,* seem to have survived, but the Liberal *Expositor*'s
reports of the contest for nomination are available. That
paper said that the *Hamilton Spectator* had published a statement that Allen Good was to retire from the field in favor of
"the aspiring Lord of Holmedale. . . . Dire was the rage of
the plucky old Allen and he straightway hastened to the telegraph office and despatched a [telegram to the effect that this
information] was "a d——d lie!"

The *Expositor* provided its explanation of Mr. Good's with-
drawing: "Allen Good cast a wistful eye over the field, as he
himself confessed, but the prospect looked gloomy and dis-
heartening to the old high church Tory, and he durst not
enter the lists to cross arms with the invincible David of Dumfries. ["Old" Allen was then about fifty-eight!]" The *Expositor*
was, of course, delighted that David Christie once more
proved invincible. In the following year, 1858, Mr. Christie
resigned to campaign for a seat on the Legislative Council,
representing Brant and Haldimand counties. Allen Good
worked hard for the Conservatives, but again the invincible
David's side won. Later, Christie was senator, member of the
Privy Council, secretary of state, and Speaker of the Senate.
Allen Good remained an active worker for the Tories, but
probably never again seriously considered being a candidate
for Parliament. He was busy with too many serious problems
at home.

4

Ebb of Prosperity

Allen Good's poor harvest of 1857 came at a particularly bad time. The ending of the Crimean War the year before had reduced demands and prices for farm products. There was a depression again, almost a panic reminiscent of 1837. Mr. Good had backed his son, Charles, in a store; it failed early in 1858. He lost two thousand dollars (at least ten thousand in our money) in that fiasco. He was also involved in the expense of building the north wing of Myrtleville House. Worst of all, he had overextended himself on land purchases, and now was unable to finish paying. Anne wrote in May of 1858, "We are all in very low spirits on account of the scarcity of money, and the prospect of poverty before us." They were, however, still able to keep one maidservant; when Bridget O'Grady left, Mary Coonan came.

Why was what Anne called "the new house" built at Myrtleville? Perhaps to get more living space for a large family, but more likely to provide a home for newlyweds. Anne's journal reported about this time that "John returned from Ingersoll [where Tommy had gone to school]. He says he is to be married in a couple of months." Nothing is known about the young lady in Ingersoll, except that the wedding plans did not mature. Anne mentioned later that "John went to Ingersoll and back," and finally, after another three weeks, that John went to Ingersoll and on his return made his sisters, Anne and Eliza, gifts of jewelry. They had probably been his gifts to his fiancée. Incidentally, Myrtleville's wing had a good cellar under it, where the family kept milk, butter, fruits, and vege-

Myrtleville House and wing from the west

tables, until mechanical refrigeration came to the farm in the
1930s. Eliza Good's objection to cellars must have been overcome or overruled.

Anne's journal reflects the busy domestic life at Myrtleville.
There was a great deal of sewing and knitting to be done for a
large family who were clothed mostly in homemade garments,
manufactured without the aid of machines. And women's
clothes were far more voluminous than they had been in
Eliza's youth. Crinolines and more and more ruffles were
coming in. One could buy *Godey's Lady's Books* in Brantford for
twenty-five cents a copy, but almost the only help they offered
the seamstress was the inspiration of their fashion pictures
and the enjoyment of their articles and stories. Many afternoons and evenings Allen Good's daughters sewed or knitted
while Mamma or one of the girls read aloud. Anne wrote

repeatedly of knitting curtains, but none of them have survived.

Eliza Good was a determined woman; in spite of her many other responsibilities, she taught all of her seven daughters to play the piano, though only Charlotte and Isabella became really accomplished musicians. She was a sympathetic mother, however. A revealing story about her is that she always took a bag of cookies to church with her to beguile the youngsters during the long services and sermons of that era. The younger girls—Mary, ten; Clara, seven—were being given their schooling at home at this time; it was one of Anne's duties every morning to "hear their lessons." Before that, she usually read to herself the morning psalm and *Jay's Exercises* (daily prayers and meditations). She prayed earnestly, but felt that she was far from conquering her sins of anger and impatience. Finally, in September of 1858, she wrote one day that she had "a decided answer to prayer, in being able to teach Clara without a quarrel." In time, her prayers were more fully answered; her nieces and nephews remembered her as a person of rare serenity who never spoke loudly or crossly.

In spite of housework and sewing and lessons, there was time for a great deal of visiting, for staying in Brantford for a few days at a time, for having visitors a few hours or overnight. Eliza and her daughters often drove to town, but if a horse was not available, they did not mind walking two or three miles to make a call. Besides visiting friends, the Goods enjoyed festivities in Brantford. Anne was staying in town when the Queen's birthday came on May 24. She and her hostess drove out in the morning when "the firemen made a very pretty procession, the wagons all decorated with green boughs and flowers. . . . In the evening we drove out and saw the torchlight procession and fireworks." Often one of the features of such celebrations was the "callithumpian parade." It was made up of the less inhibited citizenry, dressed in outlandish attire, and banging on tubs, washboards, pots and pans, or whatever humble objects were good noisemakers. Traditional Old World celebrations were still carried on. Allen Good's farm laborers were given a holiday on March 17, "Patrick's Day." And on November 5, 1858, Allen Good went to a Guy Fawkes Day dinner in remembrance of the Gunpowder

Plot of 1605. This day has been little noted in Canada for
many years, but some of Allen Good's twentieth-century great-
grandchildren were taught the old English rhyme: "Please to
remember the fifth of November,/ Gunpowder, treason, and
plot."

There was a special celebration on August 19, 1858, a public
holiday in honor of the completion of the Atlantic Telegraph.
The Goods went to a picnic at Wilkes's Grove, and Anne wrote
in her journal, "We can now hear from England in a few
minutes." What a change this was from the weeks it had taken
news to cross the Atlantic by sailing ship just twenty years
before! It is true that the cable broke after a few months and it
was several years before there was reliable trans-Atlantic teleg-
raphy, but everyone knew that the trouble was only temporary, and that a new era in communications had begun.

In September 1858, fifteen-year-old Tommy began to attend Mr. Fenn's school in Brantford. Mr. Fenn was assistant to
Mr. Usher, rector of Grace Church. A fine new brick building
(still in use) was almost ready to house Grace Church, and
Allen Good, as a trustee of the church endowment fund, was
involved in negotiations with the redoubtable Bishop Strachan
of Toronto. His letters to the bishop began with the courtly
salutation: "May it Please Your Lordship." On November 17,
Anne went to visit friends in Toronto, and a few days later
young Tom wrote her. He addressed her in brotherly fashion
as "My dear Nany Goat," and told her about all the visitors at
Myrtleville since she had left. He went on: "I stayed at home
Saturday & went skating with the little children in Ewing's
swail [a swampy area of the next farm, just down the hill to
the south of Myrtleville House]. . . . I had first-rate sport
drawing and swinging the children on the ice in my hand
sleigh. Johnny has begun to train his colts, Pat and Barney.
They are awful stuborn creatures. Pat, the first time the
tackle was put on him, threw himself about 20 times, & tries to
jump on every person goes near him."

Anne spent four weeks in Toronto. She did much needlework, often played chess in the evenings, and enjoyed walking
about the town. One day she went "to the new University
through the College Avenue. We spent some time in examin-
ing the edifice inside and out & consider it a very handsome

one & calculated to do credit to the Province." One hundred and twelve years later, it was still a credit to Ontario. On April 22, 1970, there was unveiled in front of it a plaque, erected by the government of Canada, which reads: "The building of University College in 1856–59 largely assured the future of the University of Toronto and drew it, in time, into a federal pattern which was widely followed in Canada and the Commonwealth. Here was realized a major nineteenth century aspiration: the establishment of a non-denominational institution of higher learning supported by Government. The building was designed by F. W. Cumberland and demonstrates his skill in freely adapting the Romanesque style to the purposes of a College in the new world."

University College is now part of a large university in the middle of a metropolis; when Anne visited it first, it stood almost in the country. She wrote of walking through some "poorly built streets," and climbing over a stile onto "the College Avenue" by which she walked to Yonge Street. (There is a department store now at the corner of College and Yonge.) The new university sent out notices to newspapers. In 1857 the *Brantford Expositor* published one which read: "University College, Toronto: Examination of candidates for matriculation will commence on Thursday, September 24, at 10 o'clock A.M. The regular courses of lectures will commence on Monday, October 5. . . . courses on Classical Literature, Logic and Rhetoric, Metaphysics and Ethics, Chemistry and Experimental Philosophy, History and English Literature, Zoology and Botany, Mineralogy and Geology, Modern Languages, Meteorology and Oriental Literature."

Anne was back at Myrtleville teaching her little sisters before Christmas. Tommy went to town and bought some playthings for the children. Anne wrote in her journal, "We are becoming much reduced in worldly circumstances." In spite of money worries, the Christmas season was a gay one. John, Charles, Charlotte and her husband, young Eliza, and Fanny went to one party after another. Anne did not go to any of them, except, of course, to the one that her parents gave. She seldom went to parties, though she went to church meetings. She suffered a good deal from headaches and fatigue, and was probably thought of as a confirmed spinster who disapproved of all frivolity. Anne's physical troubles could have been caused by her psychological ones. She was tormented by feelings of inadequacy. She thought that she was not performing her mission to preach the gospel except as a Sunday School teacher; she felt that her beloved family ignored the life of the spirit and that she could not reach them. She gave way at times to anger and impatience, and she wrote in her journal, "I am not aware of being of real blessing to anyone."

The day before the Goods' party on December 29, Anne wrote: "All this day we have been very busy preparing for a large party tomorrow. I read Jay & we had Family Worship, this with a glance through the *Courier* [Brantford newspaper] was nearly all my reading. I have given Mary & Clara holidays for a few days. Tommy went tonight . . . to a party at Holleys. Nothing but parties nowadays, three this week for members of our Family. I am thankful that I was early brought to see the vanity of earthly pleasures & to seek those which are above. John gone to a Hard Times party where the Mallochs also intend to spend the evening. Oh, that my dear relatives would think of their immortal souls & strive to prepare for a blessed eternity."

Early in the new year, there was a family crisis. John and his father fell out, for some unrecorded reason, and John announced that he was going to Kansas, a stormy frontier state in those days. His mother and sisters set about getting his clothes in order, but John listened to advice from a neighbor. Anne wrote: "John dined with John Conner who went to town with him to try to make some agreement with Dada in order to remain at home. I retired to my room & prayed. . . . The matter was still undecided when they returned, Papa provoked as usual & unyielding. At last John concluded it was best to remain at home. We all spent a miserable evening as is always the case where discord reigns." The next day's entry reads: "John concluded to give up the Kansas journey & take a trip to Brockville instead; he left after breakfast, promising to be home in a fortnight. We all feel a load off our minds, though I do not know how far, for his own sake, his decision may be wise."

John returned from Brockville late in March and a few weeks later, before ten o'clock on a bright moonlit night, he and Matthew Brophy, one of the hired men, went down to the Paris Road to investigate shots they heard there. Anne wrote: "The mail carrier, an old man, was found murdered on our ground nearly opposite the black gate. He was taken into the school house & an examination of his body held. . . . He was shot through the left side of his head and afterwards thrown into the hollow, & the mail bags opened & letters opened." The following day, Mrs. Donahue, who sometimes helped with the washing at Myrtleville, was set to scrubbing the schoolhouse. Anne held her Sunday School there the next day, but noticed that the floor was still much stained with the blood of the unfortunate postman.

Six people swore that, the morning after the murder, they had seen John Moore and Robert Over, members of Brantford's small Negro colony "walking out towards the Holmedale Mill. . . . having a single-barrelled gun, and that they returned in about twenty minutes or half an hour, having each a gun, one of which was double-barrelled." Moore and Over, Harriet Moore, Emeline Sinclair, and Joseph Armstrong were arrested and their premises searched. A single-barreled gun and a loaded double-barreled gun were found, and the shot in the loaded gun corresponded in size to that in the head of the victim. At first, all the suspects claimed to be innocent, but before trial at the Assize Court on April 29, Armstrong confessed that he had gone out to steal potatoes with Moore and Over, and that Over had shot the mail carrier in spite of his, Armstrong's, objections. Armstrong, however, shared in the division of the loot, which was about fifty dollars in Canadian bills and a hundred-dollar American bill. (The *Expositor* pointed out editorially that people should use money orders rather than put cash in the mails.)

One of the lawyers for the defense was Edmund Burke Wood of Brantford, already known as one of the leaders of the Canadian Bar. He cross-examined carefully and addressed the jury on behalf of the prisoners "with great force and eloquence, and argued with much ingenuity to weaken the effect of the testimony for the Crown." His efforts were useless; Armstrong's confession held, and the jury's verdict was "Guilty." Moore and Over were hanged in Brantford on June 7, 1859, and about eight thousand people turned out to watch the grisly ceremony, including the men from Myrtleville but, of course, none of the ladies. It was the only public execution ever held in Brantford, and was commemorated by a float in the centennial parade 108 years later. Armstrong was sent to the provincial penitentiary at Kingston for life, but after assisting the guards in quelling a riot, about 20 years later, was pardoned on condition that he left the country.

During all this excitement, Tom Good was doing well at Mr. Fenn's school, as he had at Mr. King's. It was customary in those days for school examinations to be public, and Eliza Good attended Tommy's on June 30. There is a book at Myrtleville, *On the Study of Words,* inscribed, "Midsummer Examination of the Pupils of the Rev'd N. V. Fenn, Brantford, C.W., July 1, 1859, Thomas Allen Good received this book as a premium . . . together with Maury's Physical Geography of the Sea." Tom's summer holidays were for only one month, and even before he went back to school on August 1, Bella, Mary, and Clara started to the District School, as Anne called it, up the Paris Road. This was a temporary measure, freeing Anne's mornings in a busy season. She taught the girls at home again the following winter.

Money worries persisted, and the loss of two horses was both financial and emotional; the Goods loved their horses. Poor Dick was found drowned in the swamp (probably where a cow was trapped in quicksand many years later). Pirate took sick in town and the boys stayed overnight with him there. He seemed better the next morning, and John walked him carefully out to the foot of the Myrtleville hill, where he dropped dead.

The latter part of 1859 was one of those grim seasons which sometimes afflict large families; much of the time there was at least one member sick enough to cause anxiety. John was very ill with "chill fever," that is, malaria, which was fairly common until many of the swamps near Brantford were drained. Just as he was recovering, nine-year-old Clara had the measles. There were no complications and she recovered quickly, but little Maggie Smith on the next farm did not. Maggie took "inflammation of the windpipe," and died a few hours after the Smiths' hired man hurriedly came for Mrs. Allen Good very early in the morning. Eliza senior was in great demand

when there was illness or childbirth in the neighborhood, and
there was plenty of both.

Clara sandwiched an exciting trip to town between measles
and whooping cough. The whole family went to see the ascent
of a large balloon. Anne wrote, "Fanny, Mary, Clara and I saw
it from Mr. Bennett's tower. . . . The balloon looked very
pretty as it rose into the sky, but I did not envy the men, the
height looked so tremendous." The boys had some other interesting excursions that autumn. Charles went to Queenston
for the "inauguration of General Brock's monument," and
Tommy and John went to Hamilton to see the cricket match
between the "All-England eleven" and twenty-two Canadians.
Baseball had not yet supplanted cricket as a popular batting
game in Canada.

Clara was a sturdy child; she threw off the whooping cough
without a long, debilitating illness. Eighteen-year-old Fanny,
however, took very sick in November, narrowly escaping "inflammation of the lungs," that is, pneumonia. The acute stage
of the illness soon passed, but for three months the poor girl
had a bad cough and pain in her chest and side. Worry about
Fanny mingled with the grief the Goods felt at the death of
their young friend, Sally Usher Ross, daughter of their rector.
A lovely nineteen-year-old, Sally was a victim of "galloping
consumption," leaving the husband she had married only a
few months earlier. Jonathan's children had been consump-
tives too; tuberculosis was "the Great White Plague" of the
nineteenth century, top cause of death in Canada for many
years; it is no wonder everyone was very uneasy about Fanny.
To their relief, she recovered as the winter went by.

Anne was staying in town with her sister, Charlotte, in February 1860, when Brantford suffered the most destructive of
its many fires. The combination of many wooden buildings,
primitive fire-fighting equipment and lack of water mains was
deadly. Anne wrote in her journal for February 17: "This
morning between 4 & 5 . . . I heard the cry of fire in the
street & rising, perceived a very great flame in the town. . . .
George dressed & went out. The fire spread fearfully, destroy-
ing about sixteen buildings [including] the building in which
George's office was. . . . Charlotte & I went to the scene of
destruction about 7 A.M. & assisted Malloch in putting some of

his books in the Court House." The damage to George's office
and books was estimated at four hundred dollars; fortunately
he had adequate insurance. Some businesses lost much more
than George, but had no insurance.

About this time, Allen Good's last sister died, probably following a stroke. Jonathan wrote that Anne had begun to lose
all recollection of things about a month before her death. She
had lived longer than most of her siblings, and was almost
sixty-nine. She bequeathed one hundred pounds to Allen and
twenty-five pounds to his daughter who bore her name. Allen
must have hoped that the legacy would come quickly; his fi-
nances were in desperate straits. Anne, visiting friends the
other side of Brantford from Myrtleville, wrote on April 16:
"George Malloch called in on his way to Burford to look for a
purchaser for our farm. He told me that our affairs are in
such a state that we may be soon deprived of our house & all
earthly possessions."

On July 9, twenty-year-old Eliza left to pay a long visit to a
friend at Maitland, on the St. Lawrence near Brockville. She
could help with housework and sewing there, and so "earn a
living." Anne felt her departure a good deal both in the loss of
her company and the addition of much of her housework.
Pretty Fanny was still "delicate," but she was a cheerful, companionable girl, and Anne grew closer to her. Bella, almost fifteen, probably attended the new public grammar school (later
called high school), which at that time was quartered in the
upper floor of the North Ward School, up Albion Street from
Grace Church. Mary and Clara went back to the District
School on the Paris Road. At this point, Allen Good must have
been thankful for public schools; fourteen years earlier Henry
Moyle had scolded him for his lack of interest in them. About
two months after Eliza went to Maitland, a letter came from a
young farmer of that neighborhood, who asked to marry her.
Anne was not enthusiastic. She wrote in her journal, "I suppose she will become his wife & I think it is about the best she
can do in the position in which we are placed. . . . Mama &
Papa wrote to Eliza giving her permission to marry Mr.
Jones."

The Myrtleville family worked hard all summer, but on Friday, September 14, 1860, they took a holiday and joined the

Homewood, near Maitland, Ontario

largest gathering Brantford had ever seen. Anne wrote: "We locked up the house in the morning and all went into town to see Albert Edward, the Prince of Wales & eldest son of our Queen. The weather was fine. There was a very large crowd and several Beautiful Arches. At about 1½ o'clock the Prince arrived & the Procession moved towards the front street but as HRH was in a hurry he gave orders to drive fast. The consequence was that a general scramble ensued & when he reached the corner [King and Colborne Streets] where we were in the Insurance office we could scarcely see him. I did not distinguish his features at any time during the day. The Prince lunched at the Kerby House & then galloped back to the Station. It was a most exciting scene altogether. The Indians turned out in full dress, some of the Chiefs looking most extraordinary with feathers & paint . . . John was one of the Marshals immediately in front of His Royal Highness & Charles in the Brant Militia also near him. They were both on horseback & looked very nice."

There was much disappointment at the haste of the procession. The *Brantford Expositor* blamed it on the governor-general, who accompanied the nineteen-year-old prince and advised him. At any rate, His Royal Highness did not feel strongly, as does his great-granddaughter, Elizabeth, an obligation to wave and smile at the assembled crowd. The Kerby House surpassed itself that day. The bill of fare was long and elaborate. There were soup, fish, "releves," cold ornamental dishes, side dishes, vegetables, game, "center bouquets," pastry, confections, and fruits.

Brantford was extremely proud of the prince's special railway car. It had been built by the Buffalo and Lake Huron Company at the Brantford shops, and carefully inspected by George M. Pullman, who soon evolved his first sleeping car. On the outside, the prince's car was painted royal blue and adorned with his coat of arms. Inside, it was carpeted and had lounges, chairs, bunk beds, marble slab tables, and silk blinds.

A few weeks after the prince's visit, John Good moved from Myrtleville to the farm just west of it. It was one of those farms which Allen Good had purchased when his future looked very bright. John was a stock man; he had been winning prizes on his animals at local fairs for several years. Now he had a place of his own for his livestock, and a hired man and a housekeeper—and probably thought of marriage.

Eliza returned from Maitland that autumn well and happy. She brought a photograph of Andrew Jones with her, and Anne wrote in her journal that his "likeness" was "rather pleasing." Early in December, the young man himself, a widower of thirty-one, visited Myrtleville. Anne's doubts about him vanished. She wrote in her journal, "He is, I think, a very good man." Eliza and he planned to be married the following autumn, in 1861.

Allen Good was still heavily in debt, and trying to sell some of his land. He wrote to one creditor, "My difficulties do not come from extravagance, nor gambling, nor overtrading, nor high living. My fault was, I was too soft and too kind." Family tradition says that Allen Good, a convivial gentleman, was sometimes wined and dined too well before he signed notes. Many of his children and grandchildren were ardent teetotalers, using their ancestor as an object lesson. One is reminded of the bank directors' words about Allen Good almost twenty-five years before this, "Altho' a zealous and upright officer, he did not possess that calmness of temper, cool discretion and judgment absolutely needful for the post he occupied." However, he did manage to keep his home, helped by some timely remittances from Ireland—proceeds of the sale of Changetown, and a couple of legacies.

Allen continued to be a very active member of the Conservative party in Brant County. The Honorable J. A. Macdonald wrote him on May 25, 1861 (Mr. Macdonald, later Sir John A., first prime minister of the Dominion of Canada, had brought about a coalition of his Conservative party with moderate Liberals): "It has been hinted to me that Mr. Wood, the lawyer, of Brantford would run . . . and that as he is of *liberal* antecedents, would likely run well with the Reformers. I am also told that if the Conservatives support him, he will go the Ministerial ticket. . . . If Mr. Wood be available, in God's name, let us take him and let there be no splits. The period of Elections has not yet been fixed, but our friends should act as if they were to come on tomorrow. So Agitate, Organize & Electioneer. Let me hear from you in Course." However, E. B. Wood (the defense lawyer in the case of the murdered mail carrier) did not enter the lists until two years later. He was elected to the assembly then, but unfortunately for John A. Macdonald's hopes, Wood was a "Radical Reformer" and his considerable talents as an orator (he was known as "Big Thunder") were usually turned against the Conservatives.

In the spring of 1861, while Allen Good was wrestling with debts and politics and seeding, and the two Elizas were in charge of Myrtleville House, Anne paid a three-month visit to a friend in Arthabaska, a small village about sixty miles west of Quebec City. While she was gone, John was courting a Miss Duff of Elora, that picturesque town at the falls of the Grand about forty miles north of Brantford. The major topics discussed in letters from Myrtleville at this time were John's wooing and the surrender of Fort Sumter, South Carolina, to secessionist forces. Charles wrote Anne: "The principal topic of conversation here is the lamentable state of affairs existing in the U.S. It is really astonishing that the hostile attitude of one portion toward the other has not resulted in the commencement of hostilities ere this but the time is probably not

far distant when there will be some severe fighting. The
Northern people seem very sanguine of being able to coerce
the South into submission and perpetuating the Union as it
lately existed. My opinion is that the seceded states will never
again be united as formerly."

On July 7, 1861, Allen Good wrote an old friend in Cork:
"Matters in the United States are in a miserable state & I may
say without fear of contradiction that every man in Canada is
pleased & happy that he still lives under the old flag. God only
knows when the difficulties in the U.S. will end. Years may go
by before they are settled but of this you may be sure that the
U.S. are no longer the United States, but a disjointed body
ready to be split up into various governments. The time will
come when some fortunate & unprincipled adventurer will
step out, take advantage of the position in which the U.S. are
placed and perhaps form some military government or despotism as Napoleon did in years gone by. . . . We have only so
far as we are concerned to stick to our own Victoria & not in-
terfere with the squabbles or troubles of our neighbors."

Canadians could be determined noninterventionists, but
they could not ignore their neighbors' Civil War, or "revolution" as the *Expositor* regularly called it. They regarded it with
mixed emotions, and sometimes real fear for themselves. Most
of them detested slavery, and many, Allen Good among them,
had worked successfully in "the old country" for the outlawing
of slavery in British territories almost thirty years earlier. Tens
of thousands of Canadian volunteers served in the northern
states' armies. On the other hand the northern blockade cut
off England from most of her cotton supplies; England recognized the southern states as belligerents and unofficially gave
them a good deal of aid and comfort, for instance allowing the
sale and equipping of ships which preyed on northern vessels.
Union resentment naturally fell on England's American
colonies.

When Anne returned home in the summer of 1861, she
found that John's romance had collapsed and that Eliza was
"very unhappy & at last determined to break off her engagement with Andrew Jones." Anne wrote: "Mama, Papa & all of
us were sorry & vexed with her. He (Andrew) came up [late
in] . . . July and then we had some very disagreeable scenes.

Eliza first declared she would not marry him but when she saw how angry they all were she said she would. We were all busy then preparing for a wedding in two days when as I drove into town in the morning to help to buy the wedding dress what was my surprise to see a young man named Duroche who said he loved her, & her engagement with A. Jones was finally broken off. It was altogether a most extraordinary & romantic scene. A. Jones returned home to Maitland. Eliza seemed like one reprieved from execution. I never saw a person in such a state of mind & horror of marrying a man as she seemed to be & feel towards A. J. The affair was a complete town talk for some weeks, which of course, was very disagreeable." A few days after Andrew Jones left Myrtleville, Allen Good wrote him.

My Dear Sir,
    When I parted from you last Tuesday I was so perplexed and so much annoyed at the position of affairs at the moment that I was utterly incapable, and was not in fact able to tell you all I thought of you and your conduct in the unfortunate feeling between you and Eliza. On reviewing the whole transaction, looking in my cooler moments at all the circumstances of the case, I know no language strong enough to express my regret at the annoyance which you have had, nor can I conceive any language strong enough to express my admiration of the manly, the gentlemanly, the noble and generous manner in which you conducted yourself in that most unfortunate and trying transaction. You can have no idea of the general feeling of regret which we all feel, myself, wife, boys, girls and all at the abrupt manner in which this matter has terminated. As a parent I was of course anxious to ascertain as nearly as I could the position and character of the man who was about, as I thought, to be connected with my family by the nearest, the dearest and most holy tie that can bind Society together, and I am happy to say that the result of my enquiries was to more than satisfy me as to the propriety and the advantage of the engagement between you and Eliza.
    . . . I have not had the pleasure of seeing or becoming acquainted with your father and family but if circumstances should call me to your quarter my first care shall be to call on

you and them and I sincerely hope that if ever you come this
way you will give us a call. You shall get a kind and hearty welcome. I don't know what more I can say. You deserve all I have
said. We all wish you may enjoy a long life of health, prosperity
and happiness.

Anne's account in her journal continued: "The most curious
part of all was that in about a fortnight Andrew wrote to
Fanny proposing to her. Poor child, she was quite surprised &
puzzled at first but in two or three days decided to accept him.
We then commenced to work very hard to make Fanny's
clothes." Allen Good wrote Andrew again, a short and surprised note: "Fanny Anne handed me your letter to her. She
has given me the enclosed answer (which I have read) to send
to you. I do not know what further I can say than I have said
before. We all feel pleased at your views and intentions. I
must confess I did not expect it, after what had passed. Fanny
is young. She will be twenty on the eighth of December next."
Less than six weeks later, Allen Good wrote a third letter to
Andrew Jones.

11 Sept. 1861

Dear Sir,
    Fanny mentioned to me that we would have the pleasure of
seeing you on or about the 18th. . . . Under all circumstances
we would leave the matter of the wedding to you and Fanny, as
to the day, time of day, etc. etc.
    As to your movements after the wedding and as to the place
where you may choose to go you must of course be the best and
only judge. So far as Mrs. G. and myself are concerned we
would wish to have such a gathering as we had at Charlotte's
wedding, quiet but respectable, a few old and picked friends.
Mrs. G. has authorized me (and I am sure you will feel convinced that I second her views) to request you may feel yourself
perfectly at liberty to ask any members of your own family or
acquaintances to come with you. They shall be welcome—we will
do all we can to make them comfortable and happy.

Anne described the wedding in her journal. It was on September 26, 1861, and "the church was nearly full. Fanny was

Mrs. Andrew Jones née Frances Anne Good (1841–80)

dressed in white tarlatan with veil and wreath. [Tarlatan was a thin, stiff, transparent muslin, probably much like organdy.] Clara Usher, Maggie Ewing, & Bella were bridesmaids, John, Mr. Monsell & Arthur Hardy [A. S. Hardy, later premier of Ontario 1896–99] were groomsmen. We had a large party in the evening. Fanny & Andrew left with George & Charlotte about midnight. They started for the Falls the next morning. I felt very lonesome without Fanny. . . . Mr. Duroche visited at the house for about a month but before Fanny's marriage he deserted Eliza."

Fanny went to live at "Homewood," on the shore of the St. Lawrence. Some of her descendants lived there until the 1970s, in the old stone house which was built about 1800 by Andrew Jones's grandfather, Dr. Solomon Jones, a Loyalist from New York State. Fanny and Andrew were very happy together, and the Goods went on approving of Andrew Jones to the end of his long life. Tom Good's son, who knew him well, said that his Uncle Andrew was one of the most impressive persons in his memory, "the personification of kindness and courtesy. . . . One never heard other than gentle words from him."

5

Financial Collapse

Fanny Jones's marriage brought to a head the question of her Aunt Fanny Carroll's money. It had been left to Anne, Fanny, and Isabella, more than half of it to Fanny. Miss Carroll's will stipulated payment at age eighteen, or earlier if the legatee married with consent of her parents. It was argued that the Irish executor could not get a legal receipt until the legatee reached twenty-one, but Anne had been over twenty-one seven years earlier, when Fanny Carroll died, and not a penny of the Irish funds had yet found its way to her. Meantime, Mr. Crofts, the executor, had died, and his widow was hard to deal with. Some action was clearly needed.

Charles had an inspiration. He wanted work with better prospects than he had found in Canada so far. He had written his uncle about possibilities in Cork, and been roundly discouraged. Jonathan wrote Allen: "I was sorry that I could not hold out any encouragement to [Charles] to come to this part of the world in the hopes of bettering himself. We have numbers of young men here walking about for years, not able to get any situation, and [for] what are going, the pay is so small that they can hardly live out of it."

Undaunted, Charles arranged to get powers of attorney from Anne and Fanny, go to Ireland at their expense, ferret out his aunt's assets, and at the same time look over job opportunities in Dublin, Liverpool, and London. His father was not enthusiastic. He thought Jonathan could bring pressure to bear on Mrs. Crofts, and wrote him early in November, "Charles is still with me. I don't see what he can do by going to

Europe . . . I think he ought to stay with me, however, as to his movements, I know little." Nevertheless, Charles set out late in November.

Tom, now eighteen, took Charles's place in the insurance office. His small salary there would help at Myrtleville. Crops had been very poor, and Allen Good wrote a creditor, "I don't know how to thank you for your kindness and forbearance. I was in hopes of being able to pay all I owed this fall, but I cannot do so. My crops and indeed all the crops round here do not give 7 bushels to the acre."

Interesting letters came from Charles. He had gone "on the cars" from Paris to Brockville, where he breakfasted with Judge Malloch, George's father. He then spent a few days at Homewood with Fanny and Andrew, proceeded to Quebec, and sailed on the *Nova Scotian* on November 23, one day after the twenty-fifth anniversary of his parents' departure from Cork.

The voyage was too exciting for comfort. Three days out there was a fire, fortunately extinguished fairly promptly. At the end of the ninth day a great storm arose. Charles wrote: "The waves washed over the vessel which hopped round like a piece of paper. The storm continued Monday and Tuesday and on the evening of the latter reached its greatest violence accompanied with thunder and lightning. The Captain said next morning it was one of the worst he ever experienced. Every sail was torn to ribbons [early steamships had sails as well as engines], and seven of the sailors were more or less hurt. The whole crew, between 60 and 70, were on duty for over 60 hours consecutively. On Wednesday the storm abated but the sea was very rough. However the ship went gallantly forward at about 10 miles an hour. . . . About 5 A.M. of Friday 5th December we entered Lough Foyle where we had the luck to run into and smash a 3-masted Brig. The Nova Scotian however received no damage except the breaking of the railing of the forecastle." In spite of all the *Nova Scotian*'s troubles, the voyage had taken only twelve days from Quebec to Londonderry. That was certainly a great improvement over the Goods' five-week voyage a quarter-century before.

Charles spent the weekend enjoying the hospitality of Orangemen of Derry County, and went on to Cork where he

Charles Carroll Good (1835–94), Brant Militia, probably late 1850s

stayed with his Uncle Jonathan for almost three months. He wrote of his uncle's kindness to him, but there is no reference to a new aunt. Jonathan had apparently not yet married his second wife, Mary Anne, though years later she mentioned having met Charles when he was in Ireland. Jonathan must have been a lonely man in the few years between the death of his sister, Anne, and his second marriage. No wonder he was delighted to have his nephew with him and to show him the places Allen and Eliza remembered fondly. Of course, Charles was taken to the old farm, Ballinvorosig.

Charles found a good deal of war fever in Cork. A few weeks before, a United States ship had halted a British ship, the *Trent,* and removed from it Confederate States commissioners to England and France, James Mason and John Slidell. They were being held as prisoners of war at Fort Warren in Boston Harbor, and relations between Britain and the United States were strained. Charles wrote: "The great Question here now is the prospect of war with America and people are anxiously awaiting a reply to the demand made by the British for an apology and the release of Sliddel and Mason. I called to see George Strobridge but he is absent at Youghal target shooting. He will be back in a few days. The 12th Reg't to which he belongs is under orders to proceed to Canada and expect to leave in a few days so it is quite possible I may miss seeing him. If war breaks out with the U.S. I shall proceed to Canada with all convenient speed."

Three days after Christmas, Charles wrote his mother, chiefly about the old family friends he was seeing. He said, "I have about two invitations per day to dine and spend the evening." He reported also that he had seen a steamer leaving for Canada with 580 troops and 23 officers of the Seventeenth Regiment. Their band played "Dixie's Land." (Eventually the British government sent 14,000 men to Canada.)

By January 8, 1862, Charles was able to write Anne that he had "at last received a favorable answer to my demands for your and Fanny's money. . . . It will however probably be necessary for you to sign a release . . . as I fear Mr. Martin does not consider my power of attorney sufficient." He reported having seen two more transports in Queenstown Harbor waiting to embark troops for Canada, but a postscript reads, "We have just received news here that Mason and Sliddel are surrendered which has relieved the public mind from a great deal of anxiety. . . . If there is no war I may not be home for 3 months yet." (It was President Lincoln who averted war, by acknowledging that Mason and Slidell should never have been seized.)

A few weeks later, Charles wrote his father about changes in Cork, railways, steamship lines, new bridges, and so forth. He had been out to Blarney Castle, whose "romantic appearance" delighted him, "and thro' the Castle from top to bottom and kissed the Blarney Stone." He asked how the insurance business went, if Tom was proving useful in the office, if his father wanted him, Charles, back in the office, and if so, whether he might expect an increase in salary? If not, he said, "I shall try what I can do in Liverpool or London as soon as I send the girls their money, which I will get as soon as the release sent by mail is returned." He was astonished at the mild winter, no frost or snow yet, February like April in Canada.

A month later Charles wrote his father again. He was in Dublin, which he called "a beautiful city and every way superior to Cork." He had decided to return to Canada as soon as he finished his business in Ireland, and expected that would be by mid-April. He wrote also, "I see from the papers that there is a great emigration to British Columbia. There are several persons going from Cork."

Before Charles returned, John joined the migration to British Columbia. He sold his beloved stock, which brought him $650, worth over $3,000 in our money. This gave him funds for his journey and for investments in the west. Gold had been discovered in the Cariboo Mountains, and John Good, who had dreamed of Australian goldfields, set off on April 8, 1862, to seek his fortune closer than Australia, but still a long, rough way from home. He had to travel via New York, Panama, San Francisco, and Victoria. Charles's voyage to Ireland seemed short in comparison; Anne wrote that the family hated to send John off on such a "fearful journey."

John wrote briefly from New York. He had had a long train ride and was very tired when he arrived in the metropolis of America. New York was more than four times as big as it had been when the Allen Goods were there twenty-five years earlier, and in a few years would reach its first million in population. John was amazed: "The stir of this place would make anyone forget they were tired. I never saw anything like it in my life, the number of people that are on the go from daylight till dark and everyone in a hurry."

His next letter came from San Francisco. It had taken him over three weeks to get there, along with twelve hundred others, "most of them from Canada going to British Columbia to dig for gold." They had had a few hours of a Sunday morning in Aspinwall (now Colon) before taking a train across the Isthmus of Panama, and John was shocked. "There they don't know what Sunday is. . . . The shops were all open and all sorts of business going on. The people are nearly all black, some with clothes and some with none." He liked San Francisco better, though about a tenth of the inhabitants were "Chinees, the strangest looking people I ever saw."

A few days later John left for the crowded little town of Victoria, where he and his Brantford friends could not find clean and comfortable lodgings at first. Rather hastily he invested some of his precious funds in renting and furnishing a hotel, which he left in charge of his partner about a month later to try his luck in the Cariboo. He was already having doubts about his whole venture. He wrote: "A person coming out here wants plenty of brass in his face and gold in his pocket; if he has both he can make money very fast. . . . If I was at home and knew as much as I do now about this country no one would hear me say I was going to Victoria I can assure you."

Meantime, Charles had come home the end of May, just before Bella, an energetic sixteen-year-old, left to spend several months with her sister Fanny, who was expecting a baby. Anne wrote in her journal, "I shall miss [Bella] a great deal as she is becoming a very companionable nice girl, but as Charles is home, I can get on better."

Why had Charles given up his plan to seek employment in England? Letters which must have passed between him and a bright-eyed, sweet-faced Brantford girl, Kate Hardy, may have had a good deal to do with it. Two days after Charles's return he told the family that he was engaged to Kate. Although he went back to the insurance office, he could not afford a house; he and Kate would board at the Mallochs'. Young Tom worked on the farm and went to town occasionally to "train in the cavalry," and Bella reported from Homewood. She wrote her "darling Annie," that she was having a very happy and busy time. "Fanny is sitting near me mending Andrew's stockings, and making me laugh so hard that I can hardly write a bit." Andrew had taken her and Fanny to see a Cyclorama of Ireland, "the same that was in

Mrs. Charles Carroll Good née Katherine Hardy

Brantford"; Andrew had taken her across the river to see friends in Ogdensburg; many people had called on them. "I declare, Annie, they are the jolliest set of people down here that ever you saw. . . . Andrew keeps me in a fit the whole time he is in the house. . . . You never saw such a house as this for good eating." She thanked Anne for sending her off with money in pocket, and said Charlie had given her five dollars besides, so that she felt quite rich.

As the time for the baby's birth drew near, Eliza senior entrusted Myrtleville to Anne's capable hands, and joined her daughters at Homewood. Her husband wrote her on July 27: "We were in expectation of hearing from you. Your last letter was dated on the day of your arrival. You know as well as I can tell you that we feel anxious about you, Fanny, and all the family—for goodness sake do write at all events twice in the week. Never mind postage, we will pay that on arrival of your letters. . . . Our wheat field on John's farm will be cut about noon tomorrow—we then begin at the wheat behind the house." On July 29, 1862, Harold Jones was born, and his grandmother wrote that all was going very well. She would return the week of August 10, going first to Mrs. Malloch's in Brockville, then "in the cars to Port Hope [on Lake Ontario] and . . . on the boat to Hamilton." She signed herself, as she regularly did in letters to Allen, "Ever your fond and faithful wife, Eliza Good."

Fanny and Bella and baby Harold came to Myrtleville early in September and Fanny and her son stayed until after Charles's wedding on September 23. Anne described it in her journal: "The ceremony was performed by the Rev'd Abraham Nelles in the absence of Mr. Usher. The Bridal party looked very nice, the Bride in pure white tarlatan with wreath & veil. The Bridesmaids, who were Louise Hardy, Maria Smith & Josephine Strobridge had white dresses trimmed with crimson silk. Charles was accompanied to the altar by Christopher Curtis, George H. Wilkes & Tommy Good. About 11 o'clock Mama, Papa, Charlotte, George, Tommy and I went to Mr. Hardy's house where about 25 persons partook of a very nice cold dinner or Dejeuner. At one o'clock the bride and bridegroom left in the cars for Niagara Falls. We all went to the Station to see them off. The day was as fine as possible, so if it is a good omen to have the sun shine on them, they have had it to perfection." Anne also said, "I have had a very busy season but not an unhappy one. I know I have been usefully employed & have had but few temptations." It seems that the family misfortunes had worked for Anne's good; it is an old observation that human beings need to be needed.

The day before Charles's wedding, John wrote from Victoria. His trip to the Cariboo goldfield had been a complete failure. He said that over eleven thousand men had gone there during the season, but no new claims had been discovered, and now hundreds of disappointed prospectors were leaving Victoria every week on the steamers for San Francisco. He was "very sorry for ever leaving my comfortable home and family and would have gone back before now but have been trying to take home as much money as I brought away, [$650], but I think it will be more than I can do." He said that good land in British Columbia seemed to be all taken up by earlier settlers and the Hudson's Bay Company, except for areas where the Indians were hostile.

A couple of months later, John had little more than one hundred dollars in pocket. He had been working intermittently at odd jobs, mostly for a dollar a day plus board, and was lucky at that. As he wrote, "There are plenty of young men glad to work for their board in this place and cannot get it." It would take him about one hundred fifty dollars to get home; he swallowed his pride and asked his father for a loan, if he could spare "one or two hundred dollars without much trouble." Unfortunately, Allen was still heavily in debt, the sheriff was at his heels, and John had to continue the struggle to earn enough to take him back East.

At the end of 1862, Anne left Myrtleville to spend some months with Fanny Jones who had been recovering her strength very slowly after Harold's birth. Anne passed much of her time at Homewood "minding the baby and sewing." Charles wrote her that he was very busy serving as one of the auditors of the town accounts, keeping Dr. Digby's books, and also having plenty to do in the insurance office. He and his wife were still living at the Mallochs', and, he said, "Kate and I got on first-rate at house-keeping during Charlotte's absence [in Brockville]." He reported, "There is a good deal of excitement here about military affairs. Since New Year's there has been an infantry company formed in Mount Pleasant, one in Cainsville, and one in Brantford. . . . The officers of Cols. Wilkes' and Bunnell's Battallions drill regularly under

Sergeant Chinner of the Coldstream Guards every Monday and Wednesday evenings. George and I attend punctually as possible & so does Tom. There was a statement in the Hamilton Times that Joe Kerby was executed as a Spy at Richmond, Va. but it is not generally credited, altho' the letter conveying the intelligence to some person in Hamilton was from one who said he was at the execution. The Family at Myrtleville is very small now [there were only *five* of the children there] and Papa often complains about all his children leaving him. I wish Johnnie was home again—he would probably do well and be contented in Canada after all his experience of the hardships of a foreign country."

Anne came home from Maitland in June 1863 to find that the Gore District Mutual Fire Insurance Company had just been reorganized and placed under new management in Galt. Allen Good, its secretary for sixteen years, and his son and assistant, Charles, lost their positions with the insurance company. It was an awkward time for Charles, whose son, Arthur Carroll, was born the following month. Seeking employment, the young family moved to Buffalo in September. Charlie took a poorly paid job with the Erie Railroad at the Ohio Street Freight Office, where he worked six days a week from 8 A.M., to 6 P.M.

The closing of the insurance office in Brantford was inconvenient for Charles; it was a long step toward disaster for his father. There was no more salary; the trickle of money from Ireland had dried up; and by autumn the sheriff could be held off no longer. There was a forced sale at Myrtleville on November 9, 1863. Anne rescued the family. She bought enough equipment and stock to keep a small farm going, including three horses—Larry, Jack, and Kate—and "one brown cow." The Goods longed for John to come home as they could not afford to hire help; in fact, they still owed a good deal of wages. John had made it as far as San Francisco. He had hoped to go to New York by "steerage," which was much cheaper than "second cabin," but after trying that mode of transportation in a grueling eight-day voyage from Victoria, he decided otherwise. He wrote, "I would not go steerage to New York if I never went home, for they treat men as if they were so many pigs."

John's friend, William Sinon, formerly of Brantford, was very kind to him in San Francisco, and finally managed to get him a job as a guard at San Quentin State Prison. (The captain of the guard there was son of a former Brantfordite.) Unfortunately, the wages of fifty dollars per month were paid irregularly in script which brought only sixty cents on the dollar. After six or seven months, John left to drive horsecars in the city. It was a hard job; he was on his feet fifteen to sixteen hours a day, but at least his two and a half dollars per day was paid in full, and he was able at last to help by sending home a check on Wells Fargo and Company for fifty dollars.

The collapse of Myrtleville brought changes in the neighborhood. The farm on which John had lived was bought by a young Scotsman, Thomas Carlyle, nephew of the well-known writer of the same name. The little schoolhouse, where Anne had held Sunday School for so long, and where ministers from Brantford had often come to preach to the countryfolk, was converted into a dwelling house. The teacher of the local school, Mr. Greenaway, lived there with his wife and son. On New Year's Eve, Anne wrote in her journal: "This, like all the years of my life, has been one of mixed troubles & pleasures. I have very many mercies for which to be thankful, almost uninterrupted health of body & peace of mind. . . . We are now reduced almost to poverty & do not know whether we will be allowed to remain in our old home. If it would at all comport with the will of our Heavenly Father, I should wish it very much, at least so long as Mama & Papa live. I intend to do all in my power toward that end . . . so now, on the last night of the year may I close with the words at the heading of Jay's exercise, 'Thank God & take courage.' "

The year 1864 was one to try the courage of the Goods. The head of the family was insolvent. This must have been bitter for a man who had been a promising young business leader in Cork and Montreal, and a prominent farmer and businessman in Canada West. He was almost sixty-five, and feeling old and tired; he was reduced to the minor position of county auditor and small farmer of about twenty acres of land belonging to his wife and fifty acres belonging to his daughter. Anne had been able to negotiate purchase of the buildings of Myrtleville and land around them, though she had to borrow heavily from the bank. Young Tom was his father's and sister's right-hand man. Eliza senior contributed more than the skilful management of the house. Her account book records payments by friends and relatives for various kinds of needlework. Working together, the family kept their handsome house, their fine furniture and silver, and their much loved books.

Allen Good wrote to John asking if he thought two of the girls might profit by joining him at San Francisco. John wrote back, "My advice is not to come, as there are more girls here than can get employment, and I would not wish to have any ladies that I care for out here unless they were married before they came, as it is a very bad place, and the society is of the very worst." San Francisco was now larger than Toronto, but it had been a small village until the discovery of Californian gold sixteen years earlier. The rough, tough, frontier heritage of the city still dominated it.

The girls were away from home much of the time, anyway. Bella spent most of the year with Fanny. Mary was in Brantford a great deal, helping Charlotte, whose husband had a long and painful siege of "inflammatory rheumatism," probably rheumatic fever or rheumatoid arthritis, either of them a serious illness. Young Eliza also was away a good deal. One of her absences seems to have been unsanctioned by her parents. Charles wrote his mother, "I am sorry Eliza has left home, but she will probably learn wisdom from being a while amongst strangers. She will act as she pleases." There was one piece of happy news for Myrtleville the summer of 1864. Fanny Jones had another fine son born, named Allen Arthur.

Charles's letters were very welcome. They were less frequent than those from the homesick and discouraged John, but certainly more cheerful reading. On April 8, 1864, Charles wrote his mother a somewhat belated birthday letter. He apologized for not having answered various letters from home, but "I am so busy days & at night I sometimes feel tired of the Pen." He was still dubious about the North's chances of military success. "The South seem as determined as ever to maintain their idea of a separate Government and altho' the power of the North is tremendous yet it is doubtful if they can now conquer the South. The Presidential Election will take place next Nov'r. Abraham Lincoln will be a candidate for re-election and if elected the war will last four years more in all probability—But enough of Politics. As I am not a citizen here, I discuss Politics very little." There was a postscript: "Kate desires me to mention that your little grandson has cut a tooth."

In November, Charles wrote that he hoped to be able to spend Christmas at Myrtleville. He sent thanks for the apples from the farm and wrote: "I am still in the R.R. office at $50.00 per month. It is miserable pay but I cannot do better. If this cruel war was over & prices resumed their figures of 3 years ago, I could live pretty comfortably on my salary, but at present it requires the exercise of a rigid economy to make both ends meet. We find keeping house much cheaper than Boarding. . . . There are rumors of propositions of Peace just now and I sincerely hope they are well founded. Mr. Lincoln is re-elected and the Southerners are no doubt satisfied that the conflict will last 4 years more if they do not submit to a return to the union. In spite of Political feelings, the Election passed off as quietly in this city & State as it would in Brantford."

Charlie was not able to get to Brantford at Christmas; but the long-absent John returned just in time for the celebration. He had been gone for over two and a half years; he was thirty-one now, thinner than he had been, and with a receding hairline. He had acquired a bushy mustache, and his little side-whiskers had grown long. Beards were fashionable again. Anne confided to her journal her suspicion that John's sojourn in the United States was a loss morally as well as financially. "I fear . . . he has gained no good from his contact with the ungodly inhabitants of that country." Many Canadians assumed, rather smugly, that there was a higher proportion of wickedness in the United States than in British North America.

John did not stay home long; he spent the first four months of 1865 in camp with the Canadian Volunteer forces at Sarnia, on the St. Clair River across from Michigan. In the two and a half years after the release of Mason and Slidell, Canada's acute anxiety about United States intentions had subsided into chronic uneasiness. Then on October 19, 1864, a small group of Confederate soldiers, operating secretly from Canada East, made an ineffectual raid on St. Albans, Vermont. The Northern states were furious, and their politicians and newspapers roared threats against Canada. It was obvious by this time that the North had virtually won the Civil War and would soon be able to turn its attention to British North America. There was a surge of military activity in Canada and John Good was among those sent to guard the border. He found his months in camp very dull. He wrote his mother on March 16: "We are all tired and sick of being soldiers already. . . . Tell Tom to do as well as he can till I get back which I trust will be in the first week in May. I wish you would find out if Dr. Cook would rent the front field and how much he would rent it for."

Meantime, President Lincoln was calm about the St. Albans raid, as he had been about the Trent affair. The dreaded invasion of Canada did not come and the most important long-term result of the raid was impetus given to a plan of union for British North America. Before the Brantford volunteers returned home in May, the shocking news came of President Lincoln's assassination. The little four-page newspapers of Brantford normally came out once or twice a week with small, quiet headlines. But on the day after Lincoln was shot there were "extras." The *Expositor* headlined in heavy black letters: "Terrible Times in Washington The President Shot! Secretary Seward Murdered!" An editorial was headed, "A Great Crime and a Great Calamity." Lincoln had been widely admired, and Brantford was one of the places where there were large public memorial services honoring him. (Incidentally, Secretary Seward was not murdered; he recovered from his wounds.)

6

Myrtleville Regroups and Recovers

With the passing of winter, prospects looked brighter at Myrtleville. On April 20, 1865, Anne signed a lease for 102 acres of
"lot No. 26 in the second concession" of the Township of
Brantford. She rented it from Dr. Cook of Mount Pleasant,
and was to pay him $50.00 at the expiration of the lease the
following November 15. This land passed into the possession
of James Randall, and on July 26, 1865, John Good signed a
contract to buy the same 102 acres of "lot No. 26" from James
Randall. He was to pay $2,000.00 in the following manner: in-
terest at 8 percent in July 1866 and July 1867, then payments
of $285.72 per annum for seven years, plus interest on unpaid
amount. John's land adjoined Anne's 50 acres and was, of
course, part of old Myrtleville. It was the second step in the recovery of the farm.

Charlie's prospects were improving, too. He had written on
March 4 that he had left the railroad office and was working
as "an assistant Bookkeeper with a Mr. W. H. Glenny, an extensive Wholesale and Retail dealer in Crockery & Glass at 162
Main St. My present salary is not much better than with the
Railway Co. but my prospects are much better. . . . Kate went
yesterday to an afternoon exhibition of 'Cinderella' at the
Theatre. This Play is having a great run here and is a most
exquisite piece of work. The Good Fairy turns the mice into
horses and the Pumpkin into a coach with a wave of her
Wand, and at one time there appear upwards of 50 Automa-
ton Birds flying about the Stage all warbling melodiously. . . .
I was very glad to hear that Papa had got Books to Audit.

99

Every little money no doubt is very acceptable to you at present. . . . I have no doubt from what [John] told me that he will be at home this summer. Tom is a fine fellow & much to be praised for his conduct. I hope I may be able to contribute my mite towards assisting you before the end of another year." All of Allen Good's children were haunted by the fear of losing Myrtleville. They helped in various ways; for instance, Charlotte and Fanny a number of times sent money in spring to buy seed grain.

The same month that John came home to farm, George and Charlotte Malloch left Brantford and moved, more than a hundred miles, to the village of Paisley, a Scottish settlement in the Bruce peninsula between Lake Huron and Georgian Bay. It was a much newer community than Brantford, and could not yet be reached by train. The family at Myrtleville missed the Mallochs greatly. They lost Bella again for a while, too. Anne wrote in her journal: "Fanny sent me a present of $40 . . . & money to take Isabella to Maitland. I am sure I feel very grateful for the money. . . . John is at home now, but does not seem at all settled. Tom is working steadily. I do not know how I would get on without him. . . . Mary and Clara continue to go to school, Mary to the High School [in] Brantford, Clara to Mr. Greenaway [at the local public school on the Paris road]."

Now there came another crisis with the rebellious young Eliza. She decided to marry George Laird. The Goods had known him for several years, as he had worked in George Malloch's Brantford office. Eliza's parents knew him well enough to be quite sure that in spite of the gentleman's undeniable good looks and charm, they did not want him for a son-in-law. No record of their specific objections has survived, but whatever they were, Eliza refused to listen. She married on December 4, 1865, and a friend wrote Eliza senior, "I hope the poor deluded Child may not suffer for her disobedience."

John was planning marriage too, in his case with the full approval of the family. He was engaged to Mary Moir of Elora, and he carried her picture with him when he went to visit the Mallochs. Nine-year-old Lilly wrote her uncle Tom, "Do you think [Miss Moir] will be a nice Aunt? I think she will be by her picture."

John Good (1833–68), Canadian Volunteer Forces, 1865

Meantime, Lilly's aunt, Mary Good, age eighteen, was visiting the Mallochs. She was the sister who had written lively little letters to Tom when he was away at school and she was only seven years old. Now she wrote Tom again.

Paisley, March 4th/66

My dearest brother Tom,

I take up my pen to let ye ken that the weather is cold, oh so cold. . . . Do you still go *skiving* [italics mine] on Sunday? I suppose you have been very busy drawing wood since I left, as there was no good sleighing before. . . . When is Johnny to be married? Tell him to come up here for his wedding tour. There has been a great deal of wheat going through here to Southampton [on Lake Huron] lately, it (Southampton) has a very good wheat market, I believe. There is no market here, it is very inconvenient not to have one as some days we cannot get any meat in the village. Fresh eggs are just coming in, they are 15 cts. per dozen. Butter is 15 cts. per lb. & it is very hard to get good even at that price. There was division court here last Monday, it made a little stir in the village.

(What does *skiving* mean? Certainly not the dictionary meaning, which is to cut leather thinly. Could she possibly mean *skiing*? The *Encyclopedia Britannica* says that skis were an accepted mode of winter travel in mining camps of the West in the middle of the nineteenth century, and that there were skiing clubs in Plumas and Sierra counties of California in the 1850s and 1860s. Of course, skiing did not become a popular sport in America until the twentieth century, but John Good might have learned about skiing in the West, and his young brother might have been amused by trying skis instead of the usual Canadian snowshoes. I remember using snowshoes at Myrtleville. They were fun.)

Young Eliza and her husband had gone to live in Rouseville, Venango County, Pennsylvania, where George Laird was drilling for oil. Rouseville is near Titusville, where the petroleum industry really began in 1859, although there had been a small oil field near Sarnia in Canada West developed slightly earlier. There was a good deal of talk about oil everywhere; in fact, Charlotte Malloch wrote her father on May 31, 1866: "George [her husband] had a letter from old Rawlings this week and he told him that you had good signs of Coal Oil on the farm. You did not say anything about it so I hope it is not a mistake. If you could only strike ile as the Yankees say you might all get rich fast." No oil was found at Myrtleville, but soon the Goods bought oil, gave up making candles, and for almost fifty years used "coal oil lamps" for illumination.

John's wedding took place on March 28, 1866, and he and his bride set up housekeeping in the empty north wing of Myrtleville House. About two months later, the neighborhood was startled by a Fenian raid on Fort Erie. John and Tom Good probably did not join their friends who marched against the Fenians. They were very busy on the farm, and John was not likely to go "volunteering" again, unless there was acute danger.

The Fenian Brotherhood was now eight years old. It had been organized in New York by Irishmen who were violently anti-British. They took advantage of American indignation about the St. Albans raid to mount a much more serious attack in the opposite direction. During the night of May 31, 1866, about a thousand Fenians crossed the Niagara River from Buffalo and took possession of Fort Erie. The invaders fought off some volunteer troops, but most of them prudently withdrew across the border before the regulars arrived. American authorities now arrested some Fenian leaders, and seized Fenian weapons. Brantford's companies returned without having been actively engaged, but they did see service as escorts and guards for about sixty-five prisoners who were jammed into the county jail at Brantford. Part of the aftermath of the Fenian scare in Brantford was the welcome gaiety brought by hundreds of regular soldiers quartered in and around the Kerby House in 1866 and 1867. The Seventh Royal Fusiliers, in residence from October to March, had a fine band of thirty-eight pieces, which used to give concerts in Victoria Park. Each evening the bugle band played a tattoo in the Market Square.

After the Fenian danger lessened in the summer of 1866, Eliza Good went to Buffalo to visit Charlie and Kate. Charlie had been getting a salary of one thousand dollars a year since February, a great deal more than the fifty dollars per month he had made at the railroad office. Eliza enjoyed seeing more of three-year-old Arthur. He was a bright child; six months earlier, his father had written Eliza, "He often speaks of you and talks of going back to Canada. [Canada to him meant Brantford, where all his doting grandparents lived.] . . .

Please excuse my writing so much about him, but he is a very smart boy." Arthur's grandmother soon tired of city life, however. She wrote Anne, "I long for the country. I have nearly finished my jobs of work and got Kate quite clever at knitting socks and stockings."

John's and Tom's hard work that summer was not very successful financially. Allen Good wrote George Malloch in November that he had been "obliged to assist John in making first payment to Mr. Randall—he had just finished thrashing his barley which turned out rather poorly."

In the early winter Eliza Laird came home for a long visit with her tiny son, Robert Allen. George Laird's plans were unsettled, and the Goods worried about Eliza's future. The worst blow, however, was that Tom left home. Even the "steady" Tom had lost patience with his father, or John, or both. He went to Charlie's, in Buffalo, and Mary wrote him on December 18: "We get on badly without you. . . . The Upper Pump broke last Thursday and is not mended yet, and will not be until next Thursday. . . . None of us like Benjamin [a hired man] very well, he is such a goose, or gander I should say. Laird has not come yet & there has been no word from him. . . . Now, my dear Tom, you will think this is nothing but a letter of complaints but they are all true, though with all our troubles we are still surviving. . . . We have the Heater up in the hall now and it makes the house very comfortable. . . . Johnny has a very bad cough. The pigs are not killed yet." She added a postscript: "Dada says to tell Tom for goodness sake to come home and he will try to make it all smooth again. You better not come until you hear more about it, that is if you have a good situation, at least that is my advice to you."

Fanny had written to Tom as soon as she heard of the threat of his leaving home, but her letter did not arrive until after he had gone. She wrote: "I am sure that you will be very much surprised at receiving a letter from me, as it is such an age since I have written to you, but I thought perhaps you would like to hear from "Whan" once more. . . . I received Annie's letter . . . I am sorry that you thought of leaving her as she felt badly about it. I hope sincerely that you will not do so, as she depends so much on you. . . . If you could manage it I would be delighted to have you come down to see me and stay with us for a few weeks. Andrew . . . likes you very much and is always talking about you, because you are so steady. . . . We had our hog killing last week, we killed six enormous pigs. Andrew is going to commence wood drawing again as soon as the sleighing is good enough. . . . Harold and Allen are quite well but Baby [Lucia, born October, 1866] has a bad cold. . . . I would like to be at home for Christmas, would not we have fun, it is just a year today since I left home the last time."

Anne forwarded Fanny's letter to Tom, enclosing it in one of hers written Christmas Eve. She said: "I hope you will write soon and let me know what you are doing and when you are coming home. Let me know soon so that I may hire Benjamin for another month if necessary. He gets on pretty well. We had the pigs killed on Saturday, and John sold his colt for eighty dollars to the man he bought it from so he had the mare for nothing. . . . If you cannot find anything pretty good to do I hope you will be back soon, but I will not urge you to do so for you are the best judge. We have not heard from Ireland yet. [Probably in response to Isabella's application for her inheritance, since she was now twenty-one.] Eliza is still with us. Laird wrote about a week ago, & says he has been very sick & cannot come till the beginning of next month. The Mallochs cannot come for some time if at all this winter. So we will have a quiet Christmas. . . . I spent all last week in town & it did me good. All here send love to you, Charles & Kate."

Tom found work not in Buffalo, but as a laborer in Hume, New York, about forty miles southeast of Buffalo. Anne wrote him in January 1867: "I am much obliged for the $5 Greenback & will return you its value when you come home and beg you will not think of sending any more. Now, Tommy, I want you to come home just as soon as your month is up, or before it if your employer will let you off. If you were in an easy or lucrative employment I should try to get on without you for the winter but as it is I can see no use in your working so fearfully hard at such small wages. I give you the same offer I did before, $12 per month for this year, and I owe you nearly $100 as I promised you the $12 since the first of March and I will pay you when I can so that you need not think that you will lose your time. . . . It will be far better for me to have you home for I cannot see how things are conducted at the barn. I think John is doing things pretty well but Papa & Mama are fretting the whole time about your being away." Tom apparently returned to Myrtleville before the end of the winter. Eliza and George Laird went back to Pennsylvania. On April 22, 1867, James Allen, son of John Good and Mary Moir, was born at Myrtleville. It was a season of hope again.

Allen Good was planning a trip to Paisley. The list of places through which he was to drive is interesting to those who know the district. He would go by Glenmorris, Galt, Preston, Cambridge, Breslau, Bloomingdale, Winterbourne, Greenbush, Elora, Alma, Rothsay, Teviotdale, Harriston, Clifford, Balaklava, Rees Tavern, Johnson's Corner, Dunkeld Tavern, Wardshill Tavern, Hopper Tavern, Paisley. Total distance: 108 miles; projected time: two and a half days. Some of the places Allen listed have disappeared, but a hundred years later, the trip from Paisley to Myrtleville over much the same route took little more than two and a half hours by automobile.

Canadians were still worrying about the Fenians, although that Irish group never did much damage after the Fort Erie raid. The Fenian organization had not been suppressed by the United States; in fact, it was probably given tacit encouragement. And following the St. Albans raid, an angry American Congress had served notice on Canada that the Reciprocity Treaty would end in 1866. Threats of invasion, added to loss of markets, drove the British provinces together, and the home government was eager for anything which held out hope that the colonies might defend themselves. At the beginning of 1867, the Imperial Parliament passed the British North America Act, and on July 1, the Dominion of Canada came into being, made up of four provinces, Ontario, Quebec, New Brunswick, and Nova Scotia. It was named Dominion by optimistic Fathers of Confederation, who looked at the map and thought of the seventy-second Psalm: "He shall have dominion from sea to sea, and from the river unto the ends of the earth." The birth of the Canadian federation was celebrated in Brantford with "ringing of bells and discharge of firearms." The militia were reviewed on "Sandy Hill" (Terrace

Mrs. John Good née Mary Moir, with her sons James and John, 1869

Hill), and militia and others marched in a procession to the Market Square, where the royal proclamation was read. After meetings in the town hall and Victoria Square, the great day ended with a concert in Ker's Music Hall.

As the year's (1867) summer work at Myrtleville and Homewood drew to a close, Fanny Jones wrote: "We have been drying apples and making pickles, etc., for winter. Margaret [Andrew's unmarried sister] and I, with only a little help, have peeled and hung up about twenty bushels of apples since I wrote home last. . . . Andrew is busy gathering the apples, he has just finished digging the potatoes. . . . He is husking corn tonight in the barn. . . . The boys are well, and have a great time helping their papa pick apples." Tom wrote to Charlie about chances of work in Buffalo. Charlie answered: "If you would take my advice you would not come to this side. . . . Why do you not try your hand at Scientific farming—scarcely a day passes I do not read in the papers here of instances of individual success in various kinds of Farming & Gardening. . . . If I had a small Capital I would invest it in a small piece of land near Brantford. . . . I intend to try something else as soon as I get a chance to do so if I see the prospects are better than I am now doing. . . . A small piece of land thoroughly manured and worked will produce more than 3 times that which is half worked. . . . I shall try to find you a situation in the City if possible. . . . If you wish to get into an office you should practice writing evenings so as to keep your hand in."

Tom returned to Buffalo in the fall of 1867. He worked for Harvey and Allen, Produce Commission Merchants. Mr. Allen was of a Cork family, and probably a distant relative of the Goods. Unfortunately, soon after Tom left Myrtleville, John became very ill. Anne had to take over the management of the farm. She wrote Tom on October 16.

"I am sorry to tell you that John proves to be much more seriously ill than we were led to suppose. On Monday week he commenced coughing severely and ever since it has continued. At each fit of coughing he spits up large quantities of the most dreadful phlegm or rather yellow matter. . . . He seemed a little better two days ago but yesterday (last night) & today a fresh abscess (for such they are) has burst on his lungs and he is therefore worse. Dr. Tufford . . . seems to understand his case at last. He hopes he may yet recover as his strength remains pretty good considering his long illness, but should fresh abscesses continue to form or if the disease touches the right lung he can give him no further hopes. In any case he does not expect the present ones to heal before the 1st of Decr. & he will probably be unable to do any work during the winter if he recovers which I think is very doubtful. . . . We did not thrash till last week. Tom Brown [a neighbor] did it for us. They thrashed mine on Monday and Tuesday. We had 155 fall wheat, 20 spring, 148 Barley, 160 oats. . . . Wednesday was the Agricultural Show in Paris. They all went to it. It took them Thursday and Friday to finish John's grain, he had 175 bush. wheat, 88 barley, 104 oats. . . . On Saturday they thrashed Papa's peas. . . . On Monday Isaac [Connor] took them to town in the morning then Norman, Jack, & I cleaned up a load of Barley of John's which he took to Paris in the afternoon. . . . Today the boys are all thrashing at T. Brown's, two were there yesterday in return for his man who was here all last week. Mr. Usher [Rector of Grace Church] was up to see John yesterday. I drove him in after dinner and met Bella who was just from the Station. I called for her trunk and after some business in town came home."

Less than a week later, Mrs. Charlie Good's lawyer brother, Arthur Hardy, who had served as a groomsman with John at Fanny's wedding, came to Myrtleville from Brantford. He drew a will, providing that Anne should be executrix of John's estate, that she should sell his possessions, real and personal, pay five hundred dollars to his widow, and hold the rest in trust for his son, James Allen Good, until he reached twenty-one. In the emergency, seventeen-year-old Clara, the youngest, left the high school in Brantford and stayed home to help with the work. She missed school very much. Mary wrote Tom on November 4, after John had been ill for about a month: "I received your letter this evening and was delighted to hear from you as it is so long since I had a letter from anybody; I am much, very much obliged for the money which I assure you was very acceptable. I am sorry to tell you that John is no better but rather worse than when you last heard, he coughs nearly every night and Mama sits up with him. Annie sat up last night but Mama generally does as he

likes her to be with him better than any other person. Dr. Tufford comes nearly every day. . . . We have all the apples and
carrots in but have not commenced our turnips nor have we
our potatoes taken out of the small pits. Norman was topping
John's turnips today. I am glad Kate has her house so nice,
write me an account of the party."

On November 11, Fanny wrote an affectionate letter to
Tom, full of advice from a settled older sister: "You cannot
tell how delighted I was to receive your nice letter. . . . I am
very glad indeed that you have got such a good situation, and
I hope sincerely that you will be able to keep it and gain by
your good behavior and steadiness at your business the good
opinion and good will of your employers, and in the course of
time I have no doubt that you will be promoted. . . . I was not
angry with you when I heard you had gone to the States but I
was sorry, as there are so many wild young men there, but I
am sure, my dear brother, that if you once make up your
mind you will keep out of bad company, and I don't think
being in the States will hurt you any as I know you will be
steady. You must be glad to be earning so much money. I am
sure that the girls at home were very glad when you sent them
the money. . . . My boys are well and Lula [Lucia] too. She is
trying very hard to walk—she takes two or three steps and
then laughs as hard as she can, she is just as sweet as ever."

The following week, Eliza Laird wrote to Tom from Oil
Creek, Pennsylvania: "I had letters from Dada & Clara both
lately, they were all well at Myrtleville, except Johnnie, but
they seemed to think he was a little better. I trust he may recover, & be spared to his young wife and baby. I am very glad
to hear that you have such a good situation, *tell me all about it*
Tom, like a good fellow, & what you think of Buffalo, & the
Yankees. I know for my part I don't like either the place or
the people, as well as Canada, but still I am happy and contented for I believe there is money to be made out here but
not without patience and perseverance. George is quite well, &
busy all the time. We are living very comfortably, & sometimes
putting by a little for a rainy day. I suppose Arty is quite a big
boy by this time, tell him his little tusin Allie is quite well, that
he stands alone & walks six or eight steps alone without fall-
ing, & is altogether a fine boy, so George & I think of course.

. . . There is little or no news here. . . . We live very quietly
. . . & in hopes that we won't spend many years on Oil Creek,
away from all our kith & kin. . . . Are you going home for
Christmas, if so be sure you eat enough of plum pudding &
apples to do for us both."

Anne reported conditions at Myrtleville to Tom a little later:
"I am glad you are pleased with your situation though I miss
you sadly, however we have gotten on very well with the work,
our turnips all put away more than a week ago. We had 28
loads, John 35. The man I had left yesterday, he had not quite
finished his month but he was so saucy I am glad to be rid of
him. Norman is still here. We expect Mr. Tomison's machine
to thrash the peas on Wednesday. I must sell some to make up
the instalment due on the 5 Decr. Tell Charles I bought two
nice jackets for Mary & Clara with his $9.00 so if he gave a
high price for the apples it was all in the family. Your money
they also got. . . . I have told Chas how John is. I fear there is
a poor chance for him—and what a bill for doctors there will
be. He is able to dress & sit in an arm chair in the parlour (his
own). He has not been in this part of the house for nearly 2
months."

But John astonished the family by picking up strength
quickly now. Tom got home from Buffalo for Christmas, and
Myrtleville had its most cheerful season for months. Eliza
Laird, however, was still far away in Pennsylvania, and liking
Oil Creek no better. She wrote Tom: "George began the New
Year at one in the morning by working at putting down a new
well in which he has an interest. He works from midnight . . .
till next day at noon. . . . He takes his breakfast with him. If it
should turn out a good well, it will be a nice thing for us.
George & John Mickeljohn (formerly of Brantford) intend
putting down a well as soon as the spring opens, & if they
have luck . . . I hope our life on Oil Creek will be short. Both
Mr. & Mrs. Mickeljohn & George & I are anxious for the same
thing, to get enough . . . to go back to Canada & buy a nice
farm. . . . I am glad to hear that Annie is getting on so well
. . . and to think the homestead is still safe in the family. I am
thankful no stranger owns it. Now, Tom, my dear boy I want
you to keep me posted in the affairs of home for I know they
will tell you all about them, but they don't tell me a word, &

though I am far away, I don't feel I am one bit less one of the family than Charlotte & Fanny are. . . . I hope fortune will favor us so we will be able to help them a little . . . I am glad Fannie sent them that money. . . . Write to me soon like a good boy. Do you ever think of the days of our childhood? I often do."

Anne wrote another brief report to Tom on January 30: "John, his wife, & baby went to Elora this day week. John is (or was) much better but still suffering from pain in his side & chest. He has driven about a good deal for the last month but is not able to do anything. Norman left the first of the month & John has a little boy of Vince's at $4 per month. Isaac [Connor] is with me, he finished drawing home the wood."

Anne wrote Tom again on February 10, "We have not sold the cattle yet. They are not fattening much but I must sell one of them soon or some sheep as cash is giving out." A week later she wrote a long letter in answer to one from Tom which must have expressed his disappointment in not making more money and his plans for some kind of farming. Her letter is remarkable for a few complaints, because Anne was not a complainer. Perhaps the strain was telling on her.

"I will tell you as well as I can what I think of your farming project. If you can get board near the farm you had better not think of keeping house for it would be a great extra expense, in the first place the plainest furniture including stove etc., would not cost less than $50. Then the firm [presumably Harvey and Allen] would have to advance you provisions for at least four months. . . . If you really think you would like to try the farm for the summer you had better ask Mr. Harvey or Allen in time & if you take my advice either hire yourself and team for so much a month, or make an arrangement for one half or third, they supplying you with seed, implements and board for man & horses. Billy of course is yours and you may take Kitty also. . . . If you do not take her John will keep her driving about all the time as he is doing now & I get neither pay or thanks. . . . With regard to your coming home I think it would be only the old story, you would not be happy, so I must just endeavour to do the best I can though I have very little hope of success, but perhaps by the time I break down, you will have some place where our parents & younger sisters

may stay. . . . I have not said a word of your project to anyone in the house for I know it would not be kept secret. . . . I
hope you will not be so foolish as to marry till you have something to start on." (There was apparently a young lady in
Buffalo in whom Tom was much interested.)

Tom reacted promptly with a letter containing twenty-five
dollars and expressing concern about Anne's breaking down.
She wrote him on March 5, quite in command of herself
again: "I received your letter yesterday containing the twenty-
five dollars for which I feel very much obliged, and will take it
for the present as a loan. . . . You need not fear that I intend
breaking down (if I can help it) or selling the farm either. I
confess that sometimes I am so sinful as to become discouraged & impatient but I shall endeavor to be more hopeful &
contented and all will be well at last. I mean to work very hard
this summer (DV ['Deo volente'—God willing]) and try to get
as much as possible free of the Bank next fall. So now you
need not fret in the least about us at home. . . . If you really
wished to take a farm on shares I wish you would take ours. I
would not want to impose on you more than a stranger, but I
suppose you would not like it. . . . I do not wish you to send
me anything but as a loan for a short time till I make it off the
farm. I am glad Charles' salary is raised & that he has
reengaged, it is far better than running about." Anne's worries
and the family's poverty did not cast too heavy a shadow on
the younger girls. There is an undated letter from Clara to
Tom of this period.

> My dear Brother,
> I am perfectly ashamed of myself for not writing you ere this,
> but forgive me this time and I will try to do better in future.
> About three weeks ago two Miss Joneses, Mr. Edward, his
> brother, and Mr. Burtch spent an evening here. We had a dance
> and enjoyed it very much.
> Mary and I are going to a Quadrille Party Friday evening if
> nothing prevents. The young gentlemen in town have got them
> up.
> I saw a Miss Park's marriage in the paper, she lived in Buf-
> falo, is it your Miss Park or a relative? Please tell me when you
> write, which I hope will be soon. . . .

When are you going to pay us another visit? I hope it will be a little longer next time.

Little Jimmy is growing nicely. You would not know him at all now. Give my love to Charlie and ask him if he remembers that he has a sister Clara.

Tom was still dissatisfied with his prospects at Mr. Allen's. He wrote his brother-in-law, George Laird, in Pennsylvania, and a distant cousin, Henry Tivy, in St. Louis, Missouri. George Laird answered, "I can find nothing that you could get that will pay you better than what you are at. There is no chance here except at the [oil] wells and of course you do not understand that and it would take you some time to learn it." Henry Tivy wrote that business was "very dull" in St. Louis: "What I would advise is for you to stop in your present position until times improve here somewhat, and in the meantime I will keep my eyes open, and if anything should offer that would suit you, I will hasten to let you know. . . . It would give me great pleasure to have you here, and I think that in a short time you would learn to like St. Louis and her people. I have a few warm friends here who would give you a hearty welcome, and make you feel at home in a little time, that is if you are only 'a good rebel' and hate the Yankees sufficiently."

As spring came on, Tom's thoughts turned more and more to farming. He wrote Anne about it on March 22, remarking also about Charlie's hunting for a less expensive house to rent: "I think it is high time for them to move onto some less fashionable street, if ever they intend to lay by any money. . . . Mrs. Allen told me the other day that Isabella was coming over to stay a short time with her. I hope she will as we have got some very nice friends here now. . . . It is quite pleasant now walking in the streets, compared with what it is in the country at this season of the year, but I much prefer living there to being confined to a city life, if I could only make money as fast there as here. I hope to be able in another year or so to go back near home and rent a farm. . . . I hope you are getting on all right on the farm, and have every thing ready to commence the spring work. I suppose you will soon be ploughing now, as I think this will be an early spring and a favorable season for the growing crops. If you want any advice

in the working of the place you will write to me and I will give
you the best I can."

On March 30, Anne wrote a letter which marked a turning
point in her young brother's life.

> My dear Tom,
>   I received your letter some days ago. . . . You seem inclined
> to leave your present situation. Now I want you calmly to con-
> sider what I say. You have seen & experienced both country &
> city life & you had better make your mind up as to which you
> wish to follow. If you like the city best by all means remain in it,
> you may do well & gain a competence or scratch for a living all
> your life. You see what Charlie can save out of his salary. For
> my part I think he would have more if he had taken to farming
> ten years ago, but then it is hard work & farmers have rough
> hands & rough clothes. Now, dear Tom, if you have found a
> better situation or have any good place in view do not let what I
> am about to say influence you to your disadvantage. I want you
> to get on & hope you will not think me quite selfish if I propose
> that if you decide on farming in preference to city life you
> would come home & work the farm for me this summer. If you
> cannot do so of your free consent, do not come. . . . I want if
> possible to make up the money for the Bank this fall. I shall try
> my utmost & want to put in every available spot in crops. If you
> will come & help me I will allow you a liberal recompence. If
> you wish to commence farming next spring, I will divide the
> stock & implements with you & help you as much as I can. If the
> bank is paid I will only have Bella's interest to pay her next year,
> so could afford to help you. . . . [No doubt, Bella had received
> her inheritance from Fanny Carroll and lent it to Anne.] If you
> come home you may expect trials of your temper but I trust you
> have gained too much control of yourself to be vexed by the an-
> noyances of Papa's & sometimes John's doings. If you come we
> must quietly determine to have things our own way. I think we
> could get the field across the road from John at a small rent or,
> what Mama & Papa want, that he would give up his right to it
> instead of the money he owes Mama, as it is almost impossible
> that he can pay her the money. I fear he will not be able to work
> very much as every exertion causes the pain to return in his
> side. Please answer me as soon as you have decided.

Tom answered promptly: "I . . . think I will accept your proposal. . . . I always intended to be a farmer . . . and besides, I would be of some help to you all at home which is some consideration with me. Charley wishes me to go home again, as he thinks you will be getting discouraged and perhaps sell the farm or let it." So Tom came home to stay, and every one was happy about it, except little Arthur in Buffalo who missed his Uncle Tom and kept talking of the jolly times he used to have with him.

Miraculously, as spring came on, John at last seemed well and strong again. He was able to work all summer. His wife was pregnant again, but he made no change in his will, which left most of his estate to his son, James, with reversion to Eliza Good if the boy should fail to reach twenty-one. Probably he felt so well that he simply forgot about the will he had made when he was so sick. Crops were good, and late in October two of John's horses won prizes at the township agricultural fair. The next week, a second son was born to Mary and John. Suddenly things went very wrong. Family tradition says that John died of consumption; at any rate, he collapsed and died unexpectedly at the age of thirty-five, when his baby was nine days old. On November 10, Mr. Usher christened the child John, and the following day buried the father.

7

The New Regime

John's early death caused a painful break in a large, close family. All at Myrtleville grieved, but they had little time to brood over their loss. A friend wrote Eliza Good, "Perhaps the care of the Widow and Orphans are mercies just at this moment, as besides the occupation, there is a happiness in still doing something for those your Darling loved."

On November 24, 1868, John's will was probated, and Anne took up administration of his estate. There were debts, and the question of the land which he had only begun to buy from James Randall. About this time James Randall died too, and John's contract was assigned to Mrs. William Moyle née Martha Randall. Early in 1869 Allen Good wrote William Moyle, an executor of the Randall estate, pointing out that Mr. Randall had excused John from paying principal in 1868, and had said he was perfectly satisfied with interest. Mr. Good now asked if the executors would accept one installment plus interest in 1869, "as it is our wish that the property should remain in our family." It would be hard to raise $731.44 the following summer. Charlie was worrying about Myrtleville, also. He wrote Tom about a month after John's death, "If you buy it [the south half of the lot John owned] I will try and help you with enough at least to pay a man's wages . . . and relieve you of part of the harder & rougher work." Eventually a purchase plan was worked out. Tom contracted to buy John's land. He sold twenty-six acres of it to his neighbor on the north, and gave mortgages to Martha Moyle and to Anne Good as executrix. John's widow, whom the Goods called

"Mary John," stayed on at Myrtleville with her little boys, and received from Anne the interest paid by Tom.

Charlie was never able to contribute substantially to Myrtleville. He became cashier and head bookkeeper for Mr. Glenny's wholesale house, and worked hard to fulfill his responsibilities. His "eight-to-six" day lengthened, from seven in the morning until after six in the evening, and his salary rose, but not to a point where he was able to save much of it. He and Kate had grown up with quite high standards of living, and naturally tried to perpetuate them. They sent little Arthur to a private school, and Kate usually managed to keep a servant. Tom thought they still could have saved money if they had not insisted on living on a "fashionable street."

Late in 1869, a government decision in Toronto brought a small but welcome financial windfall to Myrtleville. The legislature voted funds for an "Ontario Institution for the Education and Instruction of the Blind," popularly known as a "Blind Asylum." The provincial treasurer at that time was Edmund Burke Wood of Brantford. There was a well-situated farm just northwest of Brantford, and Mr. Wood no doubt made sure that it was considered as a location for the new school. About sixty-five acres of it were bought by the province, and the building contractor rented from Tom Good a low-lying field between the Paris Road and the railway. The lease was for eleven months, with permission to take all the clay the renter wished. This clay was used to make bricks for the original school buildings, some of which are still in use. (The one hundredth anniversary of the school, however, was marked by the tearing down of the hilltop Tudor-style main building, the tower of which was a landmark for a century.) Two ponds appeared where the clay was taken, and the larger was one of the Goods' favorite skating places, until both ponds were filled in at the time of some railway construction about 1930.

The new regime at Myrtleville settled down. A surviving diary of Tom's gives a good picture of farm activities in the early 1870s. Tom reported on crops and weather and marketing and carefully distinguished between his produce and Anne's. Many of the farm operations were still like those of pioneer times a generation earlier. In November and December there were turnip-pulling, potato-digging, pig-killing, and

Thomas Allen Good (1843–1904), taken in late 1890s

grain-cleaning. In January and February, Tom and one hired
man cut and hauled and chopped a year's supply of firewood.
The house was kept much more comfortable with stoves instead of fireplaces, but the countryside still provided the fuel.

In March, harnesses were mended, washed, and oiled. In spring, the pork, which had been salted and "pickled" during the winter, was smoked slowly for weeks in the brick smokehouse back of Myrtleville House. Sheep were driven down to the Grand River to be washed, and a few days later they were sheared. The spinning wheel was no longer used; Tom took the wool to a mill for spinning. The machine age had taken over some field crops, too. Hay was cut with a mowing machine rather than a scythe. Grain was sown with a drill and cut with a reaper. Sheaves were still bound by hand, however, and some farm workers boasted that they could toss a sheaf in the air and have another bound by the time it came down.

Tom was an energetic young man; he plowed and seeded, hayed and harvested, repaired buildings, and cut firewood. After working hard all day, he would often make calls in the evening, or go to a Farmers' Club "debate" or a party. He took on outside responsibilities, too. By late 1870, he was one of the ward's three "fence-viewers," who constituted a citizen committee to assess damages caused by neglect of line fences. In 1871, he replaced his father on the vestry of Grace Church. He became active in the local Farmers' Club, and went to various political meetings. It must have been a great relief to Anne to have him firmly established on the farm.

The founding of the Farmers' Club was stimulated by the completion of a substantial brick schoolhouse that replaced the original little frame school at the corner of the Paris Road and the Second Concession. The new building was on the southwest corner, on land donated by William Moyle, and soon after it was finished the men of the neighborhood organized to use it an evening every week or two during the winter. Their Farmers' Club elected William Moyle, president, and Thomas Carlyle, vice-president. The object of the association, they stated, "shall be the diffusion of information respecting agriculture, horticulture, and farming operations generally, also the advancement of the members in intelligence on all matters tending to elevate the mind, with the understanding that sectarian or political matters be not discussed." Allen Good, though elderly and ailing, was greatly interested in the club and wrote an account of its first year. The programs he described were quite varied, ranging from "Will

summer fallowing pay?" (that is, leaving cultivated land un-
seeded to destroy weeds and insects) to "Which is the most admired in women, beauty or virtue?"

Tom's diary recorded much family visiting, and letters from
the absent members of the family. The railway was close to
Paisley by this time, and Bella, Mary, and Clara went to see the
Mallochs at various times. On July 7, 1870, Henry Tivy of St.
Louis, a distant cousin, came to Myrtleville for a few days. He
was casting a more than cousinly eye on Mary Good, and he
traveled from Missouri to the East Coast via Brantford. Tom
wrote in his diary that Henry had purchased a return ticket,
St. Louis to Boston, for forty dollars American. Then Anne
left for Paisley, because Charlotte was sick, but the next day
there was news that she was better. Trains and telegrams were
wonderful helps in family emergencies. Late in July, Mary
John and little Johnny left for a long visit with Moir relatives
in Princeton and Elora. By August 6, Anne was back, accompanied by the Mallochs, who stayed for almost two weeks.

Late in August, George Laird came from Pennsylvania for a
short time. The *Brantford Expositor*'s earlier statement that
Laird had "made his pile in the Oil Regions" was premature,
to say the least. George's ventures had been far from successful. Six weeks after his visit, Anne drove to town and brought
home all the Lairds, Eliza, George, little Allen, and a baby girl,
Bertie. They stayed for about a week, and then went to live in
the village of Burford, George's old home.

George Laird traveled a great deal. He often stayed at Myrtleville overnight, occasionally helping with harvesting and
barn repairs. It is not clear what he did for a living, though he
probably still had hopes of oil; Charlie wrote, "Has George
struck ile yet, or rather salt water?" Whatever his business, Mr.
Laird was certainly unable to provide transportation for his
family; sometimes he borrowed a horse and vehicle to bring
Eliza and the children to Myrtleville.

The rural peace of the neighborhood was shattered several
times the autumn of 1870. On September 23, Tom wrote in
his diary, "Mr. Hogle and Mr. Patton had a quarrel last night,
and Hogle stabbed Patton with a knife in four places and then
ran away. He did not kill him but the doctors say he is very
badly hurt. The constables have not found Hogle yet." Mrs.

Hogle carried on her tavern business nearby, and many people considered her a detriment to the neighborhood. Tom's diary tells of "drunk and disorderly boys . . . making a great noise" in Smith's Lane, on the eastern edge of Myrtleville. Early in 1871 he notes that "Messrs. Carlyle and Sanderson came over here to get a petition written out to prevent Mrs. Hogle getting a tavern license this year. My father drew one and I copied it for them and signed my name to it." There was a strong revulsion against the heavy drinking of pioneer days. (The famous Woman's Christian Temperance Union was founded in 1874.) Temperance Clubs grew up everywhere and Tom Good became an officer of the Paris Road "Sons of Temperance" group. That same autumn of 1870, Mrs. Henry Moyle, friend and neighbor of the Goods, was killed by a runaway horse, leaving a large family, the youngest only a baby. Several of the Myrtleville ladies helped the Moyles until the funeral, and Bella stayed on for some time.

Allen Good suffered a long illness in the following spring. The doctor was very anxious about him, and the Mallochs, the Lairds, and the Charlie Goods made trips to see him. But he revived with warm weather and wrote Charlie that he had been able to stroll around outside, admiring Myrtleville in its spring green. He thought seriously about his end, however, and drafted a document which he addressed "to Miss Anne & to Mr. Thomas Allen Good to be opened as soon after my death as possible." Inside, he addressed it to Anne and Tom and "to all my other children whether married or single."

"My first wish is of course as to the comfort & support of my wife. . . . She will have in her own right two lots of Land containing about 20 Acres. . . . Now she cannot attend to the work of cultivating these lands herself, and the better way would be for Tommy to give her some allowance in money in the shape of rent . . . 5 dollars per month or even 4 would enable her to supply herself with all necessary clothes, etc., and leave a little for the 2 young girls. . . . I shall say nothing about her accommodation and comfort in the old house. . . . I feel perfectly confident and assured that our daughter Anne will never deprive her of . . . anything . . . that may be reasonable in a mother to expect or for a very good daughter to give. . . .

"The next point I feel interested in is the protection, support and education of the two dear little boys left by my son John—they are young and troublesome but in a year or two they will become more manageable & the oldest, James Allen, will have something coming to him from his father, from the farm now held and occupied by Tommy, but for the next few years the little fellow will not want much. I hope that what there is in the farm will be kept for him and that the little required for his support will be contributed by our family willingly & cheerfully. Little Johnny has nothing, nor will he have anything from his father—he will depend solely on his mother & all his father's brothers and sisters. . . . After protection & support a suitable education ought to be provided for both the children—in fact I hope that all my children will look upon them as if they were their younger brothers. . . .

"If their mother should remain a widow . . . I do sincerely hope that she may continue to reside with the family as she has done. . . . I believe she and they have agreed pretty well together. . . . If, however, the widow should think proper to marry again . . . I hope the children will be allowed to remain with the family. . . . Whatever . . . I have (and the whole does not amount to much) I leave to my wife as will be seen by a document which I leave with her. . . . In conclusion I have only to hope that all my children will live in unity & love. . . . Let those who have abundance assist those who may be straitened in circumstances, and they all may depend on it that they will not regret it. . . . Given under my hand . . . the 28th day of June 1871."

The Lairds were certainly "straitened in circumstances." Fanny Jones wrote Clara that summer, "What in the world are the Lairds living on? Has Eliza any clothes for the children?" Eliza did; the ladies of Myrtleville made clothes for the little Lairds. Eliza thanked her mother and Bella "for making my Baby's dress so pretty."

As winter came on, Allen Good's health failed again. In November he resigned as trustee of the Church Endowment Fund, writing that "I find I have to give up all outside business . . . I cannot expect to be young again." He did, however, continue to act as one of the county auditors a couple of years longer. That brought in a little income.

The Christmas season of 1871 was quiet at Myrtleville; Mary was in Paisley, and the Lairds had moved to Newport and did not come, although their distance from Myrtleville was not great. (Newport was a village on the river below Brantford. Its name reflected the by-gone glories of the Grand River Navigation Company, and the time when it really was a port.) Bella and Tom were on a committee which put on a very successful "social" for 115 people at the new schoolhouse on December 21, but the only family festivity Tom records is that he went skating with little Jim on New Year's Day.

Letters came from bright, vivacious Mary, living in the Mallochs's fine new house, "Lillian Lawn," and working in her brother-in-law's law office. She found social life in Paisley very dull, not even a dance in four months. Her "conveyancing business" (drawing deeds and leases) was very quiet in the winter. She missed "wee Jim"; she would be sure to send him a valentine. As spring approached, she wrote more and more of going home, but by April George needed her in getting ready for the May Assizes, and, she said, "I like the feeling of being able to earn my own living. . . . We have been very busy . . . a great deal of conveyancing beside suits—the former I like best as I can do it all alone." She wrote Tom that she had no thought of getting married, but other people insisted on talking about her matrimonial prospects. She wrote a friend at Brantford, "It is quite true about my engagement [to Henry Tivy] being broken off, but the story about the nine proposals is perfectly absurd. I have not even been honoured with one."

Mary was home in time for Anne's fortieth birthday in July 1871. With five young people at Myrtleville, Tom, Bella, Mary, Clara, and Mary John, there was much social activity. The older children of the Moyle family up the road toward Paris were friends of the young Goods. The Ballachey brothers, who lived at Edgemount on the road from Brantford to Burford, often came after church on Sunday. They, like the Goods, attended Grace Church. Every now and then there were parties. In the 1920s and 1930s there were old ladies of Brantford who spoke in glowing terms of evenings spent at Myrtleville in those far-off days, and of how they remembered old Mrs. Good playing the piano for dancing. She thoroughly enjoyed it, but when she thought it was time for the party to end she played "God Save the Queen," and that was that. Anne thought dancing was a frivolous waste of time, but she gracefully accepted it in the house which was legally hers.

At parties which the young Goods gave or attended there were likely to be Ushers and Wyes, and eventually the younger generation of the Bell family, new neighbors of the Wyes and the Ballacheys, the other side of the river from Myrtleville. These young people were Mr. Alexander Graham Bell and his brother's widow, Caroline. Mr. Bell's father had been a distinguished teacher of elocution in Edinburgh and London, but when two of his three children died of tuberculosis, and the third was threatened with it, he brought his family to the healthier air of the hillside overlooking Brantford. The tall, thin, young Mr. Bell improved greatly in health, and was soon able to take a position as a teacher of the deaf in Boston. He still spent long summer vacations at Brantford, however, and as he lay in a hammock on the riverbank, he dreamed up a contraption which developed into the telephone. Although his Brant County friends found his scientific obsessions very strange, they thought him a most likable fellow. Mrs. Good especially admired his beautiful singing and piano-playing.

Allen and Eliza were enjoying their growing crop of grandchildren. The first, fifteen-year-old Lilly Malloch, was only twenty-five miles from Myrtleville the winter of 1872–73. She went to school in Hamilton then, and her parents were planning to take her to Europe the following summer. Their plans changed; in September 1873, Charlotte's second child, Sally, was born, sixteen and a half years younger than her sister. Eliza Laird had a baby also, little George, but, when he was only six months old, his sister Bertie died at the age of four. Allen Good wrote mournfully about her loss to his brother Jonathan in Ireland. Allen himself was far from well. He suffered greatly from bronchitis, an ailment which he and Jonathan shared on opposite sides of the Atlantic. (They still wrote each other every few weeks, and Jonathan faithfully sent a Cork newspaper every week.)

Two of Allen's daughters had physical problems, also. For several years Bella had a troublesome knee, and sometimes had to walk with crutches. People remarked on what a trial this was for one so young. It was doubly difficult for anyone with Bella's energy and drive. But Fanny's troubles were more ominous than Bella's. She wrote repeatedly of "weak lungs," of bad colds that gave her a pain in the side, of a continuing cough which made her exhausted, yet she kept saying, "I think that I'll be all right when the warm weather comes, so don't fret about me."

The Goods' eventful year of 1873 ended with a festive occasion. Their pretty and popular Mary married Sam Ballachey at Myrtleville. There is a friendly small-town editorial comment appended to the formal announcement in the *Brantford Expositor:* "The cake accompanying the above notice was excellent. We wish happy days and many of them to the adventurers upon the matrimonial sea." Mary and Sam went to live in a new house on the Ballachey farm, Edgemount—but not for long. The house had been built by Mr. Ballachey senior for the oldest son, George, and his fiancée, Augusta Gilkison. Then George and Gussie changed their minds. Sam saw no need for the place to stand "as an empty monument to miscarried plans." He made a bargain with George to use the place until a year after George gave notice. Sam told about it years later: "I thought he might never want it, but I got the notice two weeks after I married. . . . Father said the farm couldn't carry any more families and he was right. So . . . being the younger, I had to get out. . . . In the fall of 1874, we visited the Mallochs at Paisley, with the result that I bought a farm one mile, as the crow flies, east of the village. So we returned and planned to leave the old home in the Spring."

Meantime, Will Doyle, a young widower of Owen Sound, a big bluff man of Irish descent and a veteran of the United States Union Army, had become acquainted with Bella when he went to Paisley on business. Bella and Will were married on December 14, 1874. The family at Myrtleville seemed small now, though there were the parents, Anne, Tom, Clara, Mary John, and her two little boys. Tom was thirty-one, quite an "old bachelor." It was not that he was unattractive, or uninterested in the ladies. He was a good-looking young man, tall and slender, with sandy red hair and blue eyes. He had plenty of friends and seems to have been adored by nieces and nephews, but his romances had not prospered.

Tom had been quite smitten by a girl in Buffalo, whom

Clara referred to as "Tom's Miss Park." Anne hoped that he would not think of marrying until his financial prospects were better. Back in Ontario, he "kept company" with Anna Moyle, but early in 1872, sixteen-year-old Lilly wrote her "darling old Uncle," "Tom, I do not like Miss Hay well enough for you to marry her, so please do not do so. . . . I think Anna is decidedly preferable." This is the only reference in the Myrtleville documents to Miss Hay, but obviously something went wrong between Tom and Anna. Mary wrote her brother on April 12, 1872, "I am very sorry you are offended at Anna. I think you had better make friends with her again, & don't get jealous so easily, perhaps she only did it to try you." Whatever happened, the relationship cooled.

After Mary Good married Sam Ballachey, Tom saw a good deal of Sam's sister, Mary. She was a small and gentle girl, eight and a half years younger than he. She shared Tom's love of horses, and in spite of her timidity about many things, she was an intrepid rider. Tom may well have found her meekness a refreshing contrast to the "strong-mindedness" of many of his female relatives. There is still in existence a short and rather abrupt note which Tom addressed to Miss M. Ballachey on August 23, 1874: "I have made up my mind to call for you on Wednesday to accompany you at the riding party, if you will favor me with your company. I will be at your place about five o'clock, so we can take a short ride before tea. Can I depend on you, if not let me know."

By midwinter, Tom was making plans to marry Mary Ballachey. There was no housing problem; he and his bride could live in the north wing where John and his Mary had spent their short married life. The engagement was not announced until February 1875. On February 24, Fanny wrote: "I am ashamed of not answering your nice little note before this. Why did not you tell me you were going to be married? . . . I am sorry to say I could not follow your advice and get well fast, but I hope to do so now as I am sitting up again. . . . I wish I was able to go to your wedding . . . however I hope to go home as soon as the warm weather begins. Please excuse all the mistakes in this letter, but I am too tired to write it over."

Two days later, Charlie wrote Tom in a businesslike manner: "Yours is at hand & contents noted. Please accept my con-

Mary A. Ballachey, 1869 (at the age of seventeen), later Mrs. Thomas A. Good

gratulations on your proposed marriage. . . . Kate & myself will be most happy to receive a visit from you & your bride. . . . As the most of the Hotels about the Falls are closed at this Season, allow me to suggest that the 'Spencer House' on the American side is the best now open." The newlyweds could not afford a long honeymoon at Niagara Falls, as Tom had to borrow forty-five dollars from George Malloch to finance the trip.

With Tom's wedding, only the oldest and youngest of Allen's and Eliza's ten children remained unmarried. They were a generation apart in age, Anne in her mid-forties, Clara in her mid-twenties. Clara was a good-looking girl with beautiful auburn hair, and she had various male "admirers," but they came and went. It is quite possible that the young lady's affairs of the heart foundered on the tempestuous dispositon which had made her such a difficult pupil for Anne in days gone by.

About a week before Tom married Mary Ballachey, her brother George married Carrie Bell, sister-in-law of Aleck Bell, the speech teacher and budding inventor. Carrie was the young widow who had helped George to recover so quickly from his broken engagement. This wedding caused the Goods to lose their Mary from Brantford to Paisley at the same time that they acquired "Mary Tom" at Myrtleville. Henceforth, Mrs. Sam Ballachey will usually be called Molly, the name the Ballacheys used to distinguish her from their Mary. They said the name was appropriate for one so jolly.

Molly and Sam and their six-weeks-old baby, George Theodore, started for Paisley by train on March 16. On the train also were their team of horses and half a carload of farm implements and household furniture. Sam's brother, John, and his youngest sister, nineteen-year-old Lizzie, went along to help. The train should have reached Paisley by evening, but because of a blizzard it did not arrive until noon the next day. Fortunately the Mallochs were there. Charlotte wrote her mother two weeks later: "I am glad to tell you that we are all now pretty well, the baby boy much better, although he has a cough left yet. . . . I am very thankful that none of them took their death on that awful journey. Sam's horse is also better and will I hope be fit for work on Monday. The house is getting on well and if all is well they will move in sometime next week. . . . Mary, Lizzie, Lilly, & George are out at a concert, and Sam and I are minding the baby who is fast asleep in his cradle & Sally is sound upstairs."

Molly did not think much of the new farm. She wrote Mary and Tom: "I took a short walk over the farm today to see its beauties which consist at present of stumps, snow, mud and water, but I hope in the course of time it may improve. I would not be surprised if you were to see us back in Brantford yet." Years later, Sam wrote of this period: "I was deceived and cheated on every hand. First in buying the farm and then in buying a cow, seed grain, etc. I was charged outrageous prices for everything and in my simplicity I thought it a great place to farm when prices were so good. . . . I had never done any business. . . . Mr. Malloch . . . did not help me one bit in buying the farm, in the way of advice or otherwise, but later on he lent me money to tide over a bad year, and they were good to us in a number of other ways. I found out afterwards that he was supposed to be rich and as I was his brother-in-law I was rich too, and so would be a good goose for plucking. I paid $3,100 for the farm, which was a good $600 too much, and had only $700 to pay on it. I borrowed $600 from my eldest brother George, and $1800 from my father. By 'hook or by crook' . . . I managed to pay George his interest but I never paid father a cent of interest and he graciously sent me a receipt for it every year."

The family at Myrtleville was grateful for the help the senior Ballacheys gave Molly and Sam. In November, Mr. and Mrs. Ballachey visited their children at Paisley and Sam's mother wrote her daughter at Myrtleville: "Father has had the kitchen plastered and it upset the whole house . . . but it is a good thing done. I do not think they could have lived in it this winter as it was. The baby . . . is a beautiful boy . . . and can very nearly walk by himself. . . . When he hears me coming down stairs in the morning he jumps and capers and is ready to spring out of his chair."

There is little family record of the following winter except for the happy notices that Bella and Will Doyle had a son, William Russell, born on December 29, 1875, and that Tom and Mary Good also had a boy, William Charles, born on February 24, 1876. Willie Good was a big strong child, weighing twelve pounds, tradition says, and it was a very difficult birth, but all went well at last. Charlie wrote his brother: "I hope mother & child are progressing favorably. I was sorry to hear of my father being very sick. It is not probable he will ever be much better, I suppose, his chest troubles are of such long standing. . . . I suppose you have had a very open winter. The Roads have been very bad in most localities, & this has exerted a depressing influence on business." (It is hard for us to realize that "an open winter" was a disaster. The Myrtleville letters speak again and again of the problems caused by lack of snow for sleighing.) Charlotte wrote to Mary on March 5: "You will think me a long time in writing to wish you joy of your son but as I knew you had been very ill I thought I would not trouble you with letters. . . . I got Annie's card and we were all sorry to hear . . . that Papa was so very poorly. . . . I am very busy preparing for our trip. We expect to sail from New York on the 19th of April. . . . Mary, Sam & baby are well. . . . We have had a week of nice sleighing but today is soft and the snow nearly gone." Fanny wrote her sister-in-law on April 13: "I hope, dear Mary, that you are getting quite strong by this time after the fearful time you had. . . . Andrew sent Tom a bag of Oats last Monday, tell Tom that Andrew says they are very good oats and that . . . he would not sell any of them under seventy-five cents a bushel. . . . Andrew sent to England for the seed."

Myrtleville had a visit from thirteen-year-old Arthur the summer of 1876. Charlie wrote Tom on July 27: "This P.M. Arthur goes over to spend a few weeks at Myrtleville. I hope you will not find him troublesome. He has been going swimming frequently this summer in the Lake & can swim a little. I wish you would not allow him to go in the River except with yourself or some one who can swim. He is rather venturesome & I wish you would warn him to be careful around machinery and not to go into danger by climbing. You may think me overcareful & anxious but I incline to the opinion that an ounce of prevention is worth a pound of cure." A breezy note came to Tom from Will Doyle in Toronto where he and his wife and son had been living for some months: "Mollie wrote on 29th July & Sam had not commenced harvest. His fall wheat was thin & weevil was interviewing his spring wheat. . . . Bella & the thoroughbred are quite well. Bella sends love to all at home. Kiss the Phenomenon [little Willie] for Uncle & Auntie."

There were ripples of excitement over Aleck Bell around Brantford that summer of 1876. He came home with two prizes from the Philadelphia Centennial Exhibition, awards for both his "multiple telegraph" and his "telephone." The former aroused great interest; it would indeed multiply the usefulness of the very useful wire system. The telephone, on which Bell and his assistant had talked within a building in Boston, was regarded as a "clever toy." During the early weeks of August, the young inventor strung quantities of stovepipe wire along fences and to telegraph lines and successfully transmitted voices three times, from Brantford to the village of Mount Pleasant, from Brantford to the Bells' house on Tutela Heights, and finally and most impressively, from Brantford to Paris, almost eight miles.

A few people now thought the telephone had commercial possibilities, but almost no one in Brant County did. Many of the Bells' friends and neighbors were sorry later that they had spurned the chance to invest in Aleck's toy. It is well known that William Moyle, a prosperous farmer, firmly refused specially priced twenty-five-cent shares urged on him by the inventor's father. Anything the Goods could save was invested in Myrtleville, but they remembered that Aleck Bell held six-month-old Willie on his knee and amused and tested the baby with his watch. His verdict was that the child heard well and seemed very bright.

Allen Good's long struggle ended four days before Christmas of 1876. He was seventy-seven years old. Although his body was failing, his mind remained clear. Shortly before he died he wrote a nostalgic letter to his brother, whom he had not seen for forty years. The day before Allen's funeral, Jonathan wrote in answer: "I have not been at all well for some months back . . . I have a very trying cough. . . . . I still try and manage to get down to the Bank, as it is variety to me, 2 days in the week. . . . You are still affected during the cold weather. Well, I suppose we both must expect at our time of life to feel . . . the effects of old age coming on us. . . . . I believe almost all the friends you knew are gone, if you were to come here now you would see all new faces."

Charlie came for the funeral, and George Malloch. Charlotte did not come as she had Bella and baby Russell visiting her and Lilly was not well. The senior Ballacheys were staying at Molly's again, and she could have left little George with them, but she was seven months pregnant, and, as Charlotte wrote, "not nearly as well as she was before her other baby was born." George Ballachey senior, a kindly but pompous gentleman, sent a long and solemn letter to his daughter, Mary, who was much upset by her father-in-law's death.

"We are indeed gratified that, on a retrospect of your short intimacy with poor Mr. Good, your relations both from him & towards him, as so feelingly expressed in your letter, have been so satisfactory. This is the first personal experience of death in the family that you have had and we are very glad to find that by proper reflections on the uncertainty of human life, and the merciful design of divine providence in affliction, you are endeavoring to obtain spiritual benefit from this visitation. The gentleness & kindness of your natural disposition has no doubt caused you more suffering than would have fallen to the lot of a hardier nature, but we have no doubt that the pious frame of mind that you have happily experienced . . . will restore you. . . . Your mother and I followed you in solemn thought thro' all the circumstances from the death to the end of the funeral. The Christmas day following we all spent at Mr. Mallochs. . . . We dined about 5 after Mr. M's return. . . . Poor Samuel has 2 or 3 times complained despondingly to your mother. It is such a change for him both at table and in attentions upon his horses and cattle, from the unstinted plenty of his Brantford experiences, to the griping and as he calls it 'beggarly' mode of doling out the allowances of both man & beast. He has nothing to sell and is getting in debt. . . . Our advice is that he must weather through another year with as little grumbling and as little borrowing as possible. . . . He is planning and exerting himself to the utmost and is in no way deficient as far as he is personally concerned. . . . Little George is not at all shy and has taken to us very warmly. He is a fine handsome little chap and has a curious vocabulary of his own."

The day after Christmas, Charlotte sent her mother a letter written on proper Victorian mourning stationery, a small folder with a wide black border around the front page. It said, "I know how very sad and lonely you will feel now that you have [papa] no more to wait on, but . . . when you consider what he has suffered for so many years you would hardly regret to see him at peace. . . . I hope Annie & Clara are well and I am glad to hear how kind Tom is to you all." The family wore mourning clothes for some time. Fifty years later, one of Allen Good's granddaughters threw away ancient black crepe bonnets said to have been bought at the time of his death. Under the rules of Victorian mourning, a widow wore lusterless black for a year, and a bonnet, not a hat. Her daughters wore black, too, but under less rigid rules.

Allen Good's brother followed him to the grave within a few months. Now there were no close relatives of the Goods left in Ireland except Jonathan's son by his second marriage, fourteen-year-old Jonathan Morgan. Anne exchanged letters occasionally with him and his mother, Mary Anne.

8

Another Generation in the Making

Through most of the last decade of Allen Good's life, Myrtleville had been slowly recovering from his bankruptcy of 1864. The 1866 cancellation of the Reciprocity Treaty with the United States had not been serious, economically, in Canada, because, with a continuing boom of railway building and industrialization in North America and Europe, there was a continuing demand for raw materials. However, in 1873, about the time Molly and Sam married, the boom broke. Some districts were already oversupplied with expensive tracks, and many municipalities had gone heavily in debt for them. As the *Brantford Expositor* commented, "Railways can be bought too dear." By the time Allen Good died, there was a worldwide depression which lasted for about twenty years, and seemed to bear harder on Canada than on more urbanized countries. It was a trying time for struggling young farmers like Tom Good and Sam Ballachey, though both were alert to opportunities for improvement.

In the middle 1870s, an American farm movement, called the Grange, spread into Canada. Tom and Sam were both early members, and Tom was Master of the Brantford Division Grange in 1880. He served as a delegate to the Dominion Grange a number of times, and was also active in the Farmers' Institute formed a few years later. Both these organizations tried to help farmers by educating them in modern methods and bringing political pressure to bear on governments which seemed to be much more sensitive to the woes of manufacturers, merchants, and bankers, than to those of farmers.

In 1878, John A. Macdonald, Conservative prime minister for the first seven years of Confederation (1867–74), returned to power with his "National Policy" dedicated to fighting depression by protecting Canada's infant industries with tariffs. Many farmers complained that the tariff helped businessmen at the expense of farmers who had to buy expensive protected merchandise and sell their produce in restricted markets. It was probably at this time that Tom Good abandoned the Conservative party he had been brought up in and became a Liberal. By 1880 he had joined the Reform press in calling the National Policy, "National Humbug."

The economy of the little city of Brantford was encouraged, at least temporarily, by Macdonald's tariff policy. The town had grown from three thousand, at the time of its incorporation in 1847, to ten thousand in 1877, when it became a city. It was already well known for its manufacturing of farm implements—Wisner seed drills, Harris (later Massey-Harris) reapers and mowers, and, after 1877, Cockshutt plows. (Ninety years later, bricks from the wreckage of an old Cockshutt building were used to repair chimneys at Myrtleville.) Brantford also boasted the manufacture of stoves, steam engines, blankets (by William Slingsby), carriages, and sleighs. And since 1870 it had achieved marked success in fire control by means of water piped along the streets and pumped by Brantford-made Waterous engines. Many of the buildings of the town were more fire-resistant also. The village of frame structures had become a city of brick.

The long depression did not have much effect on the birthrate. Little was known about contraception, though many women nursed their babies for a year and half to two years, for the double purpose of delaying another pregnancy (this system did not always work) and of protecting the children against the dread "summer complaint," an acute diarrhea known as "cholera infantum." Also, in spite of hard times, children were welcomed as economic assets.

Molly Ballachey's second sturdy son arrived on February 20, 1877, and was named Frederic Allen. Life was still rough for Molly on the backwoods farm, but Sam's sister, Joanna, went to help with the new baby and the hard work and stayed through the summer. The "maiden aunt" in those days often

Mrs. Samuel Ballachey née Mary H. Good (1848–94)

made a most useful career of helping whatever relatives needed her most. Fanny Jones was pregnant again, ten years after her third child's birth. She was not strong, and her family worried a good deal about her, but in April she gave birth safely to another healthy boy, Carroll. Fortunately, the Joneses could afford domestic help.

Eliza Good probably worried most about her namesake, who

was also expecting a fourth child. Eliza Laird lived at this time in the village of Princeton. It was only about twelve miles from Myrtleville, but George Laird was still absent a great deal and Eliza still had no means of transportation. Her two boys, Allen and George, were eleven and four years old. She had lost her only daughter.

Eliza senior was feeling the burden of her seventy years. She had received little in the way of worldly goods from her husband, but she was still a famous needlewoman, and she set to work providing for the younger Eliza's baby. There is a letter from Eliza Laird to "My own dear Mamma," written in early June 1877: "I am sure you must think me very ungrateful for not having written to you before, & thanked you for the very handsome & valuable present you sent me by my dear Husband. . . . The flannels are the nicest I ever saw, & the little dresses are so elegantly made, indeed every article is so nice I don't know which I like best. I feel quite rich in Baby clothes. I trust & pray the little stranger may be spared to wear them. . . . I hope dear Annie & Clara are well, & I shall be glad if some of them, Mary John, or Tom can drive up to see me when I am laid up. . . . What a Grand day they must have had in dear old Brantford on the 31st. I would so like to have been there. [Eliza refers to May 31, 1877, when Brantford officially became a city. There were large public meetings, congratulatory speeches, fourteen bands performing, and an impressive display of fireworks.] I assure you I feel proud that my childhood home is so near the new & lovely City. . . . Does Fanny speak of coming up this summer to shew you her baby boy. I hope when you see mine you will see a baby girl. . . . George told me you had heard of the death of Uncle Jonathan, he was not left long to mourn the death of my dear Father. . . . Tell Annie to come & see me when she can." Eliza's hopes for another daughter were frustrated; the baby was a third boy.

Soon after Allen Good's death, Bella and Will Doyle moved to St. John, New Brunswick, about a thousand miles northeast of Myrtleville. It was the farthest any of Eliza Good's children had gone since John's journey to the Pacific, but distance had lost much of its terror since then. Overextended though the rail system might be, it took Bella quickly and comfortably to

New Brunswick, and brought her letters to Brantford more efficiently than the mail service does a hundred years later. Postage was cheap, too. John had had to pay $2.50 to send a letter from the Cariboo; letters anywhere in Canada cost only three cents in 1877 (British Columbia had been part of Canada since 1871). In June, there was bad news from New Brunswick. A terrible fire destroyed much of the city of St. John. The Doyles were unharmed, but the insurance company for which Will worked was ruined. He was unemployed in the depths of a depression. For about two years he tried one thing after another, while much of the time his family lived with relatives in Ontario.

At the end of 1877, Tom and Mary Good had a daughter. They named her Mary Elizabeth Anne after her two grandmothers and her Aunt Annie. There was already a confusing abundance of Marys in the family, and the baby soon came to be known as Mamie. Lilly Malloch wrote her grandmother from Paisley on January 8, 1878: "A little girl baby will seem nice after so many boys. . . . I was out at Sam's yesterday & spent the day. Miss Pepper was with me & we were sewing for Mary. Poor girl, she is driven to death with work, I don't know how she gets on, but the men will soon be done chopping & then she won't have so much to do."

The land-clearing process on Sam's farm was more complicated than it had been forty years earlier at Myrtleville. Then trees had been burned in great piles. Now they were carefully cut up and the surplus wood sold. Molly wrote Mary Tom about the domestic ordeal involved: "The sawing is finished. We had twelve days of it and the chopping will be done in a week or two. You can't fancy what work I have had to do this winter, Mary. We've had two men for over two months living in the house. Sawing days we had eight, sometimes ten . . . and I have had no help whatever. We've had three pig-killing scrapes, have made lots of headcheese [from odds and ends of pork], churn once a week, and make on an average thirty loaves of bread a week. . . . I have not been in town for months except Christmas day, but I expect I'll go and stay a few days after the men are gone."

Before Mamie Good was six weeks old, there was another little girl in the family, Fanny Isabella, daughter of Bella and

Will Doyle. She was born at her Aunt Fanny's house, where her mother had spent so much time years before when Harold and Allen Jones were little. Both Fanny Jones and Bella were quite ill shortly after the baby's birth. Fanny wrote her mother and Anne: "You must be satisfied with a joint note as I feel too weak to write much. . . . I had a severe attack of pleurisy, and about a week ago, I coughed up several mouthfuls of blood. . . . I feel better now but am very weak, the cupping and blistering have weakened me a good deal. My last blister is healing now. [Both of these treatments worked on the theory of counterirritation. A vacuum cup or a mustard plaster, for instance, brought the blood to the skin.] I will have to wean the baby soon. He is so heavy I can hardly carry him at all. I have plenty of nurse for him but the Dr. is afraid all my strength goes to nurse and that I will have to wean him before my lungs get strong. The little fellow is not 11 months old yet. I hate to wean him but I must. Bella is getting quite strong again. She has had a very severe attack on her lungs but I think she has quite recovered. . . . I would like to be able to go home for a visit very much indeed. . . . My boys [aged 16 and 14] are getting on splendidly at school. I wish you could all see them."

Meantime, Tom was toying with the idea of renting from Anne. His father-in-law, visiting at Sam's and Molly's, wrote advising against it: "We incline to the conclusion that it seems preferable for you and Annie to farm on shares. . . . You then would have, each of you, what really is your own. Annie, on the one hand, would want all that she has been getting, with your assistance, in the present mode, and although it may have been in excess of her real share, yet she might think a rent too low which did not realize so much as that, and on the other hand produce in general is selling so low . . . that altogether it would be very difficult to fix a proper rent. I consider the farming business at present lies under a depression. . . . Georgy is growing well both in mind & body and is a very good boy and Freddy is a fine fat jolly fellow almost too heavy to walk."

Little John Good of Myrtleville, almost ten now, was supposed to spend the school year of 1878–79 at his Uncle Charlie's in Buffalo, but just before schooltime he came down with

whooping cough. Kate wrote that he should come as soon as
he was well, but he must be entirely well or they would not
allow him in the school. He had a bad time with the cough; he
still had it at Christmas. On December 30, Charlie wrote, "I
would suggest that you do not send him for a month or two
until all remnants of his cough are gone. . . . Arthur [fifteen
years old] is studying Law. Has been so for four months past.
He is quite busy & gets no Christmas Holidays as this is the
Lawyers' busy season."

When spring came, Molly paid a longed-for visit to Myrtleville, and unfortunately was sick while she was there. Charlotte
wrote her mother: "I have not seen or heard of Mary since
her return Saturday night. She was very tired when she arrived and looks very miserable. I was so sorry she had to come
home on Saturday as she might just as well have stayed a few
days longer, but Sam and Lizzie were selfish and missed her. I
was quite cross about it when Sam said he wrote for her to
come. Poor girl, she had not much pleasure being so ill all the
time." Molly continued to find very trying the privations, the
hard work, and above all, the isolation of life on the Bruce
County farm. She wrote Mary Tom: "Lots of days this summer I have worked from five A.M., till ten P.M., but I hope to
be able to stand it. . . . I drive to town about twice a week
with the butter & go to the post but never go any where else.
. . . The children were much pleased with their trumpets &
candy & I am much obliged for them. The white sugar you
gave them is their candy yet. I give them one piece a day."

In autumn, Sam and Molly tried without success to get Tom
and Mary to visit them. Sam wrote Tom, "Yours duly received. Glad to hear that your crops were so good and that everything appears to be flourishing with you. You seem to
think it quite a mystery that our crops do not turn out well.
Perhaps if you came upon the premises you could solve it.
Our show is next week, Tuesday and two following days. Reduced rates from Guelph good for 4 days. We would like you
and family to pay us at least a week's visit. . . . Tell Mary it is
all nonsense about your not being able to afford it. Why, you
are rolling in wealth if you only think so. . . . Now, Tom,
putting all nonsense aside I would really like you to come and
pass your opinion upon this farm. If the thing is really worth-

less the sooner we clear out the better. My inclination is to hang on, Mollie's is to start for parts unknown." Molly added a note: "Do come up next week or I will have the blues terribly. I have them now pretty badly. I'm in a fearful hurry, have to go to town, so Good-bye."

In spite of his father-in-law's advice the year before, Tom had leased Anne's land on April 22, 1879, "with the out Buildings, back part of Dwelling house and one Room in the front part of Dwelling house and three fourths of cellar." He was to pay two hundred dollars per year, half in April and half in October. His farm operations would be simpler this way, and he hoped they would be more profitable.

Will Doyle eventually solved his unemployment problem. Although he had never farmed, he went pioneering in what was later Manitoba. The Homestead Laws of Canada, following the pattern of the famous American Homestead Act of 1862, encouraged settlement by giving public land (mostly obtained from the Hudson's Bay Company) in return for a small token payment and several years of residence and cultivation.

Since July 1, 1873, Canada had been a dominion "from sea to sea." Six years before that, at the time of Confederation, it had included only Ontario, Quebec, New Brunswick and Nova Scotia. West of Ontario there lay: first a rocky wilderness; then a few settlements in the Red River valley; in the third place, hundreds of miles of empty fertile prairie under the jurisdiction of the Hudson's Bay Company; and finally, the distant mines and forests of British Columbia, where John Good had hunted gold in vain. Two years later, the Hudson's Bay Company ceded most of its rights to Canada, in return for a cash payment of three hundred thousand pounds. The following year, 1870, the province of Manitoba entered Confederation. It was only a small southern part of what is now Manitoba; the rest of the modern province was part of the vast wild Northwest Territories, as were Saskatchewan and Alberta. In 1871, British Columbia joined Canada, on the promise of a transcontinental railway within ten years. And in 1873, tiny Prince Edward Island, stubbornly aloof for six years, was driven by mounting debts to become part of Canada.

When Will Doyle set off for the Northwest Territory, he left his wife and children at Homewood with the Joneses. Bella was pregnant again; she planned to join her husband the following summer, when the baby would be a few months old and Will would have some kind of house built.

Harold and Allen Jones were both big teen-agers now, able to help on the farm. Their attitudes were different, however. Fanny wrote her mother: "Harold is a great comfort and help to us. He works all the time and is so contented and cheerful that it is a pleasure to be where he is. Allen does not like farming. I think he will study law as soon as he leaves school." In the autumn the Joneses put fifteen-year-old Allen in boarding school at Belleville, but he was miserable there. His mother wrote to Myrtleville, "We had to send for Allen . . . he was so uncomfortable and starved at school." The school was not being deliberately cruel, of course. Allen Jones grew to be six and a half feet tall. The beds and the meals at school were no doubt quite inadequate for a boy rapidly growing to a great height.

Meanwhile, Will Doyle wrote Tom and Sam, his brothers-in-law in Ontario, from "Birtle P.O., North West Territory": "I am alone 3 miles from the nearest house, my two chums having left me two weeks ago enroute to Winnipeg for their families. During said 2 weeks I have been cutting roads in the woods to get out logs for my house . . . plowing the prairie sod, or breaking as we call it, and cutting hay. Tomorrow is Sunday and my supper of Prairie Chicken (stewed), boiled potatoes (bought from the Sioux Indians . . .), fried pancakes dusted with granulated sugar, tea that would send a quiver of bliss from the roots of your tongue to the ends of your toe nails (I tell you my tea is about as good as Charlotte's . . .), and the writer just tired enough and hungry enough to thoroughly enjoy it, is finished, and as my 3-mile neighbor is coming to get my Indian pony to ride to the P.O. tomorrow A.M., I am getting this ready for him to post. I have hit it, I think, in coming out here, though most of my friends thought I was foolish. . . . I have 640 acres, in a block, of splendid land, 150 or 200 acres of it timber, poplar, birch & oak. A fine spring creek large enough to drive any machinery runs for two miles through my land & there are splendid water powers on it. I am in sight of Assiniboine River and my family can come by steamer within 1½ miles of our house. We have plenty of game."

In that autumn of 1879, Bella went to Myrtleville to await

the birth of her third child. Tom and Mary were expecting a third also. The house was very full and busy, and it was just as well that little John was finally sent to school in Buffalo. He was lonely and homesick, however; Kate wrote that "he does not seem to know what to do with himself." He sent a letter to Eliza Good in his childish scrawl.

My dear grandmother,
    I am going to take the pleasure of writeing to you today. I have not much to tell you but I will tell you all I can I went out to dinner on Sunday. Art went out to Mrs. Baxters on Saturday. . . . My knew suit is poor cloth we have no school today here, did Jim and mother get my letters and valitines that I sent them. . . . How are they all at home I hope they are all quite well . . .
    I remain your affecanet grandchild

John Good

Both the Myrtleville babies were born in January, Clara Louisa Good, known as Louie, and Sarah Eliza Doyle, who was always called Lily.

Tom Good was very much involved with the Grange at this time, serving as Master of the Brantford Division. He wrote an angry letter that winter to the *Farmer's Advocate,* a London, Ontario, magazine, which had published letters and editorials attacking the Grange. He was particularly annoyed at an anonymous letter from "Brant," which claimed that the Grange had failed in all it had set out to do. The principal objects of the Grange, Mr. Good said, were "to make the farmers more independent of other classes; to give them a more thorough knowledge of their occupation . . . to teach them to take part in public discussions . . . and not be led away by oily-tongued lawyers and politicians to go against their own interests, and also to show them the benefits of dealing without the aid of middlemen and of paying cash for their purchases. . . . I know of Grangers getting more for their produce by selling direct to large houses or sending direct to Europe. . . . Has the Grange failed in enabling the farmers to buy . . . reaping machines for $88.oo that are retailing for $110.oo, to

Back of entry hall and staircase, Myrtleville House

buy ploughs for $12.00 that others paid $20.00 for, . . . to
buy harrows for $11.00 that I know were sold for $22.00? . . .
Let him answer. . . . I do not write over an anonymous name
but sign my own, which I would like 'Brant' to do likewise."

When spring came there was quite an exodus from Myrtle-
ville. Mary Tom was not well, and she and her baby went to
Paisley for a visit. Mamie went to her Grandmother Balla-
chey's, and four-year-old Willie stayed with his father and
Aunt Annie. Bella was preparing to join her husband in the
West. Tom wrote his wife the end of May: "I was in Paris on
Friday shipping Bella's freight, she has 3740 lbs. Her fare to
Winnipeg & freight on her goods is $100.00 except 10 cts.
. . . I have now paid Anne everything except $100 on the
cattle which will be due next fall. I will be able to send you
some money in about a week. . . . Do not stint yourself in
anything, get what you want & take care of yourself & see if
you cannot get better. Harold Jones came up on Friday night
to go with Bella; he is a big strong boy & will be a great help to

Bella on her journey. His mother is coming up here to stay in about two weeks. She is very sick. I am afraid she will never get strong. She has an abscess on her lungs [that is what they had called John's illness] & the doctor says she must have change of air. . . . I was not able to go to the Division Grange on Thursday. . . . I expect they have elected me as delegate again to the Dominion Grange but I do not know for certain yet. I hope to be able to go to the Grange Picnic on Wednesday next, the fare to Port Stanley [on Lake Erie south of London] is only $1.00. George & Carrie [Ballachey] are going."

About a week later he wrote again: "I think I will bring Mamie home next week as I am very lonesome without her. . . . Willie is very well & not near as much trouble since Bella & the children went away. . . . I went to the Grange Picnic. . . . There was a very large turnout, from 10,000 to 15,000 persons. . . . I met a good many old acquaintances." Tom was miserably lonely for his wife, and longed to join her in Paisley. He wrote her a touching letter on June 10: "I now send you $5.00 so you can come home any time you wish. If I can go up on excursion ticket to Paisley I think I will do so in about a week. If I cannot get return for two or three dollars I will not go, or if you wish to come home next week let me know a few days before so that I can meet you at Harrisburg. I think you had better come as I can ill afford the trip to Paisley, but I am getting very hungry for your arms about my neck & your kiss on my lips. I do not want you to hurry home on my account if you are getting better & stronger."

Meanwhile Mary Tom was in the middle of an unfortunate family situation at Paisley. Molly and Charlotte had fallen out. George Ballachey senior had written his daughter from Paisley in April, "Molly . . . and S. attribute the whole rupture to Mrs. M. It appears at all events to be a quarrel originating between her and Molly. Mr. M. and Saml transact business matters as usual but all intercourse of a more friendly nature has ceased."

No explanation of the quarrel can be found in the Myrtleville documents. It is known, however, that Molly was pregnant, overworked, and thoroughly miserable. Charlotte was eleven years older, relatively rich, and of a bossy disposition. Had she tried to give orders or even too much advice to an

overwrought young woman? There is a strong hint of resentment at the Mallochs' airs in a letter Molly wrote her mother:
"I do not care at all for our old minister . . . but I believe he
will get on in Paisley, he is an old Irish blarney & suits the
common people very well & will suit Lord Malloch well
enough if he praises him up considerably."

The situation was very strained in June. In every letter Tom
told his wife that she must be sure to visit Charlotte. Finally
she wrote on June 12: "I went to the Mallochs. They were exceedingly kind to me & they were all so fond of baby. . . .
Mary & Sam are not any more friendly to the Mallochs than
they were. . . . Oh, how I have wished that I was rich since I
have been here. I would give them a Rocking chair & a set of
tea trays & a new teapot & ever so many things. . . . They are
so very short of meat, they only have a little pork." The Tom
Goods were far from rich but they did send a welcome gift to
the Sam Ballacheys. Molly wrote her brother on July 3:
"Thank you for the things you sent us. The meat will save us a
good deal of cash this year & the dollar will come in useful
some day. I am very much obliged to you for both things &
hope you are not robbing yourself too much. . . . I hope
Mary is better for her small rest. I suppose you are very busy
as we are. I quite dread the work this summer, there will be
such a hurry but I hope we will all get through & have good
crops. . . . I will say good-bye now as I can't keep my eyes
open any longer."

Fanny Jones did not get to Myrtleville in June. By now, the
family knew she was consumptive, but they still avoided the
dreaded word. Charlotte wrote her mother from Brockville on
July 4: "I went down to see Fanny on Friday and staid all
night. I found her looking rather better than I expected. She
is up and about the house but takes a lie-down morning and
afternoon. Her cough is pretty bad and she can eat but very
little. She has had a fresh cold this week and her side and lung
are very sore." Charlotte wrote again about two weeks later: "I
went to see Fanny. . . . She had again been very ill with fresh
cold on her lungs. . . . I really think we may all conclude that
she is not long for this world. She can eat nothing without
being sick at her stomach after it and she has high fever all
day and heavy perspiration at night. . . . Andrew is such a

kind man he does not let Fanny want for anything. . . . Carroll is a lovely boy and Lucia and Allen are nice children. They spoke of writing for Harold to come home, and indeed he should never have gone and his mother so ill." Meantime, Harold was seeing the Wild West. When he was an old man, he wrote his recollections of it.

"In the spring of 1880, I got the urge to go west to see the prairies of Manitoba, so I went out with my Aunt and her young children who were going out to their new home in the west. The Canadian Pacific Railway was not built but a short distance west of Ottawa at the time, so we went via Chicago, St. Paul and Minneapolis, to Emerson at the International boundary between Dakota and Manitoba, reaching Winnipeg by boat and rail.

"Winnipeg at that time was a settlement of small houses, tents, and one brick building (Ashdown's Hardware Store). The Hudson Bay Trading Post, Old Fort Garry, at the junction of the Assiniboine and Red Rivers, was a long log building which partly enclosed the parade ground of the Fort. The gate at the entrance to the Fort faced the Assiniboine River. At each side of the gate were two small brass cannon and the parade ground was surrounded by the Officers' quarters and Soldiers' residences.

"The store or trading post sold or bartered for furs—everything from a needle to an anchor that might be required by the voyagers on their annual trips through the wilds of the north. Here I bought my first pemmican which was very palatable and tasted somewhat like old cheese. The pemmican was made by the Indians from Buffalo meat. The meat was jerked or stripped and hung to dry in the hot sun, and then was pounded into shreds between stones and packed in the skin of a fresh killed Buffalo calf—first a layer of meat pounded solid, then boiling tallow poured in, then meat and tallow until the hide was full and then sewed up tightly with rawhide thongs. [Pemmican was already getting scarce; a few years later, the buffalo was almost extinct.] Traps, guns, powder, shot, bullets, blankets and long twists of tobacco were the chief features of the stock in trade.

"Winnipeg was noted for its mud. It was as fine as pipe clay and when it once dried on your clothing, it was there to stay.

When the main street was first paved, they laid planks on the mud and then placed paving blocks about 8 inches long on end, filling the cracks with a tar preparation.

"After spending a few days in Fort Garry or Winnipeg, I was able to sail on a Mississippi stern-wheel boat that sailed about every two weeks up the Assiniboine. It took most of a week to reach Birtle Landing, a distance of about 225 miles west of Winnipeg, which was nearer 600 miles by river, as the river was like the letter S.

"I eventually reached my Uncle's homestead with his wife and children, and spent the summer helping him to get out logs for his house. In the meantime, we lived in a small log cabin with one door and one window which later was used for a stable.

"I had an interesting summer hunting prairie chickens, ducks and some muskrats. The prairie chickens were very tame and we did not shoot any more than we required for food, and the same with the ducks. The ponds were swarming with muskrats and I skinned some in season at 8¢ a piece. Mink were plentiful but harder to trap and skins very cheap.

"That fall, I started for home, traveling the 200 odd miles in Ox Cart to Winnipeg. I then took the American railroads to Duluth and sailed to Owen Sound on an old wooden vessel and then home."

Bella wrote home that summer of 1880: "Well here I am . . . in my log house on the Northwest prairies, though I hardly call it a prairie, as the woods are all about us. We are at present in the stable, and when our house is up it will be in a much nicer place out on a little height with a pretty grove behind in which our spring water is, and I don't suppose you ever tasted better. It is just like ice, & lovely for butter. I hope to have a dairy built over it some time. . . . I never had so little time for writing or reading, and as for sewing I can just keep the mending done. . . . I suppose you have had lots of fruit now, cherries etc. How I envy you all the fruit, I miss it dreadfully, but when we get some vegetables it won't be so bad. I have no news for you as I have not been out since we moved here, but one day for a little walk to our hill at the back of the house. Tell Tom that his present is a most acceptable one, the very delicious shoulders of bacon, & tell him that

Russie and Fanny talk of him every day, & Fanny often wants to go to Uncle Tom's house. . . . I must now close as I have to make up my bread . . . tonight, and it is late now." Will Doyle wrote Tom on September 23.

"We were pleased to receive yours of Aug. 11th. I can now realize why farmers have so little time to write letters. My harvest is now all cut and one day more will finish stacking and as Harold left in the midst of it & I was alone since, it has been slow work especially as I have never swung a cradle before, but I have managed it about an acre a day, cutting, binding, & shocking besides doing all my chores, cutting wood, getting vegetables for the table, going off on the prairies at night for the cattle. . . .

"My wheat is poor as is usual in first crop off sod, but the oats headed grandly and though thin on the ground promised a fine crop, but the infernal blackbirds came down on them in myriads & have taken 10 or 13 bushels per acre, perhaps more. . . . You can imagine what hordes they fly in when I tell you that Harold & I fired two shots into a flock & picked up 18. . . . When we get a larger area under crops I don't think their inroads will be perceptible.

"My potatoes, carrots, turnips, & other roots are good. I have (or rather had, for my old ox got in & ate it) a turnip 31 inches in circumference 10 days ago. The early frost nipped our melons, cucumbers, & tomatoes. We only got one pumpkin & one squash. I planted nearly everything too deep & they were very late coming up & that with the late spring kept them back till this Sept. frost did the business. . . .

"We got Harold off on the 12th. He went to Rapid City with a neighbor & on arrival found that the Winnipeg Stage owner wouldn't take him 130 miles under $20 so he was at last accounts waiting a few days for a chance down at a cheaper rate. Teams are going nearly every day so he won't be delayed long. . . .

"There are a few reapers & mowers but as most of the settlers are cutting their 1st crop they do not need them. I intend to get a reaper and mower next year if I can manage it without going in debt. I can get a good deal of cutting to do for others & thus help pay for it. . . .

"It is very difficult to get a man to work here. If I can't get help to put up the house, Bella wants me to remain in the stable for the winter, which is a really good building and would be very warm, but I am determined not to do so unless I am obliged. . . . Russie . . . is continually criticising my mode of operating & says 'Now, papa, Uncle Tom don't do it that way.' . . . He spends much of his time afield with me and is delighted to ride the pony & the oxen. He is loud in his praises of Willie but don't seem to think much of Jimmy who he says is a 'great nuisance.' [Was thirteen-year-old Jimmy such a nuisance to the four-year-old boys at Myrtleville because he was at loose ends with his brother Johnny in Buffalo?]"

Harold Jones had come home after almost four months' absence. His sick mother rallied enough to go to see her mother at Myrtleville. When the Joneses returned to Maitland, Clara Good went with them. Soon she wrote her family: "I am sorry to tell you that we all see Fannie failing very fast. I can scarcely write tonight she seems so sick. She has just had another bad faint-fit & we just saved her from getting into hysterics. Harold is sitting with her now and I thought I ought to let you all know she is failing, for she may go off sooner than we expect. . . . You must not look for me home as long as you get on nicely without me. . . . If Annie can find my good overshoes . . . & can send them by parcel post I would be glad." Fanny wanted very much to live. She was not yet thirty-nine; she had a devoted husband and four children, age eighteen, sixteen, fourteen, and three. Energetic and cheerful by nature, she fought her losing battle hard.

It was a dark season at Myrtleville, too. Anne had her hands full; Clara was gone, and her mother was "frail and weak" and had had a second bad fall. Even sturdy little Willie got sick, and Mary Tom could not get domestic help. The one bright spot was news of the birth of Molly's third son, Samuel Francis, "Frank," on November 15. "Aunt Jo" Ballachey was on the spot to help again. She was with Molly for two months before the baby came, and three months afterward.

Fanny "died by inches." Clara wrote in November: "Fanny . . . is sinking every day. . . . Her limbs are paining her very much now and that is a bad sign. She suffers very much in all ways, her cough hurts her a great deal & she has a mustard blister on some place nearly every day. Her back aches badly. I rub it frequently but the bones are so near the surface I do not wonder they get sore. It is a puzzle to know what to get her to eat or drink rather. . . . Fannie will try to write to Tom some day but she can scarcely hold a cup her hand shakes so. This letter must do for all of you for some time, for I do not like to take time to write much." Fanny clung to life week after week. She sent out "Season's Greetings," a custom taken up by her generation. The Goods kept one of her cards at Myrtleville, a picture of flowers and grain, with a verse headed "Christmas," and the inscription, "For Mary & Tom, with Fannie's best love. Christmas, 1880." Finally, on Christmas Eve a telegram came to Thomas A. Good. It said, "Fannie died last night. Put notice in Brantford papers. Andrew Jones."

Because of Fanny's youth, hers was a sadder death than her father's four years earlier, but like him, she had been so ill so long that the family were relieved to have her suffering over. They buried her in the graveyard at the little "Old Blue Church" at Maitland. Family tradition tells that there was a "body-snatching" epidemic at that time (medical schools often had to buy bootleg cadavers), and for some nights Andrew Jones and young Harold took turns guarding Fanny's grave with rifle in hand.

9

A Lasting Attachment

After Fanny Jones died, Andrew's unmarried sister, Margaret, took charge of his house and children. Clara Good went home to Myrtleville, warmly welcomed by her tired sister and sister-in-law there. Mary Tom wrote her brother, William Ballachey, who had been taken to England as a child and did not remember any of the Goods: "Clara . . . is my main stay. . . . She is a bright, clever, energetic, generous, quick-tempered & warm-hearted Irish girl, which qualities belong more or less to the whole family. Mrs. Good is now over seventy & suffers from pain nearly all the time. About three years ago she had an attack of shingles since which she has suffered very much. The Drs. say it is neuralgia of the skin. She has tried many things but with no relief. She also suffers from Rheumatism. She is stout and sits too much which is not good for her but it pains her so to move. She is most industrious & knits & sews & sometimes makes beautiful netted neckties. Her sight is excellent & all her faculties clear. She is of a very practical turn of mind, orderly & dignified in all she does & is a good woman waiting for her Lord's call to go from this world of pain & suffering. She is extremely fond of her children, which affection is warmly returned by them all. I never saw a mother more esteemed."

Mrs. Allen Good taught her grandson, five-year-old Willie, to read. He learned very quickly—and asked questions insatiably. His mother described him as "a merry child . . . chief pet with his Aunties . . . and in danger of being somewhat spoiled." All her children, she said, were very healthy and lively, with rosy cheeks, blue eyes, and light hair.

Molly's children were lively, too, but unfortunately she had no sister-in-law under her roof at this time, and Sam had to go to London on business, making a side trip to Brantford. Molly wrote Mary Tom on April 5, when spring should have been coming: "I am having a fearfully lonesome time & we have all been miserable with colds since Sam left, but are rather better today. I find it almost impossible to get on with my work. . . . Baby [Frank, age five months] is more troublesome than either of the others & he cries so piteously that I have to take him, he is a sweet little fellow. . . . Yesterday I tied him in the high chair and left Georgie [age six] to push it round to amuse him while I hung out the clothes. In about two minutes I heard a fall and scream. G. had upset him on his face. I got a dreadful fright & George, baby & Fred cried for some time & I almost cried so we had a lively time of it. He was not much hurt, cut the inside of his upper lip a little & it bled which frightened the boys terribly. . . . I will be so glad to have Sam back again. Did you ever know such weather as we are having? This has been one of the stormiest days this winter, snowing, blowing & very cold. The kitchen is the only warm place in the house. I'm afraid we'll almost freeze tonight. If Sam goes back to Brantford, tell him we are getting on all right & he may as well stay as long as his ticket lasts. My back is no better, I don't know what I will do with it."

That summer Anne took a much needed vacation at Paisley. She wrote her mother from the Mallochs' on July 14, her fiftieth birthday: "I thought I would not let today pass without writing to you. I hope you are bearing this hot weather without feeling much worse. I have been feeling very well the last few days, the air here (though hot in the sunshine) is so cool and bracing. They are all so kind to me, this morning at breakfast, I found my plate covered with a napkin on which were presents from all of them, a note from George containing a five dollar gold piece, two pairs of fine white stockings from Charlotte, a nice purse from Lilly & a comb from little Sally. . . . Mary is to come in for Miss Macdonald and me after dinner to spend the afternoon if it does not rain. There was quite a gala day here on the 12th. [Celebration of anniversary of 1690 Battle of the Boyne]. The Orangemen looked very well and all went off without any drunkenness that we know of. . . . If all goes well I intend going to Elora [home of Mary John's family] next Tuesday and going home the Saturday after. . . . Love to all." There was a postscript: "I finished reading the *Siege of Derry* yesterday." (Anne loved to read history. She enjoyed Macaulay's long *History of England*.) Her mother answered by return mail. She was expecting "poor Eliza," who had written asking to visit Myrtleville "to see if it would do her any good." This is the first mention in the surviving documents of the younger Eliza's chronic illness.

There is no reference in the 1881 letters to the Charlotte-Molly disagreement. Things were definitely more comfortable at the Sam Ballacheys'. Sam was getting the farm under control with clearing and fertilizing, and Molly acquired a most satisfactory "lady help," Ruth Stow. Molly herself was able to visit Myrtleville in the fall of 1881. The "lady help," who was definitely not a servant, was a product of economic distress and an educational system which gave girls little vocational training beyond the household arts. As her children grew up, Mary John sometimes worked as a "lady help." In suggesting a friend's sister to Mary Tom, who was expecting a fourth child, Molly wrote: "If you get her you know you must remember that she is a lady & give her all the liberties that it is possible, & let her have as much change as possible. That sort of thing goes a long way in making girls contented & I advise you not to be too particular in little things because you know every one has a different way of doing things & we cannot expect every thing to be done as we would do it ourselves. You must excuse me speaking in this way, Mary, but I speak from experience & I think if you could get a nice respectable girl to live with you & treat as one of the family & one who could teach the children & help with the sewing & keep things comfortable, it would be a great comfort both to you and Tom. [Miss Julie] has been very much knocked about & wants a comfortable home & I don't suppose she has been used to very hard work, but if she is strong & willing I should think she would get on all right."

Late that year Mary John married again. The groom was a well-known business man of Paris, Samuel Qua, a middle-aged widower. Mary Qua had a good home of her own to offer her boys now, but they stayed on at Myrtleville; it had always been home to them, and besides they were already useful as farm workers. Sometimes Jimmy, the older, went for long periods to the Sam Ballacheys'; sometimes, at Myrtleville, he went back to school for a while. The school curriculum may have been limited and rigid in those days, but a great deal of individual instruction must have gone on. Both boys and girls from the country attended school quite irregularly because in summer they had to help at home and in winter the weather was often too bad for long walks.

Charlie wrote Anne a long letter on November 21, 1881: "I am quite ashamed that I have not sooner answered your letter. I was sorry to miss seeing you last summer, & yet glad you had the rest & enjoyment you so much needed. We are very quiet this season. Arthur [age eighteen] is away at College at Ithaca, N.Y. I presume you heard he obtained a Scholarship which gives him his Tuition free. The course is four years at the end of which if he passes he will obtain the degree of Bachelor of Science. Cornell College is one of the best in the U.S. tho' one of the younger, not yet being 20 years old. . . . Many years ago the U.S. Congress gave each state 30,000 acres of land for each Congressman to be applied towards Educational purposes. New York state having 35 Congressmen received over 1,000,000 acres and turned it over to Cornell College on condition that the Hon. Ezra Cornell (father of the present governor of this state) should give $500,000. Mr. Cornell gave that sum and subsequently about $300,000 more. . . . Arthur purposes studying Law after graduation so it will be six years yet before he will have his profession. It seems a long time but the years roll away, fast. . . . I often think if I had studied Law & worked as hard at it as I have at Book keeping for the last 20 years I would have been much better off. . . . So after long and careful consideration we decided to help Arthur get a profession & then let him paddle his own Canoe. . . . I was so glad Arthur got acquainted with the Jones'. He had a delightful visit there. I hope some day the boys will return his visit. Write soon & give me all the news."

Three months later there was news of another baby at Myrtleville, a round-faced, towheaded little girl whom Tom and Mary named Ethel Isabella. News came also from the child's Aunt Isabella and her husband. Will Doyle's horizons were not limited by his farm for long. No sooner had he built a good-sized, comfortable house than he turned his attention to insurance business and municipal government. Early in 1882, little more than a year from living in a log stable and harvesting his first crop, he wrote Tom Good that "[I] would have written you sooner but for the fact that I have more writing than any one man should be obliged to do." He then went on to describe what those obligations were.

"I have now taken charge of a much larger District as Crown Timber Agent and do considerable Insurance business as well. Then I have prepared & compiled all the bye laws of the municipality of Shoal Lake County & this has involved a great deal of labor & study of the consolidated statutes in order that no conflict could occur. Then for the past 3 mos. I have been fighting a very lively municipal battle with the citizens of Birtle & Shoal Lake over the subdivision of our old County.

"By a division of our County, Beulah would be . . . the seat of County business, and again by securing the division we of the South half would be in a position to vote a bonus to a Railway if we desired to do so without interference by the North half. . . . I had to go to Winnipeg twice & tho' the Gov't was beset by deputations from Shoal Lake & Birtle, I carried my point . . . and we now have a new county of 21 Townships, known as Miniota (Sioux for well-watered). The result of my work was a . . . call for me to take the wardenship (wardens are here elected by the people, not by the Reeves) & my election was by acclamation as I declined to stand otherwise. . . . We must thank you very much for your kindness in remembering us so handsomely as you have done this Xmas. I look forward to the time when I can return all your kindness."

Will also reported that the Doyles had enjoyed a short visit from Andrew Jones who was "delighted with the country," and invested considerable money in the new county of Miniota. Harold Jones was working for his Uncle Will and "standing the winter pretty well." Temperatures were much more extreme than in Ontario, but the Doyles always maintained that forty degrees below zero in the West felt no worse than zero in the East.

Will's thriving insurance business had some drawbacks. Bella was often left alone with the children on the farm. Usually she "coped" magnificently; she was a strong, active, self-reliant woman, and, like her mother before her, a tower of strength to neighbors in trouble. But now she was pregnant again, feeling worse than she had before, and lacking the company of husband, or mother, or sisters. She wrote Mary Tom a most uncharacteristic letter: "I have intended writing to you for a long time but want of time kept me from doing so. . . . I have never felt so poorly as I do this time. It must be from having so much to do . . . Will says he will get a servant if there is one to be got, but I don't know. . . . I am glad little Ethel is such a fine child & I hope she may be a comfort to you. To tell the truth, Mary, I don't ever feel as if I would have any comfort with my children & I wish with all my heart I never had any. I do my best to make them obedient but it seems almost impossible. . . . God grant I may never never have any more after this trouble is over. . . . I look forward to the time when I can go back to Ont. & send them to school. I am sorry to write you such a blue letter . . . but I feel dull & lonely today. Will has gone away to be gone till Friday. He is away nearly all the time. . . . As far as travelling goes he might better be in Ont., for there he could go by rail, but now he has to drive through bad roads & storms." The baby, born March 23, 1883, was named Clara, and she did grow up to be a comfort to her mother and many other people.

Molly's fourth and last pregnancy went much more smoothly than her third. She had Ruth Stow to help her, and sixteen-year-old Jimmy was there to help Sam. Molly must have made her peace with the Mallochs; she was able to accept their kindness again. She wrote that George, age eight, was going to school in the village and doing very well, and it was so nice having him go to the Mallochs' for his dinner. He liked to go and the Mallochs liked having him. In the spring of 1883, Molly and Ruth did a great deal of sewing on that wonderful invention, the sewing machine. Molly wrote Tom about it: "This week have been fixing Jimmy up, made him two pairs of working pants, covered two neckties, & fixed the necks of two shirts his mother sent him & they did not fit. We have George's best suit all ready for him to wear, all navy blue except hat that is white straw with navy blue ribbon. I have not to get any new things for Fred & Frank which is a comfort but we have lots of fixing and altering to do for them. We turned Sam's best summer coat & it is a great success, it looks as good as new, I have not got anything for myself but a hat which is a very pretty black chip poke with blue inside & all black outside. I think it is becoming." Molly's baby was born in August, her youngest child and only daughter. She had really forgiven her sister, Charlotte Malloch, for whatever had caused hard feelings three years earlier, and she named the baby Charlotte.

Eliza Good sat in her big chair at Myrtleville and sewed and knitted for her many children and grandchildren. Her body was stiff and sore, but her mind was active. She read widely, and Charlie continued his long practice of sending her a subscription to *Harper's Magazine* for Christmas. (It was founded in 1850, the earliest of the "quality" illustrated magazines. The Goods usually had their numbers bound, and there is still a row of *Harper's* volumes on the library shelves at Myrtleville.)

Mrs. Good knew clearly that she was living "on borrowed time." Her husband had left her all he had, but it was not much. She also had a little property which had always been hers. She thought a good deal about how she could best bequeath her small estate, and she had a will drawn which said: "I leave to my daughter Anne the eight acres of ground on the South part of the front field. I wish the land on the Paris Road to be sold for as much as it will bring, and to be equally divided between the five others namely Eliza, Thomas, Mary, Clara, and my grandson John Good, also to Clara the 270 dollars for which I hold the note. . . . I leave to Anne and Thomas the pew no. 25 in Grace Church, Brantford. I wish that whatever share may come to my daughter Eliza may be given to Anne for the use of Eliza so that her husband may not get any of it. I leave Anne entire Executrix of this will. At her death I wish her to divide the Books, Plate, and China among Charles, Thomas, Mary, Isabella, Charlotte, and Clara, and a few books to the grandchildren as keepsakes. . . . In case of the death of James A. Good before the age of twenty-one the sum of 450 dollars left to me by my son John Good I leave to his brother John Good."

Drawing room, Myrtleville House, showing Victorian fire screen of flowers and fruit painted on velvet

In the spring of 1885 there was startling news from the Northwest Territories, causing the Goods anxious weeks. The railway which had been promised British Columbia when it joined Canada in 1871 was being built slowly in sections. Part of it was pushing into the valley of the Saskatchewan west of the Doyles. This was a wild country inhabited by Indian tribes and a few half-breed settlers. To the Indians the railway meant the end of the great buffalo herds on which they depended for food. To the half-breeds it meant difficulty in keeping their land, to which they often had insecure title. The country had been spared much of the lawlessness which afflicted the American West, because of an efficient mobile force, established in 1873, the Northwest (later the Royal Canadian) Mounted Police. But in 1884 the French and Indian settlers of the Saskatchewan Valley begged Louis Riel, the leader in a Manitoba revolt of 1870, to come back from Montana and help them. On March 24, 1885, a group of them attacked a party of mounted police near Prince Albert, killing fourteen and wounding twenty-five. They appealed to the Indian tribes to join them and drive out the white settlers.

As quickly as possible, eight thousand troops from the East went to suppress the rebellion. The railway from Lake Superior to Winnipeg was still unfinished and the soldiers had to cover uncompleted sections on foot in bitter weather. By May 15, Riel was taken prisoner, and the worst was over, at a cost of about two hundred lives. The disturbances had not affected the Doyles except for the worry that they might spread eastward.

Sometimes Tom Good wondered if he should follow Will Doyle's example and go West. Could he provide better for his growing family on a prairie farm? After more than fifteen years of putting a great deal of physical and mental energy into Myrtleville, he was still making little more than a bare living. But all Canada, East and West, was as depressed in the mid-eighties as in the mid-seventies. A burst of economic improvement in the early eighties had been small and brief. Even the longed-for completion of the transcontinental railroad did not pull Canada out of its slump. People drifted off to the United States with its more varied opportunities and its more accessible frontier. For three decades in a row—the seventies, eighties, and nineties—Canada had more emigrants than immigrants. There was a slow increase in population (mainly urban) because there were more babies born than disappointed immigrants—and natives—leaving the country, but it was not a situation to stimulate demand for farm products.

Ontario farmers continued to make efforts to help themselves. The Farmers' Institutes sprang up in the mid-eighties. They brought professors from the O.A.C., the Ontario Agricultural College at Guelph, to lecture on their fields of study; they invited prominent farmers to share their knowledge. In one of Tom Good's annual reports as secretary-treasurer of the South Brant Farmers' Institute, he listed the speakers of the past year: President Mills of the O.A.C. on "Education"; Mr. Thomas Elmes on "Rust and Blight"; Mr. Thomas Good on "Farm Buildings"; Mr. W. H. Metcalf on "Fruit Growing"; Mr. George McLaughlin on "Horse-Breeding"; Professor Robinson of the O.A.C. on "Dairying"; Mr. Thomas Brooks on "Manures"; Mr. Francis Malcolm on "Some Mistakes"; Mr. Brethour on "Shorthorn Cattle"; Mr. I. F. Smith, veterinary surgeon, on "Diseases of Farm Stock"; Mr. William Thompson on "Sheep Husbandry."

Tom Good was an expert on farm buildings at this time. He had just rebuilt and enlarged the north barn at Myrtleville, using material from the old barn, mostly white oak from pioneer days, and probably also material from Fanny Carroll's little schoolhouse at the gate. It was torn down about this time. Nine-year-old Willie was tremendously interested in the building project, and remembered it all his life. He was always a boy with marked manual dexterity, and no doubt began to practice building skills that summer. Incidentally, the 1885 barn is still in use at Myrtleville.

At Christmas, Molly wrote that she had hoped they could get to Myrtleville, but they really could not afford it. She said: "I am sorry Phillip Laird [probably George Laird's brother] is dead as I suppose he helped Eliza somewhat. I wish I had something to send her this year but I feel that it would be wrong to do it as we are pretty sure we will not be able to get through without borrowing. I am sick of this grinding poverty & the sooner we give up farming the better pleased I'll be, but

Tom Good's "cement silo" built in 1902 and north barn, rebuilt and enlarged in 1885

I'm afraid that will not be, as I suppose Sam would not be fit for anything else." Eliza Laird had been in poor health for years. Her nephew Johnny had not been strong, either. Now his "weak lungs" finally made him an invalid too. Willie remembered him mainly for his terrible cough. Older members of the family realized that "the great white plague" of tuberculosis was upon Johnny. This was a time when newspapers still reported that "consumption" was the top-ranking cause of death in Canada; after it came "old age."

Eliza Good felt that Johnny and she were not long for this world. She was also concerned about Molly's poverty and the lack of resources of her youngest daughter, the spinster, Clara. She had already sold her land on the Paris Road and given Clara her share, one hundred dollars. Now she wrote a postscript to her will: "If John Good dies before he is twenty-one years of age, the one hundred dollars bequeathed to him I leave to be divided equally between my daughters Mary H.

Ballachey and Clara C. Good. . . . If both the boys die before twenty-one, I leave the Four Hundred & Fifty dollars between Mary & Clara."

About this time the wreck who had been the handsome, vivacious Eliza Laird came home to stay—alone. She was almost unable to walk. The Goods, who had never liked George Laird, said that he abandoned Eliza when she became helpless; at any rate, her brothers and sisters supported her for at least the last ten years of her life. It must be said in justice to George Laird that he does seem to have taken responsibility for his younger sons; they did not come to Myrtleville to live. Allen Laird was a grown man now and worked on some traveling job. One of his letters to his mother survives. In it he expressed regret for having given her such a hard time when he was growing up, and he said that when he had a house of his own, she was to come live with him. Eliza's youngest was still a child; perhaps some of his father's relatives cared for him.

Tom Good struggled on with the farm work, missing Johnny's help. He had five children to support now; little Fanny was born in March of 1886. Clara adored her and called her "little Pansy." The lively children from the north wing must have been welcome entertainment in the front of Myrtleville House, which was virtually a hospital by 1887. In the southeast bedroom, Eliza Good, eighty years old and lame, was helped in and out of the high four-poster which had been her bed for fifty years. In the hall bedroom next door, Johnny coughed his young life away. Downstairs, Eliza Laird, miserable and shaky, occupied the northwest room, behind the long pantry. Anne, calm and cheerful, was head nurse; Mary Qua, busy with a little son by her second marriage, could not do much for her consumptive child.

Johnny died on July 23, 1887, not yet nineteen years old. He was sadly missed, but Willie, though only eleven, was already doing easy farm work that had been Johnny's task. His usefulness caused him and his father a terrifying experience that summer. Seventy years later every detail was still burnt into his memory.

"One day in harvest time, my father sent me to rake the stubble in one of our fields. I had an old buggy horse hitched to a one-horse dump rake and in proceeding to the field to be raked had to go through a somewhat narrow gate on our lane-way going to the public road. Going through this gate I caught one end of the axle on the gate post. It was probably not more than a half inch overlap, since the rake passed through immediately. But the jolt was sufficient to throw me off the seat and release the hook that held the rake up. I fell down on the ground near the horse's hind feet, losing the lines, and noticed to my dismay that the teeth were down. There was, therefore, nothing I could do except hang on to the rake and be dragged along under it. If I had relinquished my hold I would have been torn to pieces and speedily killed by the sharp steel teeth. The natural reaction of a child under such circumstances is to call for help. There was no human being near, so I immediately dispatched a prayer, unformulated and unspoken, to the Heavenly Father. This, of course, resulted in no miraculous intervention, but it did allay my anxiety so that my wits did not leave me.

"The old horse was startled by the jolt at the gate, but not frightened. Breaking into a jog trot he followed the beaten path down the road towards the public highway about a quarter-mile distant, indifferent to any calls from me, and subject to no control by the lines. So I kept hanging on to the foot board, my heels dragging along the ground. Fortunately, the road gate was closed, and when the old horse reached it he stopped. I then crawled out, somewhat bruised and shaken up, but uninjured, and held my horse by the bridle. Looking up, I saw my father running down the road. He must have been watching to see if I had succeeded in getting safely through the gate, and, noticing the accident, followed me on the run. He must have had a great fright, for he said when he got near, 'Are you dead?' I assured him that I was not injured, but I was not a little humiliated by my carelessness. I do not recall doing the raking that day" (W. C. Good, *Farmer Citizen: My Fifty Years in the Canadian Farmers' Movement* [Toronto: Ryerson Press, 1958]).

A few weeks later, Mrs. George Ballachey senior made one of her periodic visits to Myrtleville. These were always happy occasions; she was a warm, merry person whose children, even when they were old, remembered the sound of her happy laughter. Her grandchildren adored her but they were some-what afraid of her austere husband. On her way home to Edgemount, Mrs. Ballachey called at a friend's house in Brantford. There she had a severe stroke, and died the next morning without regaining consciousness. She had married very young, and was still only sixty-one years old. Her death was a terrible blow to all her family.

After that summer of deaths and near-disaster, the winter passed peacefully at Myrtleville, except that ten-year-old Mamie hurt her knee sledding and it would not get well. Willie was in his last year at Moyle's School, but Mamie could not go regularly. She was taught at home, if anyone had time to teach her. There was news from Buffalo that Arthur was trying his first important case in one of the higher courts, and that Allen Jones, who disliked farming, was staying at his Uncle Charlie's and doing very well in medical school. Mary Tom's brother, John Ballachey, forty-year-old father of four, gave up his farm near Brantford and went to work in a store at Madison, Dakota Territory, hoping to better himself financially.

Eliza Good failed noticeably in March. Molly came to see her, and Charlie wrote anxiously. She died on April 6, 1888, two days after her eighty-first birthday. She was the last of the first generation to live at Myrtleville, and an era was over. She had lived there fifty years, seen land cleared, a house and addition erected, barns built and rebuilt. She had seen Brantford grow from a village of less than a thousand people to a city of thirteen thousand. She had traveled from Ireland to America in the age of sailing ship and stagecoach, and before her death for many years had traveled by steamship and railroad. She had brought up ten children at Myrtleville, and by the end of her life had had twenty-seven grandchildren, two of whom predeceased her.

Jim Good was twenty-one the month his grandmother died. He settled some money matters with his Aunt Annie, executor of his father's estate, and, like so many other young men, took off for the West. Johnny was dead, and Willie was a twelve-year-old schoolboy. Tom Good was heavily dependent on hired help, and the farm was not very profitable. His dissatisfaction with Myrtleville came to a head, and he wrote his western brothers-in-law for advice. John Ballachey answered in May: "In regard to your queries re country etc., 'tis hard to advise anything. Some farmers seem to be doing well, a majority not so well. You see they nearly all came here poor. As a rule, you know, those who are doing well east stay there & those who come here do so as a last resort, & when it happens as it sometimes does that a Farmer does not get a crop for a time, as one man told me the first year a Cyclone took his House away, the next Prairie fire burnt his Barn & grain, the next the Hail destroyed everything, you may imagine his condition coming here without money. The money Loaners have him solid & will make him die hard. . . . If I remain here I shall not think of farming. . . . I hear Iowa well spoken of, no Cyclones or Blizzards and Land is cheap they say."

Will Doyle wrote on July 2, on paper with the letterhead "The Miniota Farmers' Mutual Fire Insurance Company. W. A. Doyle, manager & secretary": . . . "I would have replied to yours of 23rd May sooner had I been able to make up my mind how to advise you. I have now made up my mind not to advise you at all further than to say that you should stick to your farm if you can even hold your own. Of course, if you find yourself steadily losing money, it would perhaps be wise to sell out, invest the proceeds in safe mortgages and go into some light business which would supplement your income from investments. . . . If you will write and tell me what you could have clear if you sold out land & chattels & wound up your business, I would have an idea as to what you should do with your capital in Manitoba."

Willie was horrified when he overheard some friends urging his father to give up the farm. Tom did not really want to leave, and his brothers-in-law did not encourage him to do so. He decided to keep on trying at Myrtleville, and in time pass it on to his son.

10

Education—In and Out of School

The summer of 1888, following Mrs. Allen Good's death, a great change came over Myrtleville House. Tom's family moved out of the wing into the front section. Anne spent a long time with the Sam Ballacheys; Molly was very ill for weeks with "jaundice," a form of hepatitis. At Myrtleville, the summer work, combined with the care of the five children and their invalid Aunt Eliza, bore heavily on Mary Tom and Clara. The family took advantage of Brantford's first regular hospital, a forty-five-bed building on Terrace Hill, presented to the city three years earlier by John H. Stratford, a prominent businessman. Charlie sent money in four monthly installments from mid-June to pay Eliza's hospital bills. There is a pathetic scrawled note from Eliza to Mary Tom: "I want to tell you what I should like you to bring me from the farm. Please bring me a nice pat of butter as the butter we get here I can't eat. . . . Also if you can spare them bring me 4 or 5 of your buns. . . . I hope you have good news from Molly and Sam. Give my love to Clara & tell her to be sure & not go to Manitoba till I see her. I hope dear Mamie is feeling better everyway. I long to see you all."

Willie took the entrance examination for high school early that summer. He was twelve, almost two years younger than the average candidate, but he ranked fourth among ninety-four county children. When the new term opened, he attended the Brantford Collegiate Institute, a fairly new building on George Street near the Grand Trunk (now Canadian National) station. This was not the present station; it was a low building with a Gothic peak in the center front, and beginning to look rather old-fashioned. The school was described as "elegant and commodious"; it had arched windows and two towers and housed several hundred students to whom it offered good college preparatory courses. It was a far cry from the two-teacher high school that Mary and Clara Good had attended little more than twenty years earlier.

Willie either walked about three miles to school, or rode a horse which he left at a livery stable back of the station. His special companions were Arthur Lyons, a boy he met at the Collegiate, who shared his interest in things mechanical and electrical, and his childhood playmate and cousin, George Melville Ballachey of Edgemount, who was somewhat less scientific, but also good with his hands. (George M. Ballachey was usually called "George M." to distinguish him from his cousin, the Sam Ballacheys' "George T." He was distinguished also as the first farm boy to have a telephone in his home, his "Uncle Aleck's" invention.) Together, George and Willie built a forge in the workshop at Myrtleville, learning to lay bricks in the process, and so provided the means for shoeing horses without a trip to the neighborhood blacksmith shop.

Arthur Lyons and George M. enjoyed Willie's lathes, which he made when he was about fifteen. He wrote about them many years later: "I built a wood lathe, out of odds and ends about the place. I think the only bit of machine work I had done on it was the shaft in the head stock. I then tackled a small metal lathe which I mounted on an old sewing machine base. This involved several patterns for castings, the making of which involved careful woodwork. A little of the machine work, turning and planing I got done in Brantford at insignificant cost. . . . About the time I built the forge, I built a simple device for boring holes in metal, which has been used off and on for about sixty-five years." Willie used part of the empty north wing of Myrtleville House for a private workshop. There is a story that during one of Aleck Bell's visits to Brantford, Mary Tom proudly showed the inventor her son's contrivances. He was interested in the boy's ingenuity, and said, "How I wish I had a son!"

When Anne came back to Myrtleville from Paisley she fitted into it in a new role. Her household duties were now of a sub-

ordinate nature, sewing, knitting, dusting, gardening. She re-
sumed her nursing of Eliza, and had more time to teach the
lame child, Mamie, both book learning and needlework. In
1891, her pupil won a prize at the Toronto Exhibition for
"Best dressed doll (under 15 years)." This baby doll and its
clothing are still in the possession of Mamie's daughter. It has
a pretty round-featured bisque head, golden-haired and blue-
eyed, attached to a surprisingly long slim body encased in
white kidskin. It wears a very long, elaborately embroidered
and tucked dress of the type Mrs. Allen Good made for her
children. The underclothes are hand-knitted shirt and boo-
tees, a long flannel "band" wrapped around the abdomen (a
practice that went on for at least another generation), diaper,
ruffled diaper cover, and long flannel petticoat. Outdoor
clothing consists of a lace bonnet and a flannel "wrapper" with
matching shawl. Both wrapper and shawl have edges embroidered in scallops. Now yellowed with age, the whole outfit was
no doubt once snowy white.

Clara Good went West soon after her mother died, but
Anne and Mary Tom lived together affectionately for thirty
years, with the younger sister-in-law operating the older's
house. Fortunately, they were congenial in many respects;
both were deeply religious and attached to the Low Church
aspect of Anglicanism. Mary Tom, more than Anne's brothers
and sisters, shared her aversion to dancing, intoxicating
liquors, and frivolous books. Anne had more imagination than
Mary, it seems, and therefore more tact. Mary admired Anne
greatly; she wrote her brother, William, overseas. "Miss Good
is quite the best woman I know. She is a true Christian."

Anne had her own Bible class again, her nephew and nieces
at Myrtleville. Willie wrote much later: "I became familiar with
a good deal of the Bible through having it read to us children
by our Aunt Annie, who also diligently instructed us in the
Church of England Catechism. She had the good sense to con-
fine her Bible reading for the most part to Bible history. My
mother was a great student of the Bible but found herself
baffled by much that she found in it. And it has been my
opinion that her bewilderment was increased rather than di-
minished by certain books she read that purported to 'explain
the mysteries.' "

The "Good Girls" of Myrtleville, taken about 1902. Left to right: *Mamie, Fanny, Louie, Ethel, and Carol*

George Ballachey senior died in 1889, and his youngest grandchild, the Tom Goods' sixth child and fifth daughter, was born on August 23, 1890, and named Caroline Ballachey. The following year, Tom was one of the founders of the North Brant Dairy Association. This group built a cheese factory a few miles north of Brantford on what is now Highway 24. Ontario farmers increasingly emphasized livestock and dairying rather than wheat-growing (which was the special strength of the fertile western prairie). For years Tom Good, working hard as a dairy farmer, also served as secretary of the cheese factory. Willie remembered his father's "enormous amount of clerical drudgery."

Tom did not keep his only son's nose to the grindstone, however. In the summer of 1891, Willie and his Aunt Annie visited Homewood. They took the boat from Hamilton to Prescott. It was Willie's first experience of travel by water, and the farthest he had ever been from home. The visitors had a fine time at Homewood. Anne wrote approvingly of Andrew's sister-housekeeper, "Margaret Jones keeps everything in the greatest order & is very kind to everyone." Willie and Carroll, who was about his age, helped with farm chores, but had a great deal of fun rowing and fishing on the river. Willie found the St. Lawrence fascinating. Uncle Andrew's right-hand man was Harold, back to stay at Maitland after three years of homesteading near the Doyles.

The following summer it was Mary Tom's turn to have a vacation. She and fourteen-year-old Mamie went to Paisley. Molly and Sam were living in the village now. Sam's inheritance from his father had cleared the farm of debt; he had sold it for a good price and gone into partnership in Paisley's general store. The oldest son, "George T.," had been sent at the age of fifteen to his uncle in Buffalo, who got him a job in the W. H. Glenny office where Charlie Good had worked for twenty-five years. The boy was bright and attractive and did very well. It is an interesting sidelight on the proud "Lord Malloch" that he is the one who gave young George some pocket money for the trip to Buffalo. Sam Ballachey, like his sister Mary, was not very good at putting himself in the other fellow's shoes.

Molly had never recovered her strength after that dreadful summer of jaundice four years earlier, and she was very glad to leave the farm and its hard work. Her gregarious nature had a chance to blossom again. George T. came from Buffalo while his Aunt Mary was in Paisley. She wrote her husband: "Sam & Mary have a most comfortable house, so neat & nice & they like living in the village. . . . I have been twice to the store & it is quite an extensive one, such a lot of goods & very cheap (of all kinds except hardware & stationary). They one day lately handled over a thousand dollars worth of butter, & Sam says their stock of butter has greatly exceeded that. George is enjoying his holiday very much, says he never liked Paisley so much before, & is out visiting about every day & Mary gave a party for young people on Monday, & on Tuesday we were all invited to Mrs. Saunders'. The Mallochs too were there. We had a very pleasant evening. The church picnic was yesterday afternoon & Mary & I & the children went & Sam got there in time for the tea."

Tom wrote news from Myrtleville. Louie and Ethel had gone back to school the last week of August. The children had had a birthday party for two-year-old Carol, "all by themselves." Six-year-old Fanny was staying with "the Aunts" (Jo and Lizzie) at Edgemount and going to school with her cousin, Meg Ballachey. Willie wanted to go to the Toronto Fair to see "the Electric machines and other machinery," but Tom felt he could not afford to go this year.

Twelve-year-old Louie wrote her mother: "Aunt Annie & I got letters from Aunt Clara night before last and she is very homesick & lonely. Aunt Lizzie has cut Fannie's hair all off close to her head, and her teeth are all coming out in front so she looks pretty queer." Louie wrote Mamie about schoolwork, and fun with the Carlyles, who lived on the next farm toward Paris: "We have begun French, alegbra [sic], bookkeeping (but I have not got my book yet), and we are at the Isles of Greece in the fifth book. For about four verses of The Isles of Greece we have about two pages of notes to learn, and we have been having a lot of figures of Speech to learn as antithses [sic] Apostrophe, Simile, Synedoche, Metaphor, Metonymy, Climax, allusion, irony, Epizeauxix, and some others. In arithmetic we have begun Discount. Last night we asked Blanch Carlyle to stand in their garden and watch for us looking out of the place above the pig-pen. So Ethel and I when we were hunting eggs got up through the holes in the roof and sat on the roof and Blanch was in their garden and Tom & John too and we had quite a conversation. We could hear each other quite plainly. . . . Blanch . . . said she heard our hens cackling and we could hear theirs quite plainly."

Tom wrote his wife the following week, "Anne has taken a pew in St. Jude's church for three months; we went there yesterday." Apparently this was the beginning of the final break with Grace Church. Anne had run out of patience with the unorthodoxy of the rector, who showed his liberal theological leanings in a series of sermons on "the Wider Hope." All the adults at Myrtleville were also uneasy about liturgical innovations at Grace Church, which seemed to them tinged with "popishness." Tom was worried about his poor harvest, but he could not resist Willie. He wrote on September 18, "Willie wanted to see Toronto Fair very much and did not wish to go alone, so I went with him. We were away two days. . . . The show was immense and Willie enjoyed himself a good deal. I was sorry to spend the time and money but wanted Willie to see the show."

The "Electric Machines" Willie wanted to see were all the rage. Electricity was an answer to many problems. Brantford had had a horse-drawn streetcar system for six years, but the light cars kept running off tracks, the horses' feet wore dangerous trenches in the streets, and snowstorms simply eliminated service. Now electric cars were coming. The first arrived in October 1892, about a month after Tom's and Willie's trip to Toronto Fair. It was honored with a detailed description in the newspaper. It had a "body of the very best cedar, . . . The conductor will stand at rear and the motorman at the front." Soon there were six cars providing twelve-minute service in town, and before the end of the nineties there was an hourly service from Brantford to Paris, with a stop near the tollgate only a mile from Myrtleville.

Clara Good was in San Jose, California. She had gone there to work, probably as a practical nurse. She did not like the place, said it was "nasty and dirty," and wrote that she longed to see "her dear little girls" at Myrtleville. She sent money for Louie's music lessons. Later, she nursed in Oakland for some years and there she married John Matthews, from Indiana, who worked in a government office. She was in her mid-forties at that time.

Two years after Willie's trip to Maitland on the St. Lawrence he had an even more exciting trip in the opposite direction. His Uncle George and Aunt Carrie Ballachey took him along with their boys to the World's Columbian Exposition in Chicago. Its fascinating exhibits made a great impression on him, as did the huge city, America's second largest, with its pioneering "skyscrapers."

"George M." and Willie were seventeen now. George attended a fine old private school in Toronto, Upper Canada College, but Willie, needing to earn money, left the Collegiate when he reached what was called "Junior Leaving" (later Junior Matriculation). He took the three-month training course at the "Model School" in Brantford, and then, not yet eighteen, started teaching at Howell's School, a one-room country school four and a half miles from Myrtleville. He walked this distance twice a day, and was paid at the rate of three hundred dollars a year without board, perhaps fifteen hundred a year in 1970 money. By the end of his first term, he had decided to resign. He would go back to the Collegiate for Upper School work, and try to get a university scholarship. His cousin, Arthur, had done it.

Meantime, Arthur's father, Charlie Good, had left his long-time employer, Glenny and Company, and become manager of the American Bit-Brace and Tool Company of Buffalo. He also bought a good-sized house across the river in Fort Erie, Ontario. He already had a "bungalow" (summer cottage) at Erie Beach. Now he still worked in the United States but lived the year round in Canada. Before long, he was not well enough to enjoy his new job and his new house. Kate and he went to Bermuda in the spring of 1894; and Bella wrote to Myrtleville, "I am very sorry to hear of [Charlie's] health failing; he has always been so well, but we can't expect people to last forever."

Bermuda did not help much. A Myrtleville scrapbook contains a clipping from a Buffalo newspaper of August 23, 1894. It begins: "Charles C. Good of 721 Front Avenue died at his summer residence at Erie Beach yesterday afternoon. His illness had been pronounced serious several days ago and his family had been summoned. . . . Mr. Good was 59 years old." There is another clipping which describes his funeral: "The pall bearers were six employes of the Bit-Brace and Tool Company. . . . The mourners were Hon. A. S. Hardy, T. A. Good, A. D. Hardy, Brantford; Arthur Good, son of the deceased, Dr. Allen Jones and George Ballachey, Buffalo, nephews."

Two months after Charlie's death, Molly died. She was only forty-six. She had been having more and more frequent spells of the illness, described as "jaundice," which had afflicted her for six years. It is unfortunate that so many of her children's memories of "Molly the jolly" were of her sickness. Her Ballachey nephews saw her on her rare and happy visits to Brantford. One of them said, when he was a very old man, "I loved Aunt Molly. She was the pick of the Myrtleville people, the prettiest and the nicest." There is a sad contrast between the photographs of Molly as a young woman, and as a middle-aged woman soon to die. The pretty round-faced girl of the earlier pictures is almost unrecognizable in the strained and emaciated appearance of the latest picture. Toward the last, Molly lay in a coma; her family felt about her death as they had about Fanny's, fourteen years earlier, that it was "a blessed release."

Sam Ballachey's unmarried sisters at Edgemount took his

younger children under their wings. Fred, Frank, and "Lottie" (Charlotte) made their home with "the Aunts" until they had finished high school in Brantford. By the autumn of 1895 there were enrolled at the Brantford Collegiate three of Tom Good's children, Willie, Louie and Ethel, and four of their Ballachey cousins: Panay and Alec, sons of George and Carrie; Fred and Frank, sons of Sam and Molly.

Mamie never attended high school, and yet her daughter, a college graduate, says, "knowing my mother was a liberal education." Much of the credit goes to Mamie's teacher, Anne Good; much, of course, to her own quick and eager mind. To be sure, it was unfortunate that she had to rely so much on books for her entertainment. She was lame for years, suffering perhaps as much from the treatment as from the disabling. For quite a while she wore a heavy metal brace, discovered in the 1966 removal of a storage space at Myrtleville. It was anchored at waistline and foot, and looks like an instrument of torture.

At fifteen, Mamie was very ill with measles, and had severe digestive trouble for a long time. The doctors put her on a diet of zwieback and pepsin-treated milk or buttermilk, and she stayed on it month after month. Such a diet does not provide adequate nourishment for an adolescent (or anyone for long); it is not surprising that Mamie continued to be thin and weak and sickly and caused her parents great anxiety.

In 1895 Willie Good entered his final year of preparation for university scholarships. He took every course offered except Greek. Louie, though not yet sixteen, was in her last year of preparation for teacher-training. Tom Good's daughters were to be educated for professions, but the only "ladylike" profession available without considerable expense was school-teaching. (Clara repeatedly wrote her "dear girls" at Myrtleville, that they must stick to their studies and avoid all the difficulties she had had in earning a living.)

Louie had entered the Collegiate at thirteen, a year older than her brother, but with the highest score among the hundred and ninety candidates for high school entrance. She was proceeding through her courses with record speed. Ethel, like Willie, "passed the entrance" at twelve. She felt the pressure of her teachers' expectations; she complained defensively of feeling "lazy and stupid" and her performance was apt to be spotty. However, one of her reports for 1895 survives, and it bears the remarks, "one of the most promising pupils in the class," and "is doing admirable work."

Willie Good at nineteen was a serious-minded young man. He had no aptitude for "small talk" and prided himself on not learning to play cards or dance. There is a reflection of this in a note from Carrie Ballachey to her niece, Louie, late in the summer of 1895: "The boys are going to have a little dance on Friday, and would like you to come. If Willie would care to come, we will be glad to see him. If Willie does not bring you, be at the Wyes' at seven. The boys will be there."

In the spring of the next year, Willie took the scholarship examinations for the University of Toronto. He more than fulfilled his and his family's and his teachers' hopes. There is a yellowed newspaper clipping at Myrtleville which reads in part, "The success of Mr. W. C. Good . . . at the scholarship examinations in Toronto University beats any record hitherto made by any one scholar in this University. Mr. Good was prepared in the Brantford Collegiate."

The article goes on to say that W. C. Good had passed, with first-class honors in each subject, examinations in English, French, German, history and geography, mathematics, natural science, biology, and chemistry and physics. It then lists scholarships won by him—general proficiency and Prince of Wales Prize, Edward Blake Scholarship in mathematics, Edward Blake Scholarship in science. He had ranked first for other scholarships in modern languages, science, and mathematics, but these had gone to others by reversion. Willie's proud father must have wished that he could tell all this to Charlie, whose son had gone to Cornell on a scholarship years before.

Sixteen-year-old Louie, almost ready to teach school, left the Collegiate at the same time as Willie. People said, "She's as clever as her brother." Besides being a good student, she was a very pretty girl with big blue eyes and golden brown hair described as "sunny." Out in Manitoba, Fanny Doyle, Bella's oldest daughter, had been teaching since she was seventeen. (Schools had grown up so fast in Manitoba that Bella had not brought her children back to Ontario for education.) Fanny wrote Mamie in June 1896.

"I . . . have had this winter two candidates to prepare for second class certificates [presumably for teaching in elementary schools]. . . . It is a lot of care and bother to look after a school properly and do justice to scholars writing for certificates as well, but I managed it pretty fairly. . . . [Rural teachers in those days often had to keep the stoves going, as well as the building clean and tidy.]

"We had a grand Foresters' picnic at Beulah yesterday. Speakers for the three political candidates (the Tory, Grit and Patron) [Conservative, Liberal and Patron of Industry, similar to the Grange], were present, and the Conservative was there himself. I did not hear much of the speaking, for there were football and baseball matches and races, etc., to watch and last, but not least, there was an ice-cream stand, which draws the people on a hot day.

"What does your mother think of the plan for you to come out and see us? I think that it would do you a world of good if you could stand the journey, and we will give you a pleasant time, I can promise that. . . . I should like you to see all of my friends and companions out here, even in the 'wild West,' and I long to see some of my relations, and have done so more than ever since Fred and George were out to see us. . . .

"Lily and Clara are growing very fast. Lil is half an inch taller than I, now, and Clara is catching up. People will soon begin to call us 'those enormous Doyles,' for we are all large, Russell being over 6 feet in height, and myself 5 feet 8 inches, Lil 5 feet 8½ inches, and Clara 5 feet 5 inches at 13 years old."

Mamie was not well enough to make the trip to Manitoba, and, if she had been, her parents probably would not have felt that they could afford to send her. With all his hard work as an up-to-date dairy farmer, Tom Good still had trouble making ends meet. He had plenty of company; agriculture in general was still not doing well, either in Canada or the United States. The farmers' cry in Canada was for markets, for "free trade," or at least for reciprocal trade with the United States. Canada's railroads and "infant industries," however, were terrified of competition from south of the border. Sir John A. Macdonald had died in office five years before this summer of 1896. He had been prime minister of the Dominion of Canada for twenty of the twenty-four years since Confederation, and his famous "National Policy" of protective tariffs survived him. Even when the Liberal party under Wilfrid Laurier formed a new government in July 1896, the principle of protection was upheld, though in 1897 some duties were lowered in the interests of farmers and consumers. The farmer was becoming less important politically, the urban laborer more important. It is significant that Brantford began to celebrate Labor Day in 1894.

Tom Good wrote John Ballachey in August 1896. From John's answer it is clear that Tom had written bitterly about agrarian troubles in Ontario. In the United States, many people, especially in the agricultural and mining West, had clutched the hope that free coinage of silver would ease their problems. As in Canada, business and industry opposed agriculture. At the Democratic National Convention of 1896, William Jennings Bryan thundered at them, "You shall not crucify mankind upon a cross of gold." He was nominated for president as the champion of "free silver." John Ballachey was now secretary of the Iowa Loan and Trust Company in Sioux City. He wrote his brother-in-law from a business point of view:

"Prices are very low, yet after all the Farmer is making his living, which many in this city are not doing today. If he can meet 'cash rent' and 'Interest and taxes,' the farmer is all right, and I believe it should be the aim of every person to secure a piece of soil free from encumbrance. The Farmer who owns his Farm has nothing to fear. The day will come that he will not be the serf you speak about, but the Lord of creation. . . .

"The Banks and Loan Companies are in a very critical state in the U.S. today owing to this Silver question. I am for sound money and protection—protection so long as we cannot get free trade—but the tariff is not in it this time, silver has sidetracked everything; such crowds block the streets in arguments about the money question. I have not had much time to study it up, but all the populists and anarchists, etc., and worthless debtors are for free and unlimited coinage of silver and, if for no other reason, I would oppose it. . . . These men have an idea that they can pay off their mortgages in 50¢ dollars, a silver dollar having only 53¢ worth of silver in it.

They don't mind robbing their creditors of this 47¢, yet they preach Honesty and down on Capitalists and monopolies. . . . I don't understand in what way a Capitalist can make an improper use of his wealth. He certainly tries to increase it, and in doing so must give employment to labor, or he will become poorer if he locks it up. . . . The only thing labor can and should do is to support and encourage the Capitalist all he can so as money will circulate and he can get a day's pay for a day's work—every man who works is a creditor for at least one day's pay. . . . What this country requires is eastern Capital to develop it and a loosening of the Purse strings of those who have money here. Don't you know that a country is always prosperous and lots of work and money for all, until some unpatriotic crank or cranks get up some new cry or scheme against capital? . . . This locks up capital and destroys confidence, then the honest Farmer and laborer suffers, and capital rests up until . . . confidence [is] restored as it will be next November when I feel sure the silverites will be defeated."

Tom Good must have given his son the letter quoted above. Within a week the young man had expounded his views to his uncle. They were quite radical. He wrote, "I consider that a man has no real right to anything except that which he produces by labour from capital—natural capital." Four days later Uncle John fired a letter back at him, and in another four days Willie sent another long missive to Sioux City. Both of his letters came back to Myrtleville; probably Uncle John thought them worth sending to Willie's parents. They are quite impressive productions for a boy who had not yet gone to college, and they bear clearly the marks of the idealist and reformer Willie was always to be. Here are a few passages.

"You say that in the burning question of the U.S. you are partly influenced by the class of men who advocate a cause. Not referring to the Silver question in the least, I would like to ask you if you think that anyone should found his opinions regarding a certain principle upon the class of men (from a worldly point of view) who support this principle? Go back to the agitation re the Slave Trade in England about the year 1770. Who opposed the abolition of the slave trade? Why, the Aristocratic, the respectable, the worldly-wise, the merchant, the man of business, etc., the great majority of the country.

And who supported it? Only a few then-called cranks. And the same will apply to the great reforms of the English law and revolutions in various senses. Look at the Reform Bill of 1832, the Repeal of the Corn Laws, the Puritan uprising, the first scientists, Copernicus, Galileo, etc. And go back to the time of Christ. Who were His opponents and those of the Gospel dispensation? Why, the so-called respectable, the Pharisees, the Sadducees, the chief priests and all who were looked up to as wise and right. And His supporters were the poor, the publicans and sinners, the poor fishermen, etc. From these and other evidences it seems to me that no one should ally himself to a certain cause simply on account of the class (social) of men who advocate that cause. And we can hardly classify men on moral bases. Is not the only policy in such a case to know something about the cause, to judge as freely from prejudice as is possible the merits of the case and to decide on these? Every man should think for himself and not simply follow the crowd. . . .

"You refer to the saying, The survival of the fittest. This may be a law in the doctrine of Evolution, but it should not be a law governing human action. Are we to let our weaker brothers go to the wall because they are weak? . . . St. Paul . . . commands the strong to bear the infirmities of the weak; yet in our competition, the strong crush the weak. . . .

"You say that in the U.S. the people govern. Do they really govern? You know that the greater part of the wealth of the U.S. is held by a few people. This wealth represents so much useful human labour, it has the present power of governing labour and the people who labour. Not long ago Mr. Depew of New York boasted that fifty men could upset all the great industries of the country and yet he calls the country democratic. It is not really so; it is an oligarchy; a monied aristocracy control an immense amount of undeserved power. The U.S. now looks very like Rome in the time of the Optimates—the rich men, the mighty money men. Let us hope that the result will not be like that of Rome's policy. . . .

"I am teaching in the B.C.I. at present, but do not expect to do so long, as I am only a substitute until the new man comes. In the recent exams, I got a little money from Scholarships and I intend to try to go through the University of Toronto;

expect to start in October. I will be down there with Panay and Fred, who are going to the Dental College, and that will be pleasant. I intend to take up mathematics and science in the University. I would like to take up the political science and metaphysics, but they only allow one to take two honour courses."

A couple of weeks later, he wrote his uncle that he had been reading and thinking about the silver question. He said: "As far as my present knowledge goes [I] have come to the conclusion that the silvermen are wrong. They seem to believe in the childish fallacy that . . . by increasing the medium of exchange, the real articles of value will be increased, too."

A majority of American voters thought the silver men wrong, also. They elected McKinley president rather than Bryan. Economic conditions improved markedly in both Canada and the United States in the late 1890s, but probably for reasons other than the rejection of silver and the continuing of high tariffs. Historians point to a combination of technological development, gold from the new fields of Alaska and the Yukon, growing urbanization, and a series of years with increased rainfall which greatly improved the wheat economy of the West. Unfortunately for our family at Myrtleville, the boom in agriculture was much more pronounced in the West than in Ontario.

11

The Third Generation

In the autumn of 1896, Willie and his cousins, Panay and Fred Ballachey, entered the University of Toronto. Panay was the second son of George and Carrie, Fred the second son of Sam and Molly. The former's unusual name, Panayoti, was an inheritance from an eighteenth-century ancestor, a Greek political refugee who had gone to England to live, and whose descendants by now were largely English in blood. The three Brant County boys were the only boarders at the house of Mrs. Rowlands, 160 Major Street, somewhat northwest of the University. There was very little college residence space available; hundreds of out-of-town students lived in boarding-houses.

In spite of the long depression, Toronto had grown fast. Its population was about two hundred thousand, five times as great as when Anne Good explored the city forty years earlier. It seemed large indeed to Brantfordites, whose town then counted about sixteen thousand people. But in many ways it was simply Brantford magnified, very British, very Protestant.

The university area was now surrounded by city, but the country was still not far away. A short walk to the north took Willie out of town, and he found "quite a bush" about two miles in that direction. The university grounds (the use of the word "campus" was frowned upon) adjoined Queen's Park; there were few college buildings as yet, and spacious lawns studded with great oaks and elms combined with the park to give welcome vistas for city-dwellers' eyes. The new Parliament Building, a massive pile of red brown Credit Valley sandstone, was on the edge of a slope at the southern end of Queen's Park, commanding a fine view of a heavily wooded city with many church spires. The legislative building itself was greatly admired in the 1890s; in our day it seems heavy and overornamented with its "carved surfaces following the Celtic and Indo-Germanic schools." Willie Good did not admire it excessively; his taste always ran to the plain and practical.

The university itself was dominated by the fine 1859 college building Anne had approved many years before. It was now completely restored after a devastating fire in 1890. There was a little old observatory near it, built even earlier, and to the south the School of Practical Science, almost twenty years old, but only recently accepted as the engineering division of the university. The growing importance of science was attested by separate new buildings for biology and chemistry. A library and a gymnasium had also been built, and an Anglican theological school, Wycliffe College. At the northern end of Queen's Park was another new building, Victoria College, formerly a Methodist institution in Cobourg. It was now "federated" with University College as part of the Faculty of Arts. Like the Parliament Building at the other end of the park, "Vic" was of red sandstone in the fashionable turreted Romanesque style. There were nine university buildings in an area now occupied by at least thirty. And one's vision did not encounter any of the high-rise structures which in our time serve as background on all sides.

Panay and Fred attended the Dental School down on College Street, not part of the main campus. There were about seventy in their class. Willie was enrolled in University College, studying mainly science, mathematics, and English. He was one of about one hundred and fifty freshmen candidates for the Bachelor of Arts degree. Although he was officially a science major, he carried "Honours English" courses through his undergraduate years, and, of all his professors, the one who became a lasting friend was W. J. Alexander, head of the English department.

The students were an action-oriented group, great believers in progress. B. K. Sandwell, a journalist who passed through the university a year behind Will Good, remembered his col-

Dining room, Myrtleville House

lege mates as people who felt that things needed to be done, and quickly. They were in search of a practical education to fit them for leadership in professional services and political institutions. Some of the students were female; women had been admitted to the university since 1884, but they were still a small minority, very able and highly motivated.

Willie did not suffer from any lack of home news. Panay's parents sent the daily *Courier,* and every week several members of the family at Myrtleville wrote, and mailed their letters in one envelope to save postage. They called the bunch of letters a "budget," the original meaning of the term, going back to the time when officials took documents and accounts out of their "bougettes," an old French word for little bags or folders. From the "budgets" one gets a picture of evenings in the "parlor" (the old dining room) at Myrtleville. The family gathered around the table, where there was a big lamp, the children doing schoolwork, their mother mending, their father reading a newspaper or a farm journal, or chuckling over something amusing like Thackeray's "Book of Snobs," Aunt Annie reading also. The family in those days was held together partly by the need for common use of a warm, well-lighted room.

Willie's letters home were also written every week, usually on Sunday evenings, when he could tell his mother and Aunt Annie about the church services and Bible classes he had attended. His mother was doubtful about the propriety of letter writing on the Sabbath unless it was "religious," but Willie's comments on sermons made his letters quite acceptable.

The family at Myrtleville were relieved to hear that their freshman had been virtually unscathed by the rough "hazing" many first-year men suffered at the hands of upperclassmen. No details of his minor harassments have survived, and the Dental College does not seem to have been afflicted with such "childish nonsense."

Willie wrote about attending the opening of Parliament, and seeing the new premier, A. S. Hardy, from a distance. The young man from Myrtleville had to be reminded many times by his parents to call upon Mr. Hardy, who was his Aunt Kate's brother. Arthur Hardy had been a member of the legislature for thirty-three years, a cabinet member for thirty of those, and away from Brantford a great deal. Willie would not have minded going to him on a specific mission, but he seldom relished purely social calls, and certainly not on the premier of Ontario whom he did not know well. Louie sympathized with him. She wrote, "I wouldn't like that piece of work very much."

Louie did not go to the Model School during the 1896–97 season. She stayed home to help with the housework. Mamie was very frail and weak and suffering from bad nosebleeds. Aunt Eliza was usually able to get around the house, but that seems to have been the limit of her activity. Aunt Annie sewed and knitted and dusted, and helped care for Mamie and Eliza, but at her age she could not be expected to do more strenuous work, and there was a great deal to be done. Bread and butter had to be made constantly, home-killed pigs and fowl prepared for eating. The pig-killing came only once a year, but it involved the housewife in making sausages and headcheese and lard. There was also the seasonal preserving of fruit.

Moreover, it was not easy to keep clean a house which was lighted by "coal oil" lamps constantly needing to be filled and have their chimneys cleaned, a house which for half the year had many stoves producing quantities of soot and ashes. Keeping clothes and linens clean was hard work, too. Laundry was done with tub and washboard and "elbow grease," and it was good to have two strong people available when it came to the hand-wringing of items like sheets.

Louie did not like some aspects of housework; she wrote her brother sarcastically about the "felicity" of plucking a number of chickens for sale. She wanted to keep her French up, and for a while she and Willie corresponded in that language. Often she was just too tired for the effort and soon the French letters were very rare. Ethel asked for a letter in a foreign language and her brother obliged with a Latin epistle, now lost. She wrote that Louie had had to translate most of it for her. That seems to have been the end of letters in Latin. Ethel at fourteen was still a towhead; she reported that one of the upper-class boys called out on the street, "There goes Bonus Good's sister with the white hair."

The Myrtleville letters, in the fall of 1896, reflected the season—the final garnering of produce, the children's nutting expeditions to hickory and walnut trees on Saturdays, an occasional horseback ride when there was a free animal, the fact that almost everyone had a bad cold. Tom Good worked many nights as well as days. He would be at the cheese factory one evening, the Binder Twine Company (also farmer-owned) another. (He was auditor there at $150 per year.) There were also St. Jude's vestry meetings and AOUW lodge meetings (Ancient Order of United Workmen, founded in 1868; they provided insurance for members' families).

Aunt Annie wrote Willie that she had had a letter from her nephew, Jim Good, in Montana and received a nice picture of his little boy. Willie heard also that his Aunt Kate had come to Brantford to visit the Hardys and the Goods. She had gone into business; Charlie had never been able to save much money and she was hard-pressed to pay taxes on the big house he had left her. Also, her son Arthur's law practice was not going nearly as well as his cousin Allen Jones's medical career, and he had two little boys to raise. Kate began to buy and sell what her nieces at Myrtleville called "old things." Louie wrote her brother: "Aunt Annie sold [Aunt Kate] . . . the four decanters, some old cracked china tea pots and other things and two of the drawing-room chairs. It took us nearly all morning packing the things up."

Dr. Allen Jones came to Brantford from Buffalo for a brief visit. He examined Mamie and advised treatment in a hospital, but the expense was a problem. Mary Tom had been praying hard for her sick child; the answer came in a letter from a family friend and former neighbor, the wife of a meat-packer in Toronto. Mrs. Davies née Emily Moyle could arrange for Mamie to have a private room in Grace Hospital, College Street, Toronto, for as much as twenty weeks with no charge. Allen Jones wrote Mamie an encouraging letter, telling her a little about hospital procedures, and advising her to cooperate in every way with the staff doctors. It was decided that Mamie would go to Toronto right after New Year's.

Louie wrote her brother in mid-November: "We have been busy house-cleaning this week. It is dreadful work. It seems as if we couldn't get things straight at all. Papa killed four pigs yesterday, and now we will have the lovely work of doing down lard and making head cheese. We have had such a time fixing stoves, etc. Papa cut two stovepipe holes—one in Mother's room and one in the drawing-room; and we have a stove in the drawing-room. I almost feel sorry because I do like a fire in the fireplace so much." Later Louie described a cider applesauce fiasco: "It was a dreadful bother. First we had to boil down the cider. We had a big boiler full on each of the stoves, steaming away all day with a roaring fire underneath it. Then that night we had quite a bee coring snow apples. We got George [the hired man] to peel them and all the rest of us cored away until we got the bread tin heaped up. That was Saturday night, and early Monday morning we put the apples on to boil in the cider. That had to boil all day and in the end about half of it was burnt. I was trying today to clean the boiler after it, but it seemed impossible."

Louie's brother was unsympathetic to the point of brusqueness. He wrote of receiving her "voluminous diary of daily doings of weary weekly work which you enjoy so much. Well, it will do you good: the best characters are those who have surmounted many difficulties." He tactlessly got Louie in trouble with her mother by referring to her complaints. Mary Tom was hurt that Louie was not completely happy helping her, and Louie was even more hurt by feeling that she had wounded her mother's feelings. This was an early indication of a developing conflict between Louie's strong sense of filial duty and her and her mother's inability to understand each other. Louie seems to have been a highly emotional person, like her father, but she lacked his habit of losing his temper, quickly begging for forgiveness, and at the same time forgiving himself. Louie brooded over things, and felt guilty about her resentment. Her mother was intelligent and loving, but literal-minded and not very perceptive of her children's feelings. In short, she and Louie loved each other deeply, but did not really get on well together.

There was a flurry of sewing to get Mamie ready for several months away from home. Aunt Mary Qua, recently widowed a second time, came from Paris to help with the sewing, but she had a great deal of trouble with her eyes. The doctor in Paris said he thought she was getting cataracts, and everyone was upset about this. Mary Tom was nervous about Mamie. She wrote Willie: "I feel very anxious in a way about Mamie's going. She seems so very weakly and delicate, and the feeling of handing her over to strangers to take care of makes me feel sad, but the way seems on the other hand so marvellously opened up for us, and we prayed earnestly to be directed, that it reconciles me to let her go." Mamie was in the hospital from January to May. Her treatment seems to have been mainly what her brother called "calisthenics," and being eased back to a normal diet. The hospital stay was a turning point, however. Gradually she recovered to lead a long and active life. One knee was always somewhat deformed, but there was no apparent lameness.

Soon after Mamie went to Toronto, her Aunt Bella arrived there, too. It was Bella's first trip East since she had gone to Manitoba more than sixteen years earlier. She journeyed triumphantly from Toronto to Hamilton to Fort Erie to Brantford to Paisley and so on. It was all very exciting, and Bella was always a voluble woman. Ethel wrote Mamie on January 23, 1897, "Aunt Bella came today. . . . She talks all the time." Louie thought her very like Aunt Charlotte.

Bella was greeted at Myrtleville by a cold wave with a southwest wind which piled snow to the fence tops and made the parlor unusable. The family sat in the kitchen and most of the houseplants froze, though moved away from the windows. It was, of course, usual for water to freeze in unheated bedrooms during severe weather. Little Fanny wrote to Mamie, "Aunt Bella said that she would tare down this old house and build a warm brick one."

The weather moderated enough for a successful party of old friends gathered at Myrtleville in Bella's honor. Before Bella left for Paisley in mid-February, she took Louie and Ethel to town to see the wonderful new moving pictures, the cinematograph. Ethel wrote Willie, "It was very good, only shook a good deal." Seventeen-year-old Louie was more analytical. She asked her brother for an explanation: "I don't understand how they can take their instantaneous photographs so as to represent very swift and very slow action equally well in the same view." The moving pictures aroused such interest that Bella went again, taking "the children," eleven-year-old Fanny and six-year-old Carol. Entertainment was scarce in those days for young children in the country, especially in winter. Often the high point of a week was going to church. Much later, Carol wrote about Sundays when she was small.

"It is Sunday morning and there's a great to-do getting ready to go to church. It is my turn to go, and Fanny's and Ethel's and Mother's and Aunt Annie's. My father is polishing his high boots. We are warming ours by the stove and hunting up coats, caps, leggings, rubbers, mittens, scarfs. I am in a brown and white plaid dress, Fanny in a red plaid, and Ethel in a navy blue trimmed with white braid. After a while sleigh bells are heard, and my father drives the sleigh to the front door. It is one of those boat-shaped sleighs with a back seat slanting very much, a high seat in front for the driver and a little seat facing the back that pulls up and rests on two legs in front. It is for the children. Father and Ethel sit on the driver's seat. Aunt Annie and Mother sit in the back and Fanny and I are on the little seat facing them. Mother is dressed in a dark coat and hat of some kind that I don't remember particularly. She sits up straight with a cushion behind her because the extreme slant is not comfortable for her. Aunt Annie, however, leans back in a state of relaxed comfort.

She is dressed in a long heavy cape and a bonnet with the strings tied under her chin. She says there is no reason for changing the style of her clothes just because other people do. If other people want to wear cock-a-lorum hats on top of their heads, they may.

"The horses are untied and away we go over the sparkling roads. We get all the wind there is and are glad to get into the warm church. There I amuse myself as best I can with looking at the coloured windows, stroking my black plush coat and playing with the big buttons and loops on it, and admiring my bright red mittens. Aunt Annie tells me in a large whisper to repeat the responses if I can. She does so quite loudly and distinctly but just about half a sentence behind every one else. If the other people gabble, that is no reason why she should. After a while church is over. We bundle into the sleigh again and drive home. This time we have the advantage of the others as our backs are to the west wind. It is too cold for conversation, but once home, with dinner over and our feet warming near the coal stove, we find opportunity to ask more questions.

" 'Yes,' says Nana, 'in the old days we filled two pews in church. That was in old Mr. Usher's time. Yes, the service seemed long then. My mother always carried a bag of cookies along to give the children when they got restless. There was no shortening of the service in those days. We always had all the psalms for the day, and the Litany every Sunday, and a good long sermon from Mr. Usher. You know that leather trunk under the stairs? Well, that is full of Mr. Usher's sermons. . . . When Mr. Usher died Mrs. Usher gave me most of his sermons.

" 'We used to go to church in the lumber wagon in the summertime, and in the bob-sleigh in the winter. . . . Often we would drive around to see the Ushers after church. They lived at Acacia Terrace. The house was red-brick, about half way up Sand Hill or Terrace Hill as they call it now. There were a lot of acacia trees around it—a very pretty place, but now the railway and factories and all have been built in front of it and have spoiled its appearance.' "

On February 24, Willie had his twenty-first birthday. The family sent a "budget" of felicitations. Mary Good wrote that

Will Good's five sisters and ten of his cousins. Picture taken by him December 26, 1898. Back row, left to right: *Alec Ballachey, Lily Doyle, Russell Doyle, Fanny Doyle, George M. Ballachey, Fred Ballachey;* middle row, left to right: *George T. Ballachey, Panay Ballachey, Ethel Good, Fanny Good;* front row, left to right: *Mamie Good, Carol Good, Meg Ballachey, Charlotte Ballachey, and Louie Good.*

she would have liked to have a nice big party for him at Myrtleville, with "recitations and readings and so on and no playing of cards or dancing."

Mamie must have had a good laugh from Ethel's letter of March 27. The Saturday before, Ethel and Louie had dressed up outlandishly, heavily veiled (it was a time when veils were very fashionable) and gone riding about the neighborhood, mystifying the inhabitants. Blanche Carlyle rode with them part of the time, not in costume, and the prank was blamed on "the three Miss Carlyles." Ethel sent Willie a sketch of herself, clad in black bonnet with red bows, green riding habit, purple shawl, and pink scarf. She reported that the hired man said it was no wonder Prince, the horse, shied at her.

Tom Good was busier than ever that spring. He had become treasurer of Brantford Township the beginning of the year, an appointment made by the township council of which he had been a member for several years. He resigned from the council, of course, but kept up his clerical work for the cheese factory and the binder-twine company. Then the spring farm work came on, and Willie was in Toronto studying for final exams. Tom began to have miserable stomach pains a couple of hours after meals. His appetite failed and he lost weight and strength. Rest made him feel better, but there was little time for rest. Whether he had an incipient ulcer, or an intestinal virus, or nervous indigestion, the doctor's prescription of "nux vomica," a stimulant to increase gastric juices, was probably not helpful. There were no diagnostic X-rays available. Roentgen had discovered the X-ray little over a year earlier (Will Good had attended a special lecture on it at the University), but it was as yet mostly a scientific curiosity. Tom Good's house was not very restful in spring, either. Spring housecleaning was worse than fall housecleaning. Stoves were taken out, stovepipes taken down, and ceilings whitewashed. This was also the time when carpets were put on lines outdoors and beaten with a wire carpet-beater to get the dust out.

Mamie was anxious to get home. She liked her doctors and nurses and enjoyed many calls from her brother and cousins, but she did miss home and the rest of the family. She wrote Carol: "Do you think it is time for you to get a letter all to your 'loneself'? . . . There are lots of dear little children go by on the street. I get quite hungry for them . . . little girls in white coats and bonnets and little sailor boys. Four little ones live two doors away. . . . They play a great deal right across from my window." She wrote her parents during a spring rain: "The cab drivers look so queer with their white oilskins over coats and hats, just like ghosts. The horse chestnut buds have burst on the tree before my window. Good-bye, heaps and loads and bushels of love to everyone and 'Pray without ceasing.' Do not think I am very homesick or fretting, but am ready to go as soon as is right."

Carol and Aunt Annie enjoyed spring together, one too young and one too old for the rigors of housecleaning. Before she went to school, Carol lacked playmates of her age. Her siblings and cousins were all years older than she. But Aunt Annie, as she was a teacher and companion to the invalid, Mamie, was friend and companion to her youngest niece, who was young enough to be her grandchild. Many years later, Carol wrote: "We were great pals, Aunt Annie and I. She was a little old lady with a sweet little face and smooth hair, golden-red turning gray, parted in the middle and brushed smoothly down with a miniature puff over each ear. Her dresses were of the tight-waisted basque style with full skirts. A white lawn tie fastened with a huge brooch, silver set with Irish diamonds, which had been some gay ancestor's knee buckle, finished the costume. Usually she wore a white apron and on very dressed up occasions a black silk one." Carol also told of gardening with her aunt.

"Spring was here; raking days were here, gardening days: swinging days were here for me. Up and down on the swing I went. The swing was tied to a large limb of an old big willow tree. The yellow-green leaves of the willow were young and lacy between me and the blue sky. Here was Aunt Annie in a pale-gray cotton dress and lilac sunbonnet coming down the slope towards me. Aunt Annie never called out too loudly or ordered us about.

" 'How would you like to make a garden?' she asked me. Make a garden—what joy! I was off the swing in a jump and was dancing along beside her. We went up in front of the house where the hedge curves around in a large sweep. Little green shoots were coming up all over. The garden was bordered with red bricks and some of them needed to be straightened. We came up to the gap near the big acacia and went out into the half-moon flower garden. Aunt Annie was digging up plants here and there which she gave me and I carried them over to my own little flower garden, beneath an east window.

"In the long sunny days of May we gardened. Aunt Annie said Star of Bethlehem made a good border because it didn't spread much. So we put a Star of Bethlehem border around the half-moon garden. At the end near the gap there were yellow lilies and iris, lily of the valley in the shade, heliotrope, verbenas, Sweet William, bachelor's buttons. Toward the far end were three rose-bushes, a pink one, a white one, and a red one. Then there were hollyhocks, tulips and narcissus, orange lilies, larkspur and Canterbury Bells. A hedge of dark green privet and light green Prince Arthur's feather swept in a long curve in front of the house. At intervals were acacia trees, and at the far east end of the hedge a Spitzenberg apple tree, white and pink in the spring, and dotted with bright red apples in the fall.

"Farther to the east was a magnificent oak tree, the only remaining native tree on the lawn. Aunt Annie said that when the oak leaves were the size of a rabbit's foot it was time to plant corn. We used to watch the little rose coloured leaf-buds uncurl and gradually turn to paler yellowish green—and just at a certain time we would know that corn planting time had come.

"The vegetable garden was out beyond the hedge and the half-moon garden and the road into the orchard. It had grape vines on trellises and a plum tree at the end of it where a grape-vine had wandered and blue grapes hung in clusters along with the big red plums. There were gooseberry bushes, and red currant and black currant and white currant bushes, and an asparagus bed, and raspberry and blackberry bushes in the corners. There was a big rhubarb bed. The biggest rhubarb leaves were very handy in covering the big baskets of butter that were taken to town periodically. The butter must be kept cool, and it was a long three miles to town, especially driving slow old Nellie. There were melon patches in the garden, and hills of potatoes and corn, cabbages, onions, beets, carrots, parsnips, lettuce and spinach, peas and beans.

"Although Aunt Annie had a hand and a voice in the vegetable garden, the flowers were her special care. Each plant seemed to have a history of its own. 'These sweet scented red and yellow tulips came from Mrs. Smith's garden,' she would say, 'and these narcissus too. Oh, it's a fine garden Mrs. Smith had. They were nursery people and kept trees and shrubs as well as flowers. . . . They lived up Smith's Lane' [Since 1957 the old Smith farm has been the North Ridge Golf Club]. . . .

Through the spring and summer and autumn we gardened. There were always bouquets for the table and for friends who came."

Mamie was home by mid-May, Willie by the end of May. He had done well in his exams, and also been elected by his peers as second-year councillor for the Mathematical and Physical Society of the university.

Willie worked on the farm through the summer, a great boon to his father. Panay and Fred worked in dentists' offices in Brantford. One day they came to Myrtleville to pull Eliza Laird's remaining upper teeth. They would make her a plate when her gums "settled." In our age of specialization the idea of a couple of boys with one year of dental training doing such work on poor Aunt Eliza is shocking, but in 1897 it seemed quite acceptable. And apparently their services were satisfactory.

The bicycle age had come to Brantford. Everyone who could afford a "wheel" had one. Panay took a bicycle to Toronto with him. When the roads were good, Mr. Wright, the clergyman, made parish calls at Myrtleville on his bicycle. Even the portly, dignified, middle-aged county judge, Aunt Kate's brother, Alexander Hardy, pedaled around town. Ethel could scarcely keep a straight face when she saw him. "He is so fat," she said, "he looks dreadful on a wheel."

The Goods bought a secondhand lady's bicycle and Louie rode it to the Model School in Brantford the autumn of 1897. She was not enamoured of the wheel; she had a couple of nasty tumbles, and endured bicycling as a means to an end, but when Ethel had a chance she would happily pedal from Myrtleville to Edgemount and back, ten miles at least.

Mamie was getting stronger and taking over a good deal of kitchen work. She made pies, puddings, cakes, and buns, but still did not tackle the big batches of bread. She was made "Scrap Editor" of the new Literary Society which met at Moyle's school, but was not expected to attend meetings as yet. Ethel and Louie were to read the paper for her.

With Louie at the Model School, Ethel was kept home a good deal that autumn to help with the work. She wrote that she and her mother had plucked and cleaned forty-nine chickens during the fall. Her letters were lively, like herself, and showed her fascination with language. She told her brother about her churning, taking out the butter when it was in little lumps about as big as peas and looking like "beautiful brilliant burnished balls of gold."

Louie got tired and discouraged at the Model School, though she was happy to be out of the "usual commotion connected with house-cleaning." Often her classes kept her from 8:30 A.M., to 5:00 P.M., and she could not get much time to prepare lessons, because, as she wrote, "I can't stay up at all late without Pa scolding me." Her spirits were greatly lifted when Dr. Kelly, the school inspector, told Tom Good that she was ahead of all the others as a teacher. Her mother wrote Willie, "Dr. Kelly said Louie's anxiety to thoroughly do what she has to do is her strongest factor for success. She showed perseverance very early in life."

As winter came on Louie usually stayed in town week-nights with her mother's old friends, the Misses Wye, who had left their family farm across the river. Aunt Annie went to visit Aunt Charlotte for about a month before Christmas. George Malloch had died, and Anne wrote that the house in Paisley was lonely without him. Louie's course at the Model School ended December 9. Christmas preparations were running late, the cake and pudding not yet made, but a friend lent them her raisin-stoning machine, which was a great help. We are so used to seedless raisins that we take them for granted, but the old kind used to cause the housewife a lot of labor. (There was a raisin-stoner in the display of gadgetry at the U.S. Pavilion of Montreal's Expo '67.)

Willie and Panay and Fred had a new boardinghouse that autumn of 1897. It was on Czar Street, described as little more than a quiet sandy lane, which ran behind Victoria College. It is now known as Charles Street West and has a good many college buildings on it. In his sophomore year, Willie's studies concentrated on chemistry and physics. He was a candidate for further scholarships in them, and found chemistry particularly interesting. He also continued to study Honours English, but not for scholarship purposes. Willie's heavy academic load did not prevent him from exploring other subjects. For instance, he attended a students' meeting of the world convention of the Woman's Christian Temperance Union, held in Toronto that fall. He wrote Mamie a description of it.

"There were delegates there from all over the world, a good many of them dressed in their national costumes. First there was some singing and the secretary (an Englishwoman) read her report, a collection of statistics from various countries concerning the progress of the W.C.T.U. . . . Miss Willard, the president, spoke for a short time. . . . She is a very clever speaker but I did not like her voice at all, especially at the beginning. She either imitates or possesses the drawling nasal conventional New England tone. . . .

"After Miss Willard finished there was a short prayer offered by the treasurer and then commenced the business of bringing forward and introducing the various foreign delegates, each of whom made short speeches. Everyone spoke in English, though some in quite broken English.

"After the presentation of the delegates there was a solo, and then in conclusion a big gaunt Yankee woman from Chicago made an appeal for money. She spoilt the effect of the meeting very much. She began talking in a loud coarse voice (meanwhile striding up and down) of the Canadian gold fields [gold had recently been discovered in the Yukon], of the way in which we taxed the Americans when they encroached upon our territory, of the great riches of Canadians and especially of Torontonians, and ended her harangue by asking for a liberal collection of not less than $ 5,000 from the audience."

About the same time Mr. and Mrs. Good went to an interesting, but very different kind of meeting in Brantford. Tom's AOUW lodge introduced among the usual songs and readings and speeches the playing of Mr. Edison's new phonograph, or as it was then called, "Gramophone." The Goods were not impressed with the quality of the sound, "it was funny, so hoarse and unnatural." Their second hearing was more successful. Most of the family went to a "social" at Moyle's School, at which the "talking machine" was featured. Twelve-year-old Fanny wrote her brother about the Gramophone: "It sung 'The Nightingale' in German, and it laughed the way the different people [do]. And another thing was 'The Morning at the Farm' and it was the dog barking, the cat mewing, the roosters crowing, the calf bawling and the horses neighing. And it sang the 'Blue Bells of Scotland' and a lot of other songs." Louie reacted to the Gramophone as to the cinematograph. She asked Willie for an explanation of the theory behind it.

Louie was not able to get a teaching job for the new year, and she stayed home while Ethel struggled to catch up with her work at the Collegiate. The principal had her in the same class as her cousins Frank and Alec who were more than a year older than she. He was pushing her hard in languages, Latin, French, and German, and she complained that she was just too sleepy to get her studying done at night. She managed to have plenty of fun at school, however. She told Willie: "I have to sit with Edith Randall because there is not another seat in the room. And I can't sit with a person without talking, so the teachers . . . are always talking to me about me talking." Another time she wrote: "I think I have a most lucky and most unlucky face, because I look at someone and set them laughing, and then, quick as a wink, I change my expression with a very innocent one and leave the other poor thing to get howled at by the teachers."

She even enjoyed the excitement of the worst flood in Brantford's history. She wrote her brother: "It was glorious. The muddy water was bubbling and boiling, crowing and capering, groaning and gamboling, howling and horrible . . . rushing and roaring, seething and sighing, foaming and frothing, dark and dreary, dreadful and delightful, etc. I never saw anything like it in my life, the way the dark turbid water dashed over the dam. I think it must have been like the white horses on the sea. . . . Blanche [Carlyle] and I walked across the railway bridge and the water was so high that it splashed up on our legs between the whatever you call the things the bridge is made of. When we got to the middle, oh, how it roared. Blanche was so frightened. I felt rather funny myself because you could see the water rushing under you. It was over West Brantford so that the Edgemounts could not get in."

February of 1898 was a festive month at Myrtleville. First, Will Doyle and his twenty-year-old daughter, Fanny, spent a week there. Fanny Doyle was a tall girl, good-looking though not pretty, with a brisk, no-nonsense air about her. Her Aunt Mary described her as "clever and capable." She was going to

Toronto to study; she wanted more education than she had been able to get in Manitoba. Mary Tom suggested to her son that he might help Fanny with languages, and he did.

Next, Andrew Jones and his daughter, Lucia, came to Myrtleville after a fine trip to New York and Washington, places which seemed very distant and glamorous to the Goods. While Uncle Andrew was with the Goods, he kept them supplied with unusual delicacies, "oranges and candies, bananas too." He took Mamie shopping when he bought beautiful presents for everyone, and her knee didn't hurt at all.

Will Doyle had bought a return ticket for Fanny. Since she made up her mind to stay in Ontario all summer, he suggested using the ticket to take one of the Myrtleville girls to Manitoba. Their different reactions were interesting. Shy Louie wrote her brother, "They think I had better go out and take the Normal training at Winnipeg and then I could get a school there. What do you think about it? I have not thought seriously of it yet as it seems such a step to take that I would be frightened of it." Ethel wrote, "Uncle Will wants me to go home to Manitoba with him on Fanny's ticket, but the people won't let me go. My, but I would like to go." In the end, neither of them went.

There were no houseguests at Myrtleville early in the spring of 1898, but there was plenty of housework. A young man named Francis Sheppard was going to work the farm on shares for three years, and Louie and her mother were busy clearing out the north wing of the house which had been used for storage and as a summer kitchen. They remarked about the staggering amount of material saved over the years by "a very economical family."

The Sheppards settled in the north wing at Myrtleville. The Goods thought they were nice quiet people, and poor Eliza Laird was almost embarrassingly glad to have them. Mamie observed, "Aunt Eliza is rather too fond of visiting, now there is someone to visit." There was an advantage, however. When Eliza could "mind the baby," Mrs. Sheppard could help with the milking, and she was a good milker. But, in general, the Sheppards did not give Tom Good the hoped-for relief from hard work and responsibility. Mamie said, "As far as I can see, Papa takes the lead, and works as hard as ever." Again, there was some relief for him when Willie came home for the summer, and his nephew, Frank, was able to help on the farm occasionally.

As usual, summer was a very busy season at Myrtleville. There was gardening, and much heavy work, haying and harvesting. There were also many houseguests, the Mallochs, Fanny Doyle and her sister, Lily, and the Sam Ballacheys. Sam, a widower for over three years, in May had married Agnes McNiven, a schoolteacher. In the midst of these comings and goings, on July 3, Eliza Laird died unexpectedly. She was about the house Friday, stricken with pneumonia on Saturday, and died on Sunday. Though she had been disabled for more than ten years, she was not quite fifty-nine. Half of Allen Good's ten children were gone now, all of them under sixty years of age.

12

Expanding Horizons

By October, Myrtleville seemed almost deserted. Fanny Doyle and Willie and Panay and Fred were all studying in Toronto. Frank was working in his father's store in Paisley. Lily Doyle went to visit her father's relatives in Owen Sound. The strangest absences were those of Aunt Eliza, who was in her grave, and of Louie, who was teaching school at Waterford, some twenty miles south of Brantford. Her departure was sudden, because a Waterford teacher had left suddenly. Often, during school hours, there were now only Mamie, her mother, and Aunt Annie in the front of the house, and Mrs. Sheppard and her baby in the north wing.

Fanny Doyle's hard work with languages bore fruit; she was admitted to the University of Toronto, and dreamed of becoming a doctor. But she had scarcely started her studies when a letter from home switched her into a six week secretarial course. Her mother would not consent to her studying medicine. "The boys," Willie, Panay, and Fred, were full of sympathy for Fanny, who wrote to Louie: "It was . . . a very great disappointment to me to have to give up my medical prospects for a time at least. I am not despairing altogether, yet. I stormed around, privately, of course, for some time. Then I went down town and walked myself tired out. I could not let it out for I had no one here to be angry with and had to keep it all to myself. I was too angry to cry about it. . . . I am awfully sorry that I cannot have my Christmas at Brantford. I have quite counted on it and hope to be able by hook or crook to manage it yet. I am never going to make any more plans, however, until I am my own 'boss' as the boys say."

Louie went to Waterford quite apprehensive about being with no one but strangers, and about managing the children, who were in what we now call fourth, fifth, and sixth grades. It was a hard job for a shy, nervous girl of eighteen, just beginning to teach. The advice of her brother, who was not particularly shy and nervous, was, "Get lots of exercise and keep your spirits up."

Louie taught her charges reading, arithmetic, Canadian history, geography, spelling, grammar, and such "frills" as singing and drawing, if she could squeeze them in. Books were expensive, and most of the school reading was done in graded "readers." These contained passages of poetry and prose on various topics, often carrying a moral message. For beginners, there were simple stories and ditties with many illustrations and a strong rural flavor. Besides pets and dolls, these children knew about horses and cows, hens and chicks, bees and sheepshearing, mill wheels and blacksmith shops. Louie's pupils were beginning to encounter the work of well-known authors, Longfellow, Tennyson, Defoe, Hawthorne, Lowell. Before they left elementary school, they would study many famous passages from the King James Bible, Shakespeare's plays, Sir Walter Scott's works, Dickens's novels, Byron's poems, even prose written by old Samuel Johnson, the lexicographer. There was great emphasis on reading aloud, an art which has fallen off sadly since then.

Soon after she went to Waterford, Louie, who was the inheritor in her family of her Grandmother Good's musical talent, found a very pleasant boardinghouse where she could have the use of a piano. She wrote her brother: "The Duncombes are very nice people. There are a great many of them here and they are some of the oldest residents of the town. I never saw such a place as this for people being related. All the acknowledged society of the town are, I think, either related or connected by marriage."

Louie grew very fond of her landlady, Amelia Duncombe, whom she described as "very gentle and quiet, very fond of reading and painting. . . . I haven't seen her out of temper in the slightest degree and she has a good deal to worry her, the baby is so cross just now (teething) and the hired girl is away working at the factory."

At rush seasons, even the school-age children of poor families went to work in the canning and evaporating factories of Waterford. And Louie once hunted up one of her pupils who had sent her a message that he was working in the brickyard and not going to school any more. It is unknown whether she persuaded him to try further education.

Louie had to cope with difficult parents as well as children. She had a peremptory note from a very protective mother.

Miss Goode,
    Please excuse Bertha for being absent yesterday. It was necessary, after this when she is absent you will know that it cannot be avoided, therefore this note will answer hereafter. Bertha is not strong and must have the fresh air, it is injurious to her health to be kept indoors so close. Bertha says you kept her in at recess for not bringing this note this A.M. If this is repeated an investigation will take place, as her health is worth looking after.

Mrs. Bentley.

On the whole Louie's teaching went well, though she felt that she was lazy about her preparations and only did what was necessary. She wrote Willie: "If only I could be more energetic in teaching and take more interest in it. I have promised the children that before Christmas we will have a little concert, but it is like pulling out eye-teeth to go to work and arrange for it. Do you ever feel an utter distaste for something you have to do? . . . I do think the hardest thing to fight against is mental laziness. Bodily laziness is nothing compared to it."

Whatever Louie's reservations about teaching, she loved having money of her own, and being able to buy gifts for the people at home. There is still an ornate little gilded clock at Myrtleville which was her first purchase for the house. And for many years the big four-poster, which had been Eliza Good's bed, had a blue and white figured canopy and a dust ruffle made of material Louie had bought. It was a pretty, romantic material with scenes from the age of chivalry.

In Waterford, Louie also had a new experience in churchgoing. "Partly out of curiosity," she said, she went to the Methodist church to hear two evangelists. The service was

Master bedroom, Myrtleville House, showing Eliza Good's bed

very unlike the dignified Anglican liturgy and preaching she was used to. She wrote: "I never saw such performances as they went through. . . . They are twins and really one could not tell them apart. . . . The subject of their discourse, they said, was on 'Unity.' First the one spoke and then the other. I suppose I should not make fun of them, but really the first reminded me of the bellowing of a bull of Bashan. He simply roared and jumped and stamped until I thought he would have a fit. When he started I had hard work to keep from laughing, but after he had kept on for a while felt more like yawning. Every once in a while he would resume his natural voice and then you could understand a little what he was driving at. . . . He would hammer away at some acknowledged fact as if someone was contradicting it. The other one would sometimes say, 'Hear, Hear, Hear.' I liked the second one better than the first. He did not talk so loud, probably because he couldn't. . . . Towards the end he said some pretty good things but I did not think the sermon at all connected. . . . I suppose such men do good, but to me it seems that their whole object is excitement."

About the same time, Will Good attended a very different kind of performance in Toronto. He went to the theater for the first time in his life. The play was Goethe's *Faust,* and he was quite disappointed; he thought the characters were played in a very unnatural manner, and the solemnity of the play was often disturbed by the "unseemly levity" of the audience. Some of the stage effects he found clever, and he enjoyed writing a description of the last scene to his little sisters: "I am afraid that if you had been there you would have been quite terrified at the scenes of chaos, tumult, witchcraft and supernatural flashes, thunder and lightning. The last scene was rather impressive. It opens with the death of Marguerite in prison. . . . Satan comes upon the stage, all suffused in a ruddy glow of dismal fires, and exults over his victory with wild and devilish glee. Suddenly the church bells chime and heavenly singing is heard. Satan is struck dumb, and slinks crouching to the back of the stage, still muttering indistinct curses. Then behold, he starts to sink down, down, down into a fiery pit, the lurid reflection of which can be seen on the gloomy walls of the prison. Hurling defiance at the powers above, he still sinks; sinks until his loud and wild curses are only faintly heard in the distance and at the same time the screen at the back of the stage lifts and reveals Marguerite ascending to heaven amid angels and sweet music and glorious light. . . . But I fear you will not quite understand all this description."

Twelve-year-old Fanny thought there was something inherently wicked about the theater. She wrote Willie, "You are a good boy to write such a long letter to us, but you should not go to theatres." Will never became much of a playgoer, but he did later see the great Sir Henry Irving do Shakespeare, and was impressed. He found the acting of most players "frantic and strained."

Like his sister in Waterford, Will Good was battling against his distaste for some of the things he had to do. He had returned to Toronto that autumn thin and tired and suffering from some lingering low-grade infection. He soon felt better physically, but had trouble settling at his studies. It was pleasant to try a variety of extracurricular activities, with cousins and friends. He went to the theater with Fanny Doyle and Panay Ballachey; he and Fred accompanied Fanny to a reception for freshmen, though he remarked that he still felt self-conscious and bashful at big parties.

The most worrisome feature of his slump was that he seemed to be losing interest in physical science, in which he held scholarships. He complained that he was finding the organic chemistry full of "memory work"; he seemed "to be getting disgusted with so many facts." His interest in literature and social science grew. He still went to church Sunday mornings and evenings, and to Bible class Sunday afternoons, and was active in the student YMCA. He was increasingly attracted to the undogmatic and humanitarian preaching of Dr. Milligan of Old St. Andrew's Presbyterian Church, and to his services which were a good deal simpler than even the Low Church Anglican. Aunt Annie hoped Willie might yet be a minister; his mother thought he might combine science and humanitarianism and become a doctor. His own inclination was leading him toward the role of social reformer, but the hard reality of his need for money kept him at the top of his science classes.

Christmas was merry at Myrtleville. Fanny Doyle did get there, along with her brother, Russell, and her sister, Lily. The day after Christmas, the Edgemount people came, including George Theodore from Buffalo. Will used his homemade camera to take a picture of his five sisters and ten cousins.

He was emerging from his doldrums, and he went back to Toronto, determined at least to organize his life, sensibly but not narrowly. "It is hard," he said, "to divide the time profitably among the many things which demand one's attention, and especially hard for me." Will bought a season ticket for the skating rink to encourage regular exercise, and tried to keep regular hours, though he still managed to work in many meetings. He wrote his mother early in the new year: "I do feel so thankful for all the opportunities and privileges which we enjoy here in Toronto, and hope I shall be enabled to bear the consequent responsibility in a worthy manner. Life seems to open out in such a wondrous manner and yet sometimes the mystery and perplexity deepen—it is a great thing for a man to have some clear-cut and definite pathway with positive beliefs to guide him in it."

He did not feel that he had made much progress on his path. On his birthday, February 24, he wrote in his diary. "Twenty-three years old today, one-third of a lifetime gone and what done or started?" (He had no way of knowing that his strong body was to carry him through a life of almost four times twenty-three.) Out of curiosity, he had gone to a Christian Science service. He wrote about the "queer system of metaphysical mysticism and delightful mental entanglement. . . . To get rid of sin through Christian Science, it is only necessary to deny its existence. . . . This is decidedly very convenient, but it seems a case of the wish being father to the thought; at all events it is very illogical."

Will had quite a decision to make the spring of 1899. He was offered a trip to England "to take over an Electric carriage for exhibition purposes." He chose instead to work on the farm in June, then go to an international students' conference at East Northfield, Massachusetts, the home of Dwight L. Moody, the evangelist. Later in the summer, he would go to Manitoba.

Mamie, who had been getting so much stronger, gave everyone a great fright by being very ill in March. She recovered slowly, while the healthy womenfolk were attacking the spring housecleaning in a great rush. Louie was glad to be out of it. She wrote her brother from Waterford: "There is such a beating of carpets going on everywhere. . . . Everyone is housecleaning. I suppose they are doing the same at home. I believe I am forgetting all about housework. I never had such a rest from it before." At Myrtleville there was need to get done quickly with all the whitewashing, filling of bedtickings with fresh straw, and taking up of carpets and down of stoves. What Aunt Clara called "The Irish Invasion" was expected very soon. It came about in this way.

During the many years since Jonathan Good's death, letters had passed occasionally between Anne Good in Canada and her only close relative in Ireland, Jonathan's son, Morgan. In 1891, he married, and in 1898, after a brief illness, he died. He left three young children, and his widow wrote to Myrtleville asking if she might take them there. Tom Good was worried about four more mouths to feed, but the family knew that Morgan had left his family ill provided-for. Anne left the decision to Tom and Mary; they would bear the burden. Mary Good maintained that it was the duty of the Myrtleville Goods to do what they could for the less fortunate, and the hospitable farm took the Irish cousins in. The children were Charlie, age seven, Morgan six, and Gwennie, four and a half.

There are some interesting early comments on the Irish Goods. Mrs. Tom wrote of Mrs. Morgan who had not been brought up to do much housework, "She does not work well, she is far from painstaking, does things very quickly but roughly, plays the piano better than anything else." She spoke of Morgan's "beaming look and sweet smile, like a cherub," but also of his "ungovernable temper." A Brantford doctor said of the child, "I like the fire in his eye." Morgan's mother alternately punished him and cajoled him, and he simply would not obey her. One afternoon when Aunt Charlotte was visiting, Morgan was so naughty that Aunt Annie sent her brother to the child's room to spank him. After that he was a model of deportment whenever Uncle Tom was around. (Aunt Charlotte, characteristically, gave money for the children's clothing, and much advice on how to bring them up.)

Gwennie, the family said, was a nice little thing, but didn't "mind" very well. Charlie was no trouble; Will wrote to Louie, "Charlie seems a very intelligent and willing little fellow." Aunt Bella offered to adopt one of the boys, and it was decided to send Morgan to Manitoba, though his Aunt Mary had some qualms about Bella's suitability as a mother for Morgan. "She is impetuous, too," said Mary Good. Mrs. Morgan soon took a housekeeping job nearby, but Gwennie and Charlie stayed at Myrtleville.

Charlie remembered getting acquainted with his new family. There was Aunt Annie, a soft-voiced old lady who never seemed to try to run things but whose influence was always felt. Many years later, Charlie was surprised to learn that Aunt Annie was owner of the house that sheltered him. She had not acted as if she was. He remembered particularly that she read the Bible aloud after supper (which they called "tea") every night. When he came, she was reading Revelation, the last book of the Bible. Somehow he got the idea that when she finished it, the world would come to an end!

Charlie remembered kind, fussy Aunt Mary, who kept

Charles A. Good (1892–1973), son of Morgan Good of Ireland, with the Canadian Expeditionary Forces about 1916

house and gave the children religious instruction every Sunday afternoon. Uncle Tom was a quiet man who spent much time working on books, or away from home on business. Years before, Tom Good had been a great favorite with nephews and nieces, but he was a rather austere figure in Charlie's memory. He must have been too busy and too tired to play with little boys as he used to. He did not do much heavy farm work any more; it was Charlie's big strong cousin, Will, and the other men, who taught the boy about farming.

Three of the girl cousins at Myrtleville seemed grown-up to Charlie. Mamie, quick and cheerful, helped keep house and "mother" him. The schoolteacher, nineteen-year-old Louie, was sweet and pretty, and took herself very seriously. Ethel was seventeen, small and pink-cheeked and golden-haired. People did not consider her such a beauty as Louie, but she was certainly fun. Fanny was a big girl of thirteen, taller than Ethel, and ready to go to high school. Carol was only a year and a half older than Charlie and a real playmate for him.

House servants having long since departed from Myrtleville, the family ate in the big kitchen, except for special occasions. There was a long table near the north wall, and, with hired men and guests, close to twenty people often sat there. The food was good but plain; plenty of homemade bread and butter, chickens and eggs, salted and smoked pork from Myrtleville's pigs, a variety of fruits and vegetables from orchard and garden.

Charlie was a little boy from the city, and he had much to learn about country life. He soon made himself useful, but he always remembered the time he went to bring in the cows for milking and saw a funny-looking black and white cat which wouldn't get out of his way. He kicked at it, and it sprayed him with some terrible stuff that made his clothes smell bad for weeks.

There were even more than the usual summer "comings and goings" at Myrtleville in 1899. Soon after Aunt Charlotte's visit, Aunt Kate came briefly. She went on to Woodstock, "still hunting up old furniture and curiosities" for her shop. Her son Arthur had left Buffalo for the West, hoping to practice law more profitably there; his family would follow him later. Mary Good thought it odd that Kate's brother, the premier of

Ontario, was unable to help her and her son financially, but Kate said that Arthur Hardy needed all his salary. No doubt he did; he had been in poorly paid public life since he was a young lawyer of thirty-six and had never used his position for personal enrichment. Brantford was proud of his legislative work, a few pieces of which were the creation of the Bureau of Mines, the Provincial Board of Health, and the Provincial Parks of Algonquin and Rondeau. It also respected him for leaving office in no better financial condition than he had entered it. Early in July, Will Good went to the student conference at Northfield. It lasted ten days, and he wrote a letter to Myrtleville about it.

"Our tents are right on top of a high bank along the Connecticut Valley and below the hill there is a fine spring and spring creek, where we wash in the morning and also obtain all our water. It is quite woody hereabouts and plenty of ferns, great large ones in clumps. . . .

"I could not begin to tell you of the meetings and addresses. I am making brief notes of most of them and you may look at them when I get home. The 'Round Top' meetings are characteristic features of the conference. They are held on a little hill behind Mr. Moody's house and are addressed by various men on subjects pertaining to one's choice of a life work. Mr. Mott [John R. Mott, born 1865, at this time student secretary of the International Y.M.C.A., later (1946) winner of Nobel Peace Prize], spoke, outlining some principles which should be guiding every man in his choice of his life work. It was a very good address and very practical. Mott is a man of great force of character.

"Last night the sun set just as the meeting was breaking up and a wonderful sight it was. From 'Round Top' one can see away up and across the Connecticut Valley, for sixty miles in one place, all a mass of green, fading into blue in the distance and brightened here and there by the shining river. The sun sinks in glory behind these hills, leaving the sky tinged with gold and crimson. How I wished I could have preserved the sunset view last night to show you all! This is my first experience of mountain scenery and it must be ever so much grander among the larger ranges."

Later in July, Will and Frank Ballachey took little Morgan

on a "harvest excursion" train to Manitoba. It was a good trip; Morgan behaved very well, and Frank was delighted to get away from his father's store in Paisley for a while. Will, however, regretted that he didn't have more geological knowledge of the country they traveled through, especially the rocky area north of Lake Superior.

The Doyles were pleased and amused by Morgan. Fanny wrote Louie: "Morgan is a splendid little fellow and we are all very fond of him already. Dad quite won his heart by giving him 'cream with sugar on it.' . . . I believe he will turn out a mechanical genius, for he has gone from lawn mower to grindstone to carpet sweeper ever since he came and seems to be very fond of them. He manufactured a plow out of the mop and an old plow coulter and was running that around the yard a few minutes but it would not go far."

Will worked at the Doyles', Frank nearby. The Doyle household was a busy one; Will remarked that there was company nearly every day and generally to stay all night. "Loneliness on the prairies cannot be thought of." He was impressed by his energetic Aunt Bella: "[She] is working continually. She often, in fact usually, gets up first in the morning, roots the two boys out, gets the girls up, etc., generally superintending. In some of her workaday toggery she is a sight to be seen, but it's just the thing for work and economy."

About a month after his arrival, Will wrote Ethel: "I don't know that I am having what you would call a regular good time or not. I have not been out (except a couple of weeks ago to Paynter's) since coming here. . . . I get up about 6 or 6:30 in the mornings and work on the average till about 8 P.M., after which I get tea and read and study. Then on wet days I get some time to read also. . . . The Doyles all work pretty hard and I expect most of those who succeed in any worthy sense do the same." He told Louie what he had been reading: "This last week, I have read three plays by Ibsen, the Norwegian dramatist, called *The Pillars of Society, Ghosts,* and *An Enemy of Society.* They are all strong, realistic modern dramas, dealing largely with some aspects of the social question. All three plays criticize very severely the conventional morality of the upper classes of Europe. . . . Yesterday afternoon I read *Othello.* It is very powerful, but a gloomy tragedy. Shakespeare's plays seem so foreign to our time and age, don't you think? It requires an effort to enter into them fully as character sketches; they are very different from Ibsen's. . . . Last week I read *In Memoriam* and some of Shakespeare, also some of *Hudibras*."

Toward the end of the summer, Will Doyle took his nephew on a long buggy ride into Eastern Saskatchewan. Almost sixty years later, Will Good (*Farmer Citizen*) wrote his recollections of the trip: "We went west from Beulah to Fort Ellice, crossed the Assiniboine River there and proceeded westward up the Qu'Appelle Valley. There were practically no settlers there at that time, but the old ox-cart trails were most conspicuous. At the western limit of our journey, there was a settlement of three families, two of the Paynters, cousins of the Doyles, and another whose name I have forgotten. They called their colony Hamona, and had it organized as a sort of self-subsisting, with a common fund, and division of labour according to individual qualifications or tastes. . . . The colony was dissolved before many years had passed."

Back at Myrtleville that August, even with Will and Mrs. Morgan and little Morgan away, there were often fifteen or sixteen people in the house. Mrs. Arthur Good (Winnie) and her two little boys were there, and Mrs. Jim Good and her small son, Harry. The family were fond of both ladies; Mrs. Jim, said Mrs. Tom, was "womanly, sensible, and cheerful . . . knows just how to do everything and makes work scarce here." Winnie was a small vivacious woman, who, Louie remarked, was both polite and outspoken. Ethel adored Winnie and bicycled around the country with her in search of antiques. Mrs. Tom wrote, "People have such a craze for old things I daresay W. may double the money she pays on them." Arthur was working in Alamogordo, New Mexico, and Winnie had many very interesting letters from him. She and the boys would join him soon, but she dreaded the five-day train trip.

Late in August all the guests left. Louie was working hard to write an essay on the late Alfred Tennyson, poet laureate for over forty years, which she was to read at the annual Norfolk Teachers' Institute soon, as she was going back to teaching at Waterford. Ethel prepared for her final year at the Collegiate to get her "first-class certificate." Fanny did not go to school with her; she stayed home all year to help with the housework. She liked housework much more than Louie did, and she and her mother were more congenial. On the first Monday in September, she enjoyed going to town with Arthur Qua to see the Labor Day parade. She wrote Louie about it: "It represented all the different trades and shops in Brantford. For instance, the tin smiths marching past with tin collars, shirt fronts and hats. Shultz lumber and stuff: a girl sitting in a rocking chair fastened to the handles of a washing machine washing clothes, and a little house with men shingling it. Water works, a little statuette of a boy and a girl holding a parasol, and a fountain at the very tip top of it spraying all over."

A note came from Aunt Clara. She and John Matthews had moved from California to Indiana. She hoped some of the Myrtleville people would come to visit them now that they were back in a "civilized land" once more. About mid-September, Will and Frank came home. Will soon returned to Toronto, but Fred and Panay were not with him this year. The dental course was only three years and both boys were practicing, Panay in Brantford and Fred in Petrolia, Ontario, near Sarnia.

Will Good was very busy his senior year at the University of Toronto. He had a chemistry research project which he was to write up in a thesis. This would be entered in the "1851 Exhibition Scholarship" competition for three years postgraduate study abroad. Will also took time to continue his classes in English Literature and to go to many meetings. He was interested in talks given at the Canadian Socialist League, and continued to think about Henry George's Single Tax theories. His YMCA group discussed the relation of the college student to the extracollege world, and he was part of a small group of senior students meeting with three top-ranking professors, Wrong, Alexander, and Hutton, to discuss academic and social problems of the university. One of their subjects was co-education and young Mr. Good was much in favor of it. Unlike the private-school boys, he had never known any other system, though women were certainly in the minority at the university.

During his senior year, Will also wrote a paper on "Aerial Navigation." He exchanged several letters with Octave Chanute of Chicago, who had been conducting many experiments with gliders. Mr. Chanute's letters were full of mathematical formulae, and discussions of "propulsion against the wind." It was about this time that the Wright brothers began to build gliders, helped by Chanute's experiences, and a few years later they flew the first successful motor-driven plane.

Every week Will wrote to Louie at Waterford, as well as to the people at home. It was to Louie that he wrote his long and philosophical missives. Once he sent her some thoughts on the Gramophone and the Kinetoscope: "The old-fashioned inhabitants believed in ghosts: surely when we see people long ago dead, moving, and hear them speaking, . . . we must believe in ghosts, too, of a certain species, anyway. But use and custom take all the wonderment out of things, and because we see a thing happen a good many times we conclude—falsely—that it is less wonderful than something we seldom or never see. You may apply this reasoning to the subject of so-called miracles."

The letters to Will and Louie from Myrtleville told about the autumn work and play. Tom Good was busy with his accounting duties and helping on the farm whenever he could. He said, "I have had to keep urging Sheppard all the fall to get the work along." The womenfolk wrote a good deal about parties. First there was Gwennie's fifth birthday. Mamie made her a three-story cake decorated with pink and white icing. Soon afterward, the little girl went to live with her mother. The family at Myrtleville hated to have her go; they had grown very fond of her. They were happy, however, to keep Charlie with them. He was a bright, good-looking, sweet-tempered little boy, and he grew up at Myrtleville as a loved member of the family in his own right, and as a special gift to Carol. Mamie wrote: "Carol and Charlie go out and play very happily together. It used to be so hard to get her out of the house."

A few weeks after Gwennie's birthday, Ethel gave a "progressive crokinole" party for about twenty young people. Crokinole was very popular at that time, and it was not tinged with the gambling associations which made Mrs. Tom Good uneasy about card games. It was played by snapping disks somewhat like checkers toward the center of a circular board, large enough to cover most card tables. There is still a crokinole board at Myrtleville, and occasionally one of Will Good's grandchildren uses it. Most people nowadays know nothing about the game.

There were several letters full of descriptions of the two big parties Aunt Carrie and Uncle George Ballachey gave at Edgemount. Both were card parties, progressive euchre, followed by dancing. Mamie stayed at her uncle's all week between the parties, and no doubt helped a great deal with the preparations. The supper, served about midnight, was ample—turkey, ham, oyster patties, pickles and olives, ice cream, Charlotte Russe, cakes, nuts, candies. Mamie described a small accident involving the food at one party. "The shanty that had the ice-cream, etc., in it, was shut up, but Panay went through and left the door open, and the drivers slipped in and took the largest Charlotte Russe. It was in a very pretty china dish. Mrs. Hardy found the dish . . . broken all to bits down by the hedge." Fortunately nothing happened to the Goods' old Sheffield candelabra, nor to the flat silver they lent Aunt Carrie to help her serve sixty to seventy people at a time.

Mamie looked very well now; she wrote her brother proudly, "I weigh 109!!!lbs. People really do not know me." It had dawned upon her acquaintances that Mamie was more than cheerful and witty; she was a pretty girl with dark hair, blue eyes, and clear skin. (As they grew up, Mamie and Fanny both acquired dark hair from their Ballachey ancestry.) Mamie wore a white skirt with a new pink silk blouse to both of Aunt Carrie's parties, and received many compliments. Her blonde sister, Ethel, was said by Alec Ballachey to be "the belle of the ball." She was in white with pale green ribbons at waist and neck. The Good girls had very modest necklines, but they noticed that many guests did not. Mamie wrote, "Minnie Strong was here in her coming-out dress and she was very much out indeed."

The "gay nineties" were almost over and the Gibson Girl look was highly fashionable. Skirts were still long and full, and a tiny waist was much admired, but ladies' clothes had a more easy and simple appearance than they had had for a couple of generations. At midcentury, women had worn tight bodices, emphasizing sloping shoulders, and immense, bell-like skirts.

Then in the seventies and eighties they had added tight, bustled or draped skirts to a still close-fitting bodice. Now there were loose-fitting "blouses" (admittedly they often had exaggerated "leg-of-mutton" sleeves) and naturally flowing skirts. Coiffures had emerged from a period of curls and bangs, following the period of the smooth center-part, which was still worn by many older women. Hair was now often piled on top of the head with a soft pompadour effect. At about seventeen, a girl "put up her hair" as an announcement that she was ready to enter the adult world. A woman's hair was her "crowning glory" and the more she had, the better.

Louie, teaching in Waterford, was not able to get to Aunt Carrie's parties, but Mr. and Mrs. Good and the Misses Good were invited to a large holiday ball at Burford. Louie wanted to go, but her mother wouldn't hear of it. In a rare expression of rebellion, Louie wrote her brother, "I don't see one bit of harm in dancing and think it would have done me more good than harm if Mother had let us girls dance from the beginning. We would have gone out a good deal more and it isn't good to be too stay-at-home. But of course I'm not going."

The Boer War broke out late in 1899, and there are many comments about it in the Myrtleville letters. The younger children found it quite exciting (there would be a school holiday when British troops came to the relief of besieged Ladysmith), and the ladies of Myrtleville started making the hospital pillows that were asked for. Most of Ontario, with its strong British tradition, wanted to send troops to help the mother country. Most of Quebec thought the war was none of Canada's business; in fact, many French-Canadians were sympathetic to the Boers in their struggle against English domination. Will Good and a few of his "radical" friends felt sympathy with the Boers, too, on idealistic grounds. Will argued his case in a letter to Louie who, he thought, had been too much affected by the "jingoistic" press.

"You . . . base an argument upon the assumed right of Britain to follow up their demand with force of the most barbarous kind. . . . Granting that Britain is so justified (which I for one do not grant) it would still remain to prove that in order to carry out this demand, the warlike patriotism is needed among us as a Canadian people. One might think in the first place that in a wealthy and populous nation like England there would be sufficient force to deal . . . with the matter. It is as if you should observe a strong man beating a small boy (who, we will grant for this argument, needs the beating) and you should feel it incumbent upon yourself to try to develop in yourself some of the same spirit which the man has, in order that you may join in the fray and assist the man. In the second place, one might see no more reason why we, who do not whole-heartedly believe that England is in the right, should be under any greater obligation to assist her than are the people to the south of us, who are almost as closely bound to the English as we are. So that I would say as I said before, that I deplore the development of the military spirit within our own borders, because . . . this spread of militarism . . . will lead to greater expenditure for military equipment . . . and will therefore retard still further the day when men of different nations may recognise each other as brothers."

The French-Canadian prime minister, Laurier, worked out a government compromise. Canada would organize and equip troops, but Britain would pay for them. Eventually more than eight thousand Canadians were mobilized for the South African war, including about twenty men from the Brantford area.

Louie's Model School certificate would expire at the end of 1900, so she decided to enter Normal College in the autumn. She hated to leave a few good friends in Waterford, but not the village itself; it was such a sleepy little place. She much preferred living in the country, with access to the relatively stirring life of Brantford, and she would have liked some of Willie's opportunities in the stimulating life of Toronto. It could be asked why she did not take secretarial training and try to get work in a city. She seems to have felt that she must be a teacher, although she was unhappy teaching. Perhaps there would have been strenuous objections from her parents and Aunt Annie to any other career for her, and Louie told her brother that she had become apathetic and weak-willed. She wrote bitterly to him in March of 1900: "I hate teaching and never dare say so even to myself. . . . I try to be agreeable here because it is expedient. . . . I'm a discontented beggar, and the pretending is trying to make other people, and perhaps myself, to think that I am contented. Trying to fit into a groove that one is not made for is a duty, no doubt, for who can choose their place in life?"

Louie's letters do not mention her Waterford admirer, a music-lover also, though later he came to Myrtleville asking to marry her. There was a young man in Brantford too with an eye on her. Uncle George's family, except for the farmer son, George Melville, moved into town for the winter that year and Louie usually stayed with them Friday nights when she came home for the weekend. Ethel said that a certain young gentleman was seen wandering around the Ballachey house every Friday evening in hopes of seeing Louie.

Early in March, Will Good handed in his thesis for the 1851 Exhibition Scholarship. Later in the month, he took a special examination for the competition. There were three applicants, but it was generally assumed that Mr. Good, head of his class throughout his college years, would win the contest. Everyone was amazed when the prize was awarded late in April to a man who had not applied until the last minute and who handed in his materials late. Apparently he was a physicist and his physics professor insisted that it was the turn of physics to get the prize. There was quite an uproar, with student petitions and faculty dissension, but the physics department prevailed. Will Good took his defeat very philosophically; he had already been dubious about three years abroad, studying science. Later, he felt that his loss of the scholarship was a clear case of "Providential intervention." He was now free to work in the field of social justice. His campus image was primarily that of a reformer. The yearbook, *Torontonensis, 1900,* described him under the quotation from *Hamlet:* "The times are out of joint." His irreverent sister, Ethel, probably teased him with the rest of the quote, "O, cursed spite, That ever I was born to set them right."

Young Mr. Good was well endowed with almost everything except money. He had a quick, retentive mind in a superbly strong body; he had energy and industry which enabled him to use his gifts very effectively. His weaknesses were chiefly lack of humor and tact, but because he had deep and varied interests, he always found congenial friends. His sisters twitted him for being so solemn; he had, however, a most beautiful smile which often broke through his severity, and he was, with all his other gifts, an exceedingly good-looking young man. He claimed not to care about outward appearances; later, his wife would say that he always managed to look as if his clothes had been slept in. He did, however, wear the fashionable full mustache; it was reddish, though his hair was blond. (None of Tom Good's six children had red hair.)

Will believed in plain living as well as plain dressing. He was much less understanding than his Aunt Kate about the modest elegance expected of the head of Ontario's government. When he went to dinner at the home of the Honorable A. S. Hardy, he was quite critical of his host's manner of living, and he professed frank disgust at the mansions, carriages, and dress clothing of certain Toronto manufacturers. There was a great gap between rich and poor in Toronto. Urban laborers were often overworked and underpaid, while Will Good was used to farms where the hired men ate as well, and usually worked not as hard as their employers.

Will was never one to follow the crowd. His classmate, and close friend, Norman Coleman (later president of Reed College in Oregon), wrote comments about Will's behavior at a public dinner in 1900: "I can imagine I see you sitting in your chair while all the rest of the diners get up and shout for the soldiers in Africa, 'the Defenders of our Empire.' You have a reserve supply of courage that will stand you in good stead in your future—has already done so many times, I doubt not— a sort of obstinate adherence to convictions regardless of majorities, not to be proud of, yet withal I think to be thankful for. It isn't strength you lack, Good, but a tenderness of manner and consideration of feeling, a power of graceful yielding in nonessentials which will keep you from antagonizing people and will make your work more effective."

Will Good learned most skills very easily, but the art of diplomacy came hard. It was even harder for him than for his father and Aunt Annie, with their quick flare-ups followed by heartfelt apologies. He was more like his mother, in that he seldom lost his temper, but did fuss, even "nag," with considerable insensitivity to the feelings of those around him, especially his family. However, as he matured, he became less dogmatic, and in public life his refusal to be deflected by anger stood him in good stead. He earned a reputation of being able to "pour oil on troubled waters."

13

Will Good—Scholar or Farmer?

Will Good's plans for the year following his graduation were indefinite for months, though his cousins of about his age were already launched on their careers. George M. Ballachey was farming at Edgemount; his brother Panay was building up a dental practice in Brantford. Fred, following a year as assistant to a Petrolia dentist, had gone to Buffalo, where he opened an office and lived with his brother George T., who had just taken the promising job of being trained to manage a large estate.

In our day, a young man with Will Good's qualifications would have a choice of fellowships, but there were few available in 1900. For a while, it seemed that there might be an opening in the chemistry department at the University of Toronto; it failed to materialize. Will worked on the farm through the summer and fall and had some outside employment with his old school friend, Arthur Lyons, doing electrical wiring in the building of the new Farmers' Cooperative Packing Company. Then he went back to Toronto for graduate study, and supported himself by tutoring. He was still very much part of the university world and active in some of its organizations.

He stayed temporarily with the three Mallochs, who had moved to Toronto. Both daughters were still unmarried. Lily was fat and fortyish; Sally was twenty-seven and "delicate." It was probably a relief to all parties concerned when Will left for a boardinghouse. Charlotte's nieces found her rather formidable, but her brother Tom's son was not easily cowed.

With the unconscious arrogance of one who was young, strong, bright, well educated, and at the same time unimaginative about the feelings of others, he was impatient with the three women. He thought his aunt kept Sally an invalid with her overprotective attitude, and he thought both his Malloch cousins were foolish. Charlotte no doubt found him opinionated and argumentative, and distressingly unorthodox in his views. The family at Myrtleville used to say, only partly in jest, that Willie was always "agin' the gover'ment."

He worked on various plans for his future, and wrote the University of Wisconsin about studying economics. A kindly dean told him that he would have to get undergraduate credits before he could hope to get graduate fellowships in political science and economics, and advised him to continue with chemistry in which he was already well qualified. Laboriously Will cut a stencil of his scholarship thesis, made blue prints of its diagrams, and used the document in applications to several American universities. In the spring of 1901, Yale offered him a tuition fellowship. He refused it because of uneasiness about the living expenses involved, and growing concern about Myrtleville. He wrote his mother: "With regard to the farm, I could easily become contented if I could once satisfy myself that it was my absolute and clearly recognised duty; but that latter is a difficult question."

Tom Good was a very weary man. With all his industry and initiative, he still found it hard to make an acceptable living for his family. He continued to give a great deal of time and energy to farm organizations and the businesses they set up in attempts to increase earnings, for example, the cheese factory, the binder-twine company, the new meat-packing plant. He also continued to be the able and conscientious treasurer of Brantford Township. Whatever he was paid for outside jobs was not enough to relieve him of farm work. John Ballachey wrote him: "You certainly have enough to do and living in the country makes it more inconvenient. . . . Should have 2 or 3,000 a year for the work you do—as long as you are willing to do it, they will be willing to let you do it. I take no office unless there is a salary attached to it."

Tom appreciated the hard work his son put in on the farm during the summers, but the young man was bursting with ideas, and his father probably found him exhausting. Willie wrote him on March 4, 1901, about plans for transforming a two-story shed into a three-story combined stable, drive-shed, and hayloft (which still stands on the east side of the barn-yard): "I hope you have been making some preparation for the building in the spring. . . . I do not think the labour will be very costly as we can do a good deal of it ourselves. We should need masons to build the wall, and carpenters to do the framing, I suppose; but the latter will be a comparatively small job. We can finish it up after that, after it is raised; can put on the roof, siding, etc., and fit up the inside entirely. There will be little new material required—shingles, a few planks, cement, etc. Have you the stones all collected, and is the building emptied of its hay? . . . Please see to it that the mulching is done in the garden before the weeds start; it will save a lot of trouble with the grass next summer if it is prop-erly done in the spring."

Will Good was always puzzled by Ike Connor's disapproval of him for having got so "uppity." Ike had worked at Myrtle-ville off and on since Tom Good was a boy. He was devoted to Tom, and it is quite possible that he thought Willie was unrea-sonably bossy—and hard on his father.

While Will was in Toronto doing graduate work, Louie spent the 1900–1901 school year at the Ontario Normal Col-lege in Hamilton, which she liked better than the Model School, and where she had a pleasant group of friends. Ethel was with her in the autumn, taking the short "model" course, as Brantford no longer offered it. Like Louie, Ethel excelled in her practice teaching. She received congratulations from Fanny Doyle, who was recuperating from typhoid fever, which she had taken in Winnipeg. With increasing population and inadequate supervision of water supplies, typhoid had become a great danger. Some farsighted municipalities already were exercising control; Brantford had had a safe public drinking-water system for over ten years, and in 1896 had undertaken to close up all the wells in town.

Ethel was now qualified to be a "schoolmarm," but she had not outgrown her love of pranks. She came back to Myrtleville from the Carlyles' one day, bringing a lady whom she in-troduced as Miss McVicar from Goderich, a Carlyle cousin.

Ethel Sirett née Good, and friends

The lady was really Blanche in a big hat with a heavy veil. The visitor was received graciously by all at the farm, including Panay Ballachey. Eventually she was asked if she played the piano, a standard social gambit at that time. Blanche and Ethel

were amazed that the disguise had worked so long, and
thought they would reveal themselves by playing one of their
old duets. They started to play, and everyone but Panay listened politely. He shocked his elders by walking over to "Miss
McVicar" and chucking her under the chin. How *could* a well-
brought-up young man be so familiar with a strange lady?
There was a stifled gasp of horror before the truth came out.

Ethel did not get a school in early 1901, and spent several
months "puttering around among the pots and pans . . . a
great waste of time as Mother and Mamie are quite able to do
the housework." She made such good bread and buns, however, that she jokingly asked her brother if he could hunt her
up a place as a cook in Toronto.

The high point of the summer of 1901 for the Myrtleville
family was their visit to the Pan-American Exposition at Buffalo. Ten-year-old Carol had written her brother in the
spring: "I am wanting to earn some money to go to the Pan-
American Show. I am to get 5 ct. every lb. ball of carpet rags I
sew, and Mamie is going to let me have the eggs of one hen to
sell and in the summer I might sell some rhubarb. . . . If you
find anything more for me to make money, tell me." The
happy memory of the long-awaited outing was dimmed by the
family's return in a terrible storm which killed four cows with
lightning.

At the end of the summer Louie went to teach at Brocksden, near Stratford. Still only twenty-one, she had gained self-
confidence at Normal School, and was happier with her teaching. She enjoyed music lessons in Stratford every Saturday;
the town was big and busy compared to Waterford. (Its chief
business in those days was railway shops; it did not establish
the Shakespeare Festival until midcentury.) Louie also wrote
home cheerfully about long bicycle rides, benefit "garden parties," and her appointment to the "exalted position of Musical
Director of the Brocksden Literary and Debating Society."

Nineteen-year-old Ethel taught at New Dundee, about
twenty miles from Myrtleville. Like Ayr nearby, it had been
named by homesick Scotsmen, but there had been heavy settlement by German-speaking immigrants. Ethel boarded with
the Lautenschlagers, and made the acquaintance of German
food. She was amazed at the bountiful table, and Charlie

always remembered the coffee cake she brought home. Ethel described the women of the Old Mennonite sect: "[They] dress very plainly, black or grey dresses, no frills, collars or ribbons, and bonnets something like the Salvation Army. In church, however, they take them off and just wear little white net caps. They pull their hair straight back. I don't believe women were intended to look so plain. They have an objection to yellow and the minister preached against the wearing of it."

She wrote to Louie that "I've been talking German tonight like a blue streak. They like to get me at it, and thus we all have a good laugh. . . . Yesterday another girl and I walked out to a church about 2½ miles from here where they were holding an Old Mennonite Bible Conference. . . . Do you have such queer sects where you are, Mennonites, Quakers, Amish people, etc.? . . . I haven't tasted the Sour Krout yet. There is some in the cellar waiting to get ready for use. I expect I will like it. I do nearly everything they have. November 30th . . . There is skating on the pond now, but I have not been on yet as it is not very safe. I bought a new pair of skates and so am all ready. . . . We had sour krout today. It is not such bad stuff. I ate a whole saucerful. They say I am a regular Deutscher." Ethel used her "Deutsch" to tell her brother to cut off the beard he was growing. "Es ist schrecklich, unausprechlich schrecklich! (It is horrible, unspeakably horrible!)"

Will was experimenting with his beard while working on the farm. The Sheppards had left and the help problem was acute. However, the young man persuaded his father to drill a new well to replace three dug wells which gave out in dry seasons. The drilling was an ordeal, and Tom Good grew almost sick with worry over the expense. His well-known "steadiness" was a matter of his dependability, not of his emotions. Given his vivid imagination and his picturesque Irish habits of speech, his periods of depression, though usually brief, were quite dramatic. All their lives his younger children remembered how scared they were of "going to the poorhouse." His wife was good at cheering him up with her simple faith that somehow "all things work together for good," even though they appear very wrong. She once wrote her son, "We seem called upon to plan & do as much as our abilities will allow & then know that man proposes & God disposes & trust entirely to a higher power." Unfortunately, in her eagerness to "plan and do" as much as possible, she fussed a good deal, especially at her children, and drove herself and them. Often she was too tired or busy to write more than a hasty scribble, but when she took time, her active, though untrained, mind produced some very interesting letters. One of them was to Louie about the well-drilling.

"The wind is howling up the chimneys tonight [Friday] and the men are taking turns at drilling . . . Mr. Frank Ridge has gone [to bed] and intends to get up at three and work. . . . It sounds like a big churn going, a continuous thumping sound about every 2 seconds. They only worked one night before, and that only till about eleven. We are feeling very discouraged, especially your Father who has had two very despondent attacks about it, and has been hopeless all the time. He was against doing it at all, he says, only W. urged it being done. . . . Willie counted it up last night with Mr. Ridge and the expenses border on three hundred dollars already, and as yet no water of any account. All the wood is burned up for fuel around the place except our firewood in the woodshed and even a good deal of that. They cut off the big limb off the willow tree by the milkstand today, where the swing was. Enough wood has been burned to have kept us a year. It is a terrible business. They struck a small vein of water about 15 feet down in the rock (which by the way is limestone) but it was but a very small quantity . . . and now they have gone 85 feet through the rock. Your Father and Willie are decided now that they are only to go 125 feet and then stop for good, water or not water. They get $ 1 a foot and we have to buy the casing which is about 60 dollars, so you see what a sad thing it seems to be, but God knows best and we do not."

The letter continued on Saturday morning: "Well, Louie, what do you think. Surely 'Heaviness may endure for a night but joy cometh in the morning.' . . . They worked all night up to 4 o'clock and lo there is water, and plenty they say. About 95 feet in the rock, 228 feet altogether. The top or surface bed was exceptionally trying and deep. . . . They are now pumping out the debris, ground up rock, etc., and have yet to see how deep the water is and of what kind. I fear it is hard. [It was.]" Two weeks later Mamie wrote Louie: "We expect the pump for the new well tomorrow. The tank is to be in the N.W. corner of Willie's room, with pipes to the barn, and after a while to the kitchen if the water is good, anyway two taps, one up and one down stairs. . . . We do not know whether Willie is appointed to the position at the College yet or not. I do not see where the money for all the improvements is to come from if he does not get it."

The "position at the college" was one in the department of Chemistry at the Ontario Agricultural College in Guelph, and Willie did get it. He was to be paid nine hundred dollars a year at first, (probably about thirty-six hundred in our money) which he hoped would enable him to hire good help at Myrtleville. He also hoped to have most of the summer free for working on the farm himself and he looked forward to learning more about the application of science to agriculture.

On New Year's Day of 1902, before Willie left, there was a reunion of the older generation at Myrtleville. All of Allen and Eliza Good's surviving children were there. They had not been together since Bella went West almost twenty-two years earlier. Willie took a picture of them with his camera. It is interesting to study the five "likenesses." Anne is seventy years old, plump and placid, with a little white cap on her smoothly parted hair. Charlotte, almost sixty-five, wears an elaborate lace cap and jabot, and seems as old as Anne. Tom looks haggard, and older than his fifty-eight years. Bella, fifty-six, is very thin, but with a healthy-looking leanness. Her hair is pulled back severely, and this emphasizes her thinness, and sharpens her features, so that she looks rather masculine and not nearly as handsome as in her youthful pictures. Clara, a good-looking woman of fifty-one, has her hair becomingly arranged and looks almost a generation younger than the others.

The pleasure of reunion was tempered by the pain of remembering how many had been lost in twenty-two years—Mamma, Fanny, Charlie, Molly, Eliza. There was a sense of change in society too; Mary Tom spoke of "these ease-loving days." Within the past year Queen Victoria had died; Myrtleville had been built the year she became queen and Anne Good had been a small child then. It was hard to think of an Edwardian rather than a Victorian era, and the Goods were

Tom Good and his sisters, January 1, 1902. Back row, left to right: *Clara Matthews, Bella Doyle;* front row, left to right: *Anne Good, Tom Good, and Charlotte Malloch*

dubious about their worldly, pleasure-loving new sovereign. Even young Will, who was so eager for social change, did not think that Edward VII was the man to help it along. He had written Mamie, "I fear that the personal influence of the new king will not be so wholesome as that of his mother."

The memory of Good Queen Victoria was kept green in Canada by the continuing celebration of her birthday. For many years, Victoria Day was a national holiday, and adults quoted the jingle from their schooldays: "The twenty-fourth of May is the Queen's birthday;/If you don't give us a holiday, we'll all run away." Now Victoria Day is simply a Monday in late May, giving a long spring weekend.

In the midst of the New Year's festivities at Myrtleville in

1902, there must have been some ruffled feelings. Will wrote Louie from Guelph the following week: "I think Aunt Clara rather too sensitive for her or others' comfort, but my short acquaintance with her lately has raised her in my estimation rather than the reverse. She is too impulsive and demonstrative to suit my taste, but I am of a peculiar type and therefore must make allowance. I think it is too bad that you should all conspire to keep Aunt C. in a state of excitement, when she is, or has been, on the verge of nervous prostration. If one comes for a quiet visit, you must ask all the neighbors, friends and acquaintances to 'parties,' and keep the house and everyone in an uproar."

The nervous and sensitive and generous Aunt Clara moved on to visit in Toronto, leaving money for Carol's piano lessons from Helen Carlyle for a three-month period. Later Clara sent money for a shiny black upright piano. Eliza Good's beautiful old mahogany instrument was scarcely playable by this time, but Anne Good kept it, probably for sentimental reasons. It was moved into the drawing room, where it still sits, and the black piano was put in the dining-sitting room. There are snapshots showing the new piece of furniture adorned in late Victorian style with embroidered drapery, vases, candlesticks, and many photographs. It was a period when even bookcases were draped.

Mary Good soon wrote Louie more family news: "Aunt Annie got a nice long letter from Aunt Kate who is now at Alamogordo. Arthur and Winnie are looking so well and the children. . . . The climate is superb . . . but food is dear, potatoes 2½¢ a lb., butter 30 cts., meat 18 cts., qt. milk 10 cts. & so on. . . . Kate says Arthur is doing very well. . . . She and Winnie were going to take a few days and cross over into old Mexico before she leaves."

Will was settling down in Guelph. The Ontario Agricultural College had been in existence now for about thirty years. It had almost eight hundred students, some of them women taking the home dairy course. Soon there would be many girls coming; a Mr. Macdonald of Montreal had recently given $125,000 to equip buildings for "nature study and domestic science." (Much later, after World War II, the institution was expanded to become the University of Guelph.)

Will found a few congenial people on the staff of the college; unfortunately, he found also that most of his salary was swallowed up by living expenses, and that he was expected to work the year round. Moreover, his laboratory was ill equipped compared to those he was used to in Toronto, and the work rather dull. He taught one class in the chemistry of insecticides and fungicides; otherwise, he spent most of his first term analyzing cheese and butter. He felt the lack of exercise; he had about half an hour's walk from his boarding-house to the college and that was all the exercise he got except "running about the laboratory." Soon he moved to another lodging, and took all his meals at the college; it was cheaper that way, and now he walked two miles before 7:30 breakfast. Later he had a bicycle, and sometimes rode it the thirty-five miles home on weekends.

His mother was concerned about his social life. She wrote Louie: "I do hope that he won't be radical and one-sided in his views, and think different from everyone else. . . . The young men up there don't seem to lack invitations and there seems plenty of sociability if they desire to avail themselves of it. I think Willie despises entertaining, 'at homes,' teas, etc., but I don't see upon what ground he can—certainly 'at homes' are the cheapest way as regards time and money, and the eating is not extravagant, and nothing objectionable such as cards, dancing, etc.—and no late hours either. If W. is not friendly, he will soon be dropped, and I think it is a pity."

The spring work at Guelph proved somewhat more interesting. Will told of enjoying some long drives around the countryside placing experimental sugar beet plots. Still, he wrote, "I wish I were able to farm this summer. This is a good deal of a slave's life, except the pay. It may get better, or I may get better used to it. If not, I shall get out when I can afford it."

Will made intermittent working visits to the farm during the summer. He was badly needed there; his father was losing weight again and suffering from chest pains and a cough. Perhaps the old family specter of tuberculosis was hovering over him. He managed to keep going, however. It was a very busy season. Besides the usual summer work, there was sometimes hand-pumping of water for the stock; the new windmill did not always operate properly. Then there was still much to be done in the finishing of the horse stable, and at the end of the summer the building of the hexagonal "cement silo" which still stands north of the barns at Myrtleville, dwarfed now by two much larger silos built by Tom Good's grandson. Charlie Good remembered helping with the 1902 silo. He worked on mixing concrete, though he was not yet eleven years old.

The silo was a novelty in the neighborhood; there were comparatively few silos in the country at this date, and most of them were of wood. Mrs. Tom Good wrote on September 2, 1902: "The cement work and plastering inside and out are finished. The roof can be put on after it is filled, I suppose. Mr. Isaac Usher wants to have it photographed, I believe, as his advertisement. . . . The silo has to be kept wet quite often which they do with the hose."

By this time Louie had returned to teaching at Brocksden, and Ethel had gone to Homewood to be governess and "mother's helper" in Harold Jones's household. There were four children, the oldest only nine, and during the winter Harold was often away for weeks at a time, lecturing on fruit-growing for the Farmers' Institutes. He was recognized as an authority on fruit-growing, and had several acres of experimental planting which for about twenty years had provincial status as the "St. Lawrence Experiment Station." (In place of some of his beautiful orchards there is now a large factory, the Maitland plant of DuPont of Canada.)

Ethel was good company for Harold's wife, Ruth, as well as a great help with the children, and in autumn with the picking, sorting, and packing of apples, some of which were carefully prepared for shipping as far as Japan. She enjoyed herself at Homewood, though she felt that she did not succeed in teaching the children much. She was genuinely fond of Uncle Andrew, "a dear old man," of Harold and Ruth, who were so kind and pleasant (though Harold sometimes made his young cousin feel very ignorant, she said), and of the children, "wild" as she thought they were. Homewood was a lovely place in good weather. There was the river in front of the house for swimming and boating; there were woods behind for walking and picnicking. Even in bad weather people managed to have card parties and dances, and Ethel did not share her mother's scruples about them. In fact, there is a note of mischievous satisfaction in her report to Louie, that she "scandalized Nana" by dancing a great deal with one admirer, when her Aunt Annie was visiting Homewood.

Soon after the girls left Myrtleville, their father had a severe attack of pneumonia. He almost died, but once past the crisis, he gradually recovered, and looked better rested than he had for months. Will wrote Louie on September 20: "I suppose you have been kept posted regarding Papa's illness. I have not heard since Wednesday when I returned to Guelph. He was then improving but too weak to get out of bed. . . . I hope to go home again at the end of next week for a few days. There is the silo to fill and the threshing to do, and Wesley [the hired man] is hardly able to manage that. I am simply nonplussed regarding the farm, and only find relief in temporarily forgetting about it." He told her about his fall work at the college: "We have been working here the last few days on the sugar beets. We get a lot of the boys in helping—today we had about a dozen—and then we can rush it through. Today we analysed nearly 100 samples. The beets have to be brushed clean, topped, weighed, sampled, pulped, juice expressed, specific gravity of latter taken, juice clarified and sugar determined therein. It is quite an interesting process, but gets monotonous and wearisome after a while."

Will's conviction grew that he liked farming better than laboratory work at the Ontario Agricultural College. The students were more numerous and the equipment still scanty; he wrote Louie that the situation was "fine torture to anyone who likes systematic and accurate work." He offered to rent the farm from his father, who could then move into town. His father answered that a good share of the rent would belong to Aunt Annie, and that there would not be enough left to make living in town feasible, as they would certainly not leave the children behind on the farm. "Another reason is that we want you to have some ready money by you before you take the place as we well know the difficulty of always being short of money, . . . and we think it will be best for you to stay in your present position for another year at least." Mary Good added a note to her husband's letter: "Your father is certainly getting stronger and if we could only get help now for a month or so Wesley and he could manage then until spring, I should think.

. . . The children are going to turn in and help with the roots when Wesley begins them, if we do not get a man before." Will now shifted his view toward spring and wrote Mamie to that effect. She immediately sent him a hard-hitting letter.

"You speak as if you thought of coming home for good (or bad) in the spring. I think it would be the height of selfish folly for you to do so. What would there be for any of us but more and more scrimping and slaving? You could not make anything like what you do up there. It is impossible. No farmers do. . . . You have never been solely dependent on the farm for your money supplies since you were a child and then did not realize them. . . .

"Mother and Papa have worked and slaved and scrimped and now, just when things have got a little easier for them, why do you want to come and take their almost only means of living, for we could not live on the rent of Papa's part of the farm, even in addition to his town work? Again, you and Papa never agree about things, there is constant friction, and that makes us all miserable and unhappy. . . . Papa will not give up the farm while he lives, and I do not see that you have any right to it as long as he and Aunt Annie live. The only thing for you to do if you want to come back before is to save enough in your present position to buy it outright. . . .

"I suppose you think you would be a better farmer than Papa but nobody else thinks so. I doubt if you would do as well. . . . Of course, if Papa gets so sick that he cannot take charge here I suppose you will be compelled to come back. . . .

"Of course there are disagreeable things to be put up with in Guelph, but is there any place outside of Heaven where there are not? . . . If you have to come back I will try to help you all I can, but in the meantime I wish you would try to put your heart and mind into your work there. . . . You would feel much happier if you would not kick against the pricks all the time."

Mrs. Tom Good took up the cudgel a few days later: "You see, Willie, how disastrous financially your coming home would be, greatly so to you, for we could not live on anything less than we had during the time Mr. Sheppard was here. They lived poorly and left in debt. . . . More than half the rent belongs to your Aunt Annie, and we, your Father and I and the children will have either to live on her charity as we do now, or yours. . . . Your Father was telling me once that he had nothing but one span of horses, not a cow, not a pig, not one sheep, no land, no implement, no good buildings. By hard strenuous work he and I have made this farm what it is. . . . I do not think you can understand what a family's expenses are." By the same mail, Will received another blast from his oldest sister.

"I received your letter on Saturday and have been thinking very hard about it ever since. I do not know what catastrophe will follow if you do not come home. I think Papa would fret himself more sick over being laid on the shelf than he would get by overseeing the farm and doing a moderate amount of work. . . .

"You seem to think that your work on the farm is worth at least $600.00 per year. I do not think that it is worth more than a good man's under Papa's direction, say $200.00, so you see we could get three men for that amount, and Papa has all his mental faculties about him yet. . . . I think your having paid the man this year has relieved him very much; of course the relief would be more apparent if all the building had not come to counterbalance it. Why can't you go on the same way for two or three years, until you have some capital to work the farm profitably? . . .

"It is a vast pity that you do not like your present work when it is what you have been spending most of your life to prepare for, and it seems a pity that a capital, in other words your University course, capable of giving you an income of $1,000 or more a year should be thrown to the winds. . . .

"I do not know how or who you hope or intend to influence here. All the young people I know in the neighborhood are honest, upright and good as far as I can see and they are quite happy without knowing Henry George's ideas on single tax, and probably would only consider you a crank if you tried to enlighten or darken them.

"If you are bound to come back some time which, as the farm is to be yours, I suppose you will, you had better try and get your B.S.A. degree. You will have far more influence in a farming community, than if they thought you were only a

school-masterish kind of fellow. . . . I think you have rea-
soned yourself into believing what you want to believe, also
'weigh well that counsel which favours thine own mind.' "

What Mamie probably did not realize was the depth of
Will's determination to work for "the farm movement," and of
his feeling that the farm was a practical base for this work,
while the Ontario Agricultural College was not. She knew,
however, that he was courting, mainly by letter, a schoolteacher who had been a classmate at the University. He was no
doubt dreaming of a career on the farm which included a
wife. At any rate, he seems to have given up his idea of coming home in the spring.

It was time to make plans for Christmas. Louie consulted
her brother and he replied on December 17: "Your letter
received today. Am sorry that I cannot help you much in the
matter of presents. I am pretty short of money and . . . considerably in debt. I owe Wesley over $100 and mother about
$90. I was intending to give mother $5 to spend on anything
she liked for the house. Beyond this I do not feel justified in
going at present. I shall get no presents for anyone this Christmas." There was a jolly Christmas at Myrtleville, anyway. Ethel
came from Homewood, and Fanny Doyle with her younger
brother, Murray, from Manitoba. The family enjoyed having
Aunt Mary Qua at the farm most of the winter; her son, Arthur, was working in Goderich, and she had rented her house
in Paris.

Will Good still planned to farm eventually. His mother
wrote him wistfully: "Perhaps I had foolishly thought of you
being the one to redeem the fortunes of the family. I believe I
would like to be rich & still choose to live simply, there is so
much misery to be relieved, people needing garments in cold
weather, & fuel & food & Drs. attention, etc. etc. . . . Surely
money is an excellent thing rightly used but who can make it?
I cannot . . . but . . . you can earn it. Many can only earn a
pittance, are not qualified to do more."

Ethel wrote her brother at Guelph: "I suppose by what you
say about not needing fine things . . . that you mean you're
going to leave. I am more sorry than I can tell, but I know it's
no good talking to you. You're throwing back the gifts of
Providence." She told about Harold Jones's adventures getting

home from the Maritimes and "crossing the straits between
Nova Scotia and Prince Edward Island. They came over in a
little row-boat, where there was water, and dragged the boat
across the cakes of ice. [This must have been the famous
winter when the ferry was marooned in the Northumberland
Strait.]"

Two anniversaries were celebrated at Myrtleville that winter. In February, Charlie had his eleventh birthday. His Uncle
Tom took him to town and they brought back a couple of his
little friends. Mamie wrote her brother about the party: "They
skated and went sleigh riding and then had tea with the small
dishes in the parlour, and a cake with candles on it, and then
they had a great time in the kitchen. I do not know what they
did, but they made a dreadful noise."

No party was given for the Tom Goods' twenty-eighth
wedding anniversary on March 12, 1903, but the couple celebrated it themselves. Mary copied for her husband a poem
which began:

We are growing old together, thou dearest of the dear,
The morning of our life is past, and evening shades appear.
Some friends we loved are in their graves, and many are estranged,
But in sunshine or in shadow, our hearts have never changed.

Many years later, after her death, this copy was found in her
writing case, along with Tom Good's letters to her, a lock of
his hair, and a well-wrapped piece of wedding cake, labeled
March 12, 1875.

14

A Scholar Comes Home

A few months after the wedding anniversary, Tom Good decided that this was his last year as a farmer. The decision was probably caused by his fatigue and his son's insistence. Will was to come home in the late summer and live in the north wing. His courting had been unsuccessful; Mamie would be the farm housekeeper, feed the hired men, churn the butter, and so on. She accepted the situation gracefully.

Ethel spent a month at home that summer, then returned to Homewood. She was restless, however, with a job which had no future. She wrote her brother, "I want to be a B.A., a trained nurse, a Domestic Science graduate, and a musician. What shall I do first?" She wrote more practically to Louie, "I simply don't know how to teach . . . I think I ought to go to Normal College next year or some place, but I can't decide what to do."

Tom Good was sixty at the end of August. About this time Will came back to Myrtleville to stay. He leased the farm, implements, stock, and so forth, for five years beginning October 1, 1903. The irrepressible Ethel sent him a letter addressed "To the Squire of Myrtleville," and his friend, Norman Coleman, wrote from Oregon, "I shall take it for granted that you are . . . a fixture on the farm until I hear that you have been elected to the Dominion Parliament on an Independent ticket." Mr. Coleman's prediction was justified; eighteen years later W. C. Good was elected to Parliament as an Independent-Progressive!

Tom Good finally was relieved of agricultural work and responsibility. It was almost a physical necessity, but father and son were not exactly congenial in their new relationship. Tom was still interested in every detail of the work on the farm where he had labored most of his life, but Will, as a very old man, remembered with sorrow how uncommunicative he had been. By this time *he* had turned over management of the farm to one of *his* sons, and finally had some understanding of his father's position.

Louie left Brocksden at Christmas and came to live at home and teach at Moyle's School. She had been very successful and popular at Brocksden, and started her new position with high hopes. There were disadvantages, however. She walked to school, and three miles and more a day in all kinds of weather proved quite tiring. Besides, there were demands made on her outside of school which would not have been made if she had been boarding with other than close family. Her desire to do her duty outran the bounds of common sense. There is a story that she kept herself awake for studying by sitting with her feet in cold water. She "leaned over backward" to avoid charges of favoring the school's "best all-round pupil," her foster brother, twelve-year-old Charlie. He was fond of Louie, but he felt acutely uncomfortable with her as his teacher.

Louie was scarcely used to her new job, when tragedy disrupted life at Myrtleville. Brantford papers of February 4, 1904, carried the following obituary notice.

> Death removed one of the most prominent residents of Brantford township this morning in the person of Thomas A. Good, township treasurer, who died at an early hour at his home, Myrtleville farm, Paris Road.
>
> Death was somewhat unexpected as deceased had been ill only a few days. Last Friday night he was working on the township books and sat up most of the night trying to make the balance. He contracted a cold, which developed into pneumonia. From Saturday morning he gradually sank, medical aid being powerless. . . .
>
> The late Mr. Good was an extensive farmer and stock-raiser. He took a deep interest in Farmers' Institute work, and, in fact, everything which stood for up-to-date farming methods. Throughout his life, he had made farming his study, and by

acute observation and reading had obtained a vast general knowledge of farming topics. During the last few years he was a prominent speaker on the board of Institute lecturers. Mr. Good was a fluent talker. His extensive knowledge, combined with a good command of English, enabled him to make his addresses unusually interesting. . . . His death makes a vacancy in Institute work which will be hard to fill.

Besides devoting much energy to Institute work, Mr. Good found time to serve the . . . township of Brantford. In January, 1897, he was appointed treasurer. . . . He filled the office ever since, to the complete satisfaction of the councils and ratepayers. In politics, the deceased was a Liberal, though he never took any prominent part.

The late Mr. Good was a strong English Church worker, having been rector's warden in St. Jude's Church . . . for a number of years. Deceased was president of the Brantford branch of the U.C. Bible Society. His character was unimpeachable, and he was always liked and trusted for his honesty and straightforward dealings. . . . The township is not alone in its loss, the city and the entire community suffers by the death of such a man.

There are more personal comments in a couple of letters Will received from friends. One young man wrote, "Your father was a great worker and lived in a few years as much as others do in many." Another said that although he had met Mr. Good only a couple of times he had been much impressed by "his kindness and evident goodness."

Tom Good left to his son his land (that is, about seventy-three acres of lot number twenty-six) and all the farm stock, implements, and tools. There were charges upon this legacy. The will read: "I give and bequeath unto my daughter, Mary Elizabeth Anne Good the sum of Three Hundred dollars and to each of my other daughters the sum of Two Hundred and Fifty dollars, to be paid to them by my said son, William Charles Good, on their respectively attaining the age of twenty-one years." The will went on to stipulate that if Myrtleville House were "rendered unfit for occupation by fire . . . my son . . . shall at once provide . . . a suitable dwelling house to be used by my wife and unmarried daughters. . . . My said son shall also provide my wife and unmarried daughters . . . with one good milking cow, my said son to feed and care for such cow, and he shall also provide for my wife and daughters so long as they shall continue unmarried all the vegetables and fruit that may be produced on the farm and that they may require for use . . . together with family flour, and . . . supply my said wife and unmarried daughters with a suitable horse, harness and conveyance whensoever required by them."

Tom Good's death was, of course, a severe shock to everyone at Myrtleville. Mamie was keeping house for her brother; it was Louie, weary and deeply upset herself, who was the chief support at home for her mother. Her old suitor at Waterford wrote a letter of sympathy, and, with her permission, came to call at Myrtleville. Several of his letters survive, and it is known that he asked Louie to marry him. But nothing came of it. One report is that Louie felt it was her duty to stay with her mother. One cannot tell whether she was in love, as he was, and would have accepted him if she had felt free.

Members of the family remembered that Mary Tom argued against all her daughters' romances. No records of her arguments have turned up, nor even recollections of what they were, just the statement by a number of people that, "Aunt Mary didn't want So-and-So to marry So-and-So." There is plenty of evidence that her own marriage was a happy one though full of hard work and worry, and that she would not have used it as an argument against matrimony. One theory about her attitude is that under her gentle exterior she was a domineering parent who wanted, subconsciously no doubt, to keep her children under her thumb. Another theory is that she was terrified of childbirth (she had certainly had plenty of grim experience with it), and hated to think of it for her daughters. Whatever the reason, her three very attractive daughters who did marry, married rather late, and two of the five remained spinsters.

As soon as school was out the summer after Tom Good's death, Louie and her mother went to visit the Doyles and get a good rest. The exhausted Louie relaxed at Beulah. At first she was hungry and sleepy all the time, she said, then she revived and enjoyed riding, tennis, picnicking. Panay Ballachey spent his summer holidays with the Doyles also. Six years before,

when he had lived in Toronto with his cousins, who were also
Fanny Doyle's cousins, he had thought of her almost as one of
his many relatives. But now he was planning to marry her. It
was the third marriage between descendants of Myrtleville
and Edgemount and brought further confusion to people who
try to figure out relationships between Goods and Ballacheys.

Back at Myrtleville, eighteen-year-old Fanny was keeping
house, but for a small family, just Aunt Annie and Carol and
Charlie. Mamie and Will had two "Fresh Air Children" from
Toronto (the kind we call "disadvantaged"). Ethel came home
at the end of the summer, but before that she sent a long account of the trip she took down the St. Lawrence with Uncle
Andrew and his daughter Lucia. Andrew Jones was seventy-
four, but still able to enjoy sightseeing, and to get up early at
Homewood to bring in the cows which he milked morning
and evening.

At the beginning of October, Fanny and Ethel went to the
Ontario Normal College in Hamilton. They wrote Louie a
request for certain books which she or her friends might be
able to lend them. The list gives some indication of their
studies: *Physiology, Latin Reader, Latin Prose Composition,* Virgil's
Aeneid, Shakespeare's *Macbeth,* Quick's *Educational Reformers,
School Law and Regulations of Ontario,* Fitch's *Lectures on Teaching,* Preyer's *Development of the Infant Mind,* Laurie's *Language
and Linguistic Studies,* Crawshaw's *Interpretation of Literature,*
Carpenter's *Exercises in Rhetoric and Composition,* Winchester's
Principles of Literary Criticism, The High School Book-keeping,
Spottan's *Botany.* They also read Browning, whose poetry
many teachers considered too difficult for study in high
schools. The course in Hamilton was harder for Fanny than
for Ethel, who was four years older, had teaching experience,
and was temperamentally quicker and more incisive. Fanny
said she tried so hard to calm herself down before teaching a
class that her lessons became slow and uninteresting.

Meantime, Will Good carried on the farm work. He had an
excellent man to help him from the spring of 1904 to the
spring of 1905, Arthur Hawtin, who had just completed a two-
year course at the Ontario Agricultural College. With health,
strength, and efficiency the two young men could get through
a great deal of work and save wages which Tom Good had

been forced to pay. Best of all, Ontario farmers were profiting from the great burst of prosperity which came to Canada in the first decade of the new century. It was largely based on the peopling of the western prairies, and the urbanization of the East, especially Ontario. The East produced goods for a Canadian population which increased almost 35 percent between 1901 and 1911, more than three times the percentage increase for the two previous decades.

Will Good made many changes in the operation of the farm. With advice from Harold Jones, he set out a new orchard. He is said to have been the first fruit-grower in the neighborhood to spray his trees regularly, though his hard-pressed father had experimented with spraying his last few years. Will and Arthur also planted many spruce trees, maples, and elms for "shelter belts" around yards and orchards and along fence lines. The elms were magnificent trees by 1960, but since then most of them have fallen victim to the Dutch elm disease. None of Anne Good's comments on the tree planting survive. It would be interesting to know what she thought of it; she remembered when trees had been enemies to be cut down and burned.

Will also undertook to drain a couple of swampy areas on the farm, one north of the buildings, one down by the Paris Road. The northern field became productive, but the field by the road never was very useful and eventually was planted in trees. One little piece of swamp was left; red-winged blackbirds lived in it and in spring there were lovely marsh marigolds. The swamp is all gone now, drained by a Brantford storm sewer, and the blackbirds and marigolds have gone too. Much of the reforested plot has been swallowed up by the Highway 403 cloverleaf.

Young Mr. Good chose to give up the pig-killing and its attendant chores, and he was forced to give up keeping sheep because sheep-killing dogs so often wandered out from town. There was some compensation from local government for the lost animals, but not enough to make the struggle and unpleasantness worthwhile.

Many years later Charlie Good wrote about this period: "We carefully put up a woven wire fence by using posts instead of stakes, and those posts had to be perpendicular! . . . During a violent thunderstorm, lightning ran along that fence and split 20 posts. Eventually the whole farm was fenced with woven wire except for the north side of the young orchard, to the west of the barns, which was left in rail fence. [Will] set about clearing the fields of stumps and rocks by using stumping powder for the former and blasting powder for the latter. It was my 'privilege' to hold the drill while [Willie] wielded the iron maul, but I don't remember that he ever missed the drill! Except for the barn work, no chore was permitted to remain for Sunday, so on Saturday evening my job was to bring in the wood, clean the shoes, bring in the water, etc., etc."

Charlie remembered Christmas at Myrtleville in those days: "For Christmas dinner, a huge table was set up to accomodate twenty persons because Brantford aunts and cousins arrived, plus the odd visitor from Paisley or Manitoba. Carol and I were elected to the small side table. I am not sure whether soup was served, but certainly there was turkey and ham, concluding with Christmas pudding, mince pie and some other variety, possibly raspberry or pumpkin. It was a feast calculated to satisfy a young boy's appetite. When the dishes were washed the younger members went for a walk in the bracing Christmas atmosphere. When all the barn chores were completed, we all sat down to another bountiful meal that consisted of cold turkey, sliced cold ham, potato scallop, some fruit such as preserved peaches or raspberries, and real Christmas cake."

In the midst of his labors and relative prosperity, Will Good remained convinced that Canada's tariff policy was unfair to agriculture, and that farmers needed much more education and organization. He attended Ontario Educational Association conferences and in September 1904, was appointed to the executive board of the Farmers' Association of Ontario. This had been organized two years earlier; many of its members had been active in the Grange or in the Patrons of Industry, groups which had declined because of unfortunate ventures. The new association was never large; it counted its members in hundreds where the Grange had thousands, but these few hundreds, as E. C. Drury says in his book *Farmer Premier,* were prominent and influential men.

The new "Squire of Myrtleville" served the cause of adult

education by arranging for a local "Reading Circle," a study club which also became in effect a social club for the young people of the neighborhood. (He still did not care for strictly social affairs; Mamie would write of parties, "I had a good time, but Willie did not.") The Reading Circle studied Ruskin's works under young Mr. Good the winter of 1904–5. Ruskin was much in vogue during Will's college days; a later critic remarked that Ruskin managed to moralize on every work of art.

The Myrtleville family were all very interested that winter in a long letter from George T. Ballachey of Buffalo, describing a rural life quite different from that of fertile southern Ontario. George was working for "The Ozark Plateau Land Company," which had its main office in Buffalo and advertised that it had for sale "in the Counties of Laclede, Camden, Dallas and Webster, Mo., 110,000 acres of agricultural, fruit and grazing lands." The letter was dated February 23, 1905.

"Two weeks ago yesterday I left for Lebanon, Mo. to testify in a law suit the Ozark Co. is interested in. . . . I spent three days there. . . . I wish I could adequately describe the 'natives' thereabouts. The caricatures of the southwestern farmer are not at all exaggerated. Of course there are exceptions to all rules, but the rule in that country is surely that the farmer is illiterate and unprogressive. Their clothes are often perfect rags; they come to town on 'gas pipe' cutters or home-made sleighs running on two timbers cut rough from the bush with no pretense to finish; their horses are thin and poor and most of the men chew tobacco incessantly.

"The court room scene was one to be described by a Dickens or a Kipling. The judge with his long yellow beard with knees doubled up nearly to his chin as he braced his chair against the wall, attorneys with their feet on the table or other chairs, or swarming around the bar of justice. They run in and out excitedly before their case comes up, conferring with their witnesses and clients. Each man seems to be a distinct individual type. None of the sameness there caused by social laws demanding conformity. The hall was well filled with interested spectators and expectorators. . . .

"The hotel was very good . . . table was excellent on the whole. . . . On Sunday, I enjoyed a very nice service at a little pocket edition of a church there (Episcopal) and had a splendid dinner and a pleasant afternoon at Mr. Nelson's house. [Mr. N. was Ozark Co. agent in Lebanon.]

"Monday morning, I got up before six to get a train for Marshfield to see our other agent. The thermometer was 24° below zero and I had to wash chiefly with a piece of ice. It was below zero almost all the time I was there and very little snow on the ground—6 inches at the most. The people there are not used to such winters and it is pretty hard on them. Monday night I went on to Springfield to enjoy a hot bath and a steam-heated room. It was quite a treat. . . .

"Arrived (at Indianapolis) about 3:15 P.M. and looked for 'John Matthews' in the Directory. They are numerous, but fate was kind, and the first one I looked up was the right man. He finished up his work and went home with me when we surprised Aunt Clara. She was delighted, of course, and we had a good visit until nearly six when I had to leave for home. Aunt Bella and Uncle Will were expected the next morning. . . . Was very sorry not to be able to wait and see them. Aunt C. has a nice comfortable cottage and they are certainly very happy.

"I got home eight hours late at 3:15 Friday. We had a hard, slow trip. First a wreck delayed us and then a heavy snow storm. I had enough of R.R. cars for once, having gone over 2,000 miles in a week, but, on the whole, the travelling was surprisingly comfortable. Excellent dining car service, good berths, a library car, and uniform heat go a long way toward making one comfortable. I regret that I could not take time to go to Sioux City [to visit Uncle John Ballachey], but perhaps next time I may."

During that early part of 1905, Will Good was in contact again with the University of Toronto world. There were repercussions of the "1851 Scholarship Scandal of 1900." Another man who seemed to be the winner had been passed over, and the senate of the University was investigating. Will went to Toronto to testify, and his friend Coleman in Oregon was asked for a statement. Eventually a Royal Commission, appointed by the provincial government, recommended changes in the administration of the university, making it independent of the provincial ministry of education. By the University Act of 1906, the president became in fact as well as in name the chief executive officer of the institution. It was of particular interest to Will Good that now one of the duties of the university senate was "to hear and determine appeals from decisions of the faculty councils upon applications and memorials by students and others."

The summer of 1905 was a cheerful season at Myrtleville. Panay Ballachey married Fanny Doyle and brought her to Brantford to live. They were both great favorites at Myrtleville. Ethel and Fanny Good graduated from the Normal College, Ethel with honors. Mary Good wrote that Willie seemed surprised at Ethel's success; it was probably hard for him to realize that his bubbly little sister had grown into an intelligent and capable young woman. Louie took a short teaching course in Toronto; it was a change for her, but unfortunately not a rest.

In July, Myrtleville had a visit from Jim Good, all the way from Montana. His Aunt Mary had not seen him for years and she noticed changes. She wrote, "Jimmy looks hearty and well, but does not seem nearly as jovial and light-hearted as in his youth. He is now about thirty-eight." He probably never came to Myrtleville again, but he did not forget it. More than forty years later, he sent a snapshot of himself, at eighty, and his only grandsons bear the names of James and John, like the two little boys who played at Myrtleville a hundred years ago.

Also during the summer of 1905, Will Good bricked in the north wing of Myrtleville House, and employed a carpenter to put in a staircase and two bedrooms upstairs. He was planning to hire a family man and move back in with his mother, Aunt Annie, Mamie, Louie, and "the children," Carol and Charlie. He hoped to get a man who would stay for years.

In the fall of 1905, Fanny Good went to teach at Fairfield Plains School, south of Brantford. Ethel taught in Brantford, and Louie, tired and nervous, struggled on at Moyle's. Will wrote articles for the *O.A.C. Review,* testified before the Federal Tariff Commission, and carried on correspondence with the secretary of the American Proportional Representation League.

Louie left Moyle's School at midwinter, the end of her second year there. The reason for her leaving was unfortunate.

Her fatigue and nervousness had become apparent, and the quality of her teaching fell so far that the trustees did not renew her contract. This was a terrible blow psychologically to Louie who had from childhood excelled at everything she tried—except for such minor household tasks as making apple butter. With her extreme conscientiousness, she felt that she must somehow have had a failure of the will to do right; she had not done her duty. The Bible and prayer had always been sources of great strength to Anne and Mary Good, but they made poor Louie feel more guilty than ever. A streak of fanaticism developed in her, and her religion hindered rather than helped her whole attitude to life.

After a pleasant visit with Amelia Duncombe, her former landlady in Waterford, Louie went to Homewood for "change of air" and to help with Harold Jones's children. Old Uncle Andrew was gone; he had died less than a year after he took Lucia and Ethel on their St. Lawrence trip. The children were quite big, Barbara, the oldest, almost thirteen. They loved Cousin Louie, who was so sweet and pretty. She went swimming and boating with them, but she just wasn't as much fun as Cousin Ethel. Monica, who was nine then, still remembers one strange thing about Louie; her father never allowed religious discussions in Louie's presence, because they would upset her.

During the summer of 1906, Ethel and her mother spent about a month with Charlotte Malloch in Paisley. The Malloch ladies had moved back from Toronto three years earlier, after Sally had been very ill, but Sally had died a few months after their return. Lily had finally married; almost fifty, fat, and short-tempered, and full of aches and pains. There were those who said that Jack Simons married her for her money, and she did buy the house in which they lived at Paisley. Mary Good wrote Louie that "[Lily] has quite a nice house, not large or fine in any way, but comfortable. . . . Ethel is over at the McFarlanes . . . playing tennis. . . . Yesterday . . . Aunt C insisted on our going down to Agricultural grounds to see the baseball match. You see it was 12th July and 9 companies of Orangemen with their flags made the town look very pretty. . . . We live here quite simply in the way of cooking, don't wash any dishes at night, sit out on verandah evenings, see people pass. Aunt C. has a friendly word with everyone, knows them all. A good many nice driving horses up here. Wish we could buy one cheap. . . . have only seen one automobile here." (There were a number of motorcars in Brantford by this time. Country people did not like them; they stirred up dust dreadfully, and frightened farm animals. Once Charlie Good had a narrow escape on the Paris Road. His horse shied at a noisy, fast automobile, and Charlie was thrown out of his cart, which overturned and needed a good deal of repairing.)

Louie was wondering about autumn plans. Her mother wrote her from Paisley: "I really can scarcely give you advice, but I think that if you do find rest in being down there, & do not think that when apple picking & packing comes on you may overdo, why I suppose you had better stay. . . . Charlotte says that if you would take a school here she would charge you nothing for your board or lodging, & you could have your salary untouched except for clothes & I believe she would give you many presents as she always does. She has given Ethel the makings of a nice white hat & a knitted cape. She is certainly very generous. . . . [Charlotte and Lily] are much better friends for being apart."

Louie stayed on at Homewood. She was well and happy there; she was usefully employed helping Ruth, but at the same time she felt that she was resting. She wrote her sisters, "The rule of this place is to be as happy and comfortable as possible, very different from the rule of our house—how right I can't make up my mind." She made several pleasant trips, Ottawa, Syracuse, and a short cruise on the St. Lawrence. She enjoyed listening to Harold, who was very fond of Mark Twain's books, read *Tom Sawyer* to the children.

In autumn Fanny went back to her little country school at Fairfield Plains, and Ethel to her teaching in Brantford. Will taught science at the Brantford Collegiate from mid-November to Christmas as the regular teacher had left on short notice; Charlie, not yet fifteen, stayed home to be, as he said, "nurse-maid and milk-maid to twelve cows." (It was not until about 1920 that Ontario children were required to stay at school until they were sixteen.) Aunt Annie spent most of the winter with her sister Charlotte, who was lonely, and nervous about being alone. Although almost six years older than her sister, Anne was more active. Charlotte, like her mother, suffered for years from arthritis.

Will Good's second serious love affair blossomed that winter. Two McCormick sisters and two McCormick brothers were members of the "Reading Circle." The youngest was Jennie, who preferred to be called Jean, as did Jane Carlyle. (Names like Jennie and Jane seemed hopelessly old-fashioned.) Jennie McCormick was a bright, vivacious girl with dark curly hair. She was quite unawed by Will Good's reputation as "a brain," and enjoyed teasing the solemn young man. Once she caught him verbally with an old trick question, "Do you say 'the yolk of an egg is white' or 'are white'?" He answered seriously, and absentmindedly, "The yolk of an egg *is* white." She said, "Oh, I thought it was yellow." After a startled moment, he turned his beautiful smile on her, and said reprovingly, "You diverted my mind!" He thrived on her teasing; eventually he asked her to marry him, and she said "Yes." They became engaged officially in the spring of 1907—and he always called her Jeanie.

That same spring of 1907, Harry Sirett, a student at the Ontario Agricultural College, came to work at Myrtleville. Everyone was delighted with him. Mamie said, "He is ever so nice," and sixteen-year-old Carol started matchmaking. She wrote Fanny, "Don't accept anyone until you have met Mr. Harry Sirett!"

Louie came home the beginning of June, in time for Will's barn raising. She said she felt ready to work at home, and to think of future teaching. She was to take Mamie's place while Mamie had long visits with the Doyles in Manitoba and the John Ballacheys in Iowa. Mamie deserved a good vacation; she had worked hard and cheerfully for years.

The new south barn at Myrtleville was the talk of the neighborhood. Will and Harry had torn down the old barn, expecting a carpenter to put up the new frame, but he backed out of the job after the old barn had gone. This caused a real emergency; the building had to be ready for the hay crop by about the first of July. Will and Harry quickly got up a frame of new design, omitting cross beams and depending on iron rods, "the bridge truss principle." Skeptical neighbors pre-

Will Good and his bride, Jennie McCormick, December 1908

dicted that the first big wind would blow the barn away, but it still stands securely, more than sixty-five years later, and most modern barns are built using the bridge truss principle.

Harry Sirett was reminiscing about the barn raising shortly before his death in 1966. He remembered that old Ike Connor shouted comments freely at Will and Harry. Jean and Blanche Carlyle helped with the supper provided for the workers, about twenty-five of them, and later Aunt Annie came outdoors and looked over the group of men still standing around talking. Her eye fell on Bert McCormick, Jennie's brother, who farmed the old Irwin place, the other side of the Carlyles. She asked if he would be kind enough to see the Misses Carlyle home. Harry was vastly amused; he thought she probably did not know, as he was sure *he* knew, that Bert was not going to leave as long as he had any chance of taking Jean Carlyle home! Perhaps Harry underestimated Aunt Annie, who may have been dabbling in matchmaking.

In general, Harry did not underestimate Miss Anne Good. He thought her a remarkably vigorous and alert old lady. She was seventy-six years old but she walked all over the neighborhood paying calls. She was still a great letter writer, and the clearinghouse for family news. About this time, her sister-in-law, Kate, wrote her from Brooklyn, New York, where Arthur Good now lived: "We are having a very pleasant summer here & I have a lovely room that looks out over the broad Atlantic & can see the ocean steamers at a distance coming & going & as I look out my window now can see Coney Island lighted up. . . . We often go out there & see the different shows & the moving pictures & listen to the music. We all go bathing often & I can lie on my back & float & the boys swim & dive like fish. . . . Mary & Allen are in the Adirondacks & I just had a card from Emma who is in Paris with four friends. They are motoring through France & Switzerland & often go one hundred miles a day. . . . How times have changed since we were young."

Mamie left for the West, and Louie tried to fill her place at Myrtleville. She felt the change from Homewood. She urged Fanny to take her place there and spoke with feeling of the "peace" in the Jones household. Louie seems to have been in a dilemma; she wanted to do her duty, but she felt strain at Myrtleville, and probably felt guilty that she did. Fanny said years later that there was always "stress and strain" at Myrtleville; her mother's hospitality, for instance, meant that there was no rest even on Sundays. In her own way, Mary Tom had the driving quality her son exhibited. She could not dominate Willie; he was more than her match. Besides, as soon as his father died, he was the head of the household. Mamie and Ethel were resilient; they listened respectfully, did what was needed, laughed off many admonitions, and kept a sense of proportion. Poor Louie was not so fortunate. She knew well Aunt Annie's motto for her nieces: "A jewel, a lily, a gem, a pearl,/A beautiful, dutiful, sensible girl." But what if you are tired and nervous, and duty and common sense conflict? Louie tried to do her duty, at whatever cost in physical exhaustion and subconscious resentment.

Lucia Jones visited Myrtleville toward the end of the barn-building. She reported to her sister-in-law, Ruth, who wrote

Louie: "My dear, I miss you terribly. . . . Lucia thought Ethel more blooming than ever, but found you looking tired. [There had been seven hardworking men to feed for weeks.]"

Meantime, Mamie traveled to Manitoba with her cousins, Meg Ballachey and Fanny Doyle Ballachey and Fanny's baby son, Alec. She wrote the family at Myrtleville about her trip: "We had dinner at a little Hotel at a little place called Brookdale. The train was not supposed to stop, but the conductor telegraphed ahead and they had dinner ready, and the train waited until we were on board again. . . . I was quite surprised to see such a wooded country as that we passed through on our way from Winnipeg. . . . I did not see a stretch of bare prairie all the way. Of course, it was flat but . . . it looked like a pale green sea dotted with darker green islands. The trees are not big, the largest only about six inches in diameter, but in the river valley Russell says there are elms a couple of feet through. We passed a great many 'sloughs,' which I thought meant swamps, but they are regular ponds or lakes, some stretching away for half a mile or more and quite deep. There do not seem to be any near here. Mr. Hull says they have rapidly disappeared as the land has become cultivated. The earth here is all black like swamp earth. Russell says he does not see how our earth grows anything, it looks so poor. . . . I have not been exploring yet. . . . There is a Beaver dam down in the creek, and the Beavers are to be seen about sundown. We were going down last night, but all felt tired."

Mamie stayed with the Doyles until autumn. She enjoyed riding and visiting and helping Lily with her trousseau, and she sometimes contributed to the production of meals, which were mammoth affairs during harvest, when the Doyles had about twenty men working for them. Late in the fall, Mamie went on to Sioux City. Lily Doyle married that winter, and Will Doyle turned over his farm to one son and his insurance business to the other. For the present, fourteen-year-old Morgan Good was to stay on the farm. Bella and Clara, her youngest daughter, went east, and Will looked over various possibilities for his retirement years. It was a good excuse for him to travel; he never outgrew his wanderlust.

Mamie had an even better time at the John Ballacheys' than

at the Doyles'. That was because of the attentions of "Mr.
Lane," who worked in the Armour and Company office. She
wrote of him at first, "He is a jolly fellow, nice and a gentleman, but he was terribly burned when a little chap and is
'homely as a hedge fence.' The school house he was in was
struck by lightning and ever so many children were killed."

A few months later, Mamie had quite forgotten that Chris
Lane was homely. She was engaged to him, and there is a
story that, although she took his ring back to Myrtleville the
summer of 1908, she kept it hidden until he was about to
come for Christmas and she had to tell the family. As she had
suspected, her mother objected, in spite of all Mr. Lane's good
qualities, which in Mrs. Tom Good's eyes included the fact
that he had been born in England and belonged to the "English" church. Mamie held her ground.

Fanny Good had not been interested in going to Homewood, as Louie had suggested. After two years of successful
teaching in a small country school, she had the opportunity of
a job in Brantford. She turned out to have a large class of slow
learners, and one year of it was enough. In the autumn of
1908, she enrolled in the University of Toronto. She did not
have her brother's scientific and mathematical aptitude; she
studied English, History, French, German, Latin.

Ethel was teaching in Burford and, with Mamie home,
Louie went to stay with Aunt Charlotte. Everyone hoped that
she would get rid of her fatigue and nervousness there, as she
had at Homewood. Poor old Aunt Charlotte was far from
well, and really needed someone with her. She had trouble
getting "live-in" help; Mary Qua had been with her for some
time, but did not want to stay indefinitely.

Will Good was working hard to get the north wing of Myrtleville House ready for his bride. The northeast room of the
main house, formerly the big farm-kitchen, was turned over to
him for a parlor. (The room which had for years been Eliza
Laird's bedroom was now kitchen for the front part of the
house, with "running water" in it.) The old fireplace where
Eliza Good had cooked was reopened and used for cheerful
and festive heat. Will built a veranda outside the parlor, facing
the orchard. He learned to upholster, and eventually finished
a "cozy corner" for the front room plus a sturdy big couch for

Myrtleville, left to right: *1837 house, 1858 wing (altered in 1905), and 1913 house built by W. C. Good*

the everyday dining-sitting room in the wing. He hired a carpenter to cut a doorway from the wing into the new parlor and to lay a modern hardwood floor over the old pine boards.

It was probably fortunate for the domestic harmony of the bride and groom that ornate Victorian furniture had gone out of fashion. The few new pieces which Will and Jennie acquired were mostly in "mission" style, adapted from the plain and heavy furniture of early Spanish settlement in California. The sturdy unadorned quality of it made it quite acceptable to Will Good. He never cared for carpeting; he thought it was expensive and hard to keep clean, but he did allow a sizable rug in the middle of his parlor. It was an imitation Oriental with conventionalized design in dark blue and rosy red, unlike the riotous floral patterns on so many floors. Will's parlor had a table in the middle of it with revolving bookshelves under the round top, and there were plenty of other bookshelves in the room too. The bedroom, instead of boasting the old-fashioned massive, highly carved wooden bed, had a light-weight bed of fairly simple design. It was of iron, enameled white, of a type "recommended for their cleanliness," "used altogether in hospitals," and much less expensive than the also popular brass beds.

Will took time off, just a few days before his wedding, to address the annual meeting of the Grange and Farmer's Association (the organizations had merged the year before) on "Direct Legislation through the Initiative and Referendum." E. C. Drury, later premier of Ontario, was elected Master of the organization at this meeting.

While the wedding preparations went on at Myrtleville, Louie lay very ill in the Bruce County Hospital at Walkerton, about fifteen miles from Paisley. She had a severe case of typhoid fever. Mamie went north to help nurse her sister, who was not well enough to travel home for two and a half months. While Louie regained strength for the trip, Mamie hurried back to Myrtleville just before her brother's marriage, a quiet Presbyterian ceremony at the home of the bride's parents, Coleman Place, near Paris, on December 3. The bride wore a high-necked dress of soft, lightweight, cream-colored wool. Aunt Annie even had a new gray silk dress for the occasion. Practically all dresses were still made at home, often by dress-makers, who stayed with their employers for a week or more at a time.

Jennie's brothers had made *their* plans; they saw to it that the newlyweds set off in a buggy decked out in traditional fashion with tin cans and old shoes. Sixteen-year-old Charlie thought it was great fun, but he noticed that the serious-minded groom seemed somewhat annoyed by all the non-sense. Unlike his father, young Mr. Good did not borrow money to take his bride on a brief honeymoon to Niagara Falls. The Will Goods drove home to Myrtleville.

15

Beginnings and Endings

Louie finally came home to Myrtleville just in time for
Christmas with the family, and its prospective member, Chris
Lane. She had been ill for over ten weeks, but now her
strength was coming back quite well. Soon she could busy herself with making needlework gifts for the bride in the north
wing, do a little housework, and even go to town, though she
felt conspicuous in public because of her short hair, imper-
fectly concealed by a cap. It was common practice to crop the
heads of typhoid fever victims; they often lost most of their
hair anyway.

Everyone was healthy and happy at Myrtleville the summer
of 1909. Chris Lane spent his holidays at the farm and left
Mamie brimming with plans for trousseau and wedding. And
the Will Goods were expecting a baby; everyone hoped it
would be a boy, a fourth generation farmer for Myrtleville.
Jennie was very well; she was hungry all the time, and people
encouraged her to "eat for two." Eventually she added almost
60 pounds to her small-boned 102-pound body. A modern ob-
stetrician would object strongly to this, but no one thought of
Jennie's even seeing the doctor until he was called to deliver
her child.

At the end of the summer, Louie went back to teaching. She
had a position near Dunnville, on the Grand River close to
Lake Erie, and could come home most weekends. Ethel's
school was at Cannington, northeast of Toronto, and nineteen-year-old Carol, after a short teaching course, taught in
West Brantford. Fanny was ready for her second year at the
university.

A great blow fell in September. The Will Goods' baby, a fine big boy, was born dead after a labor which almost killed his mother. The invaluable Mamie took care of the north wing until Jennie recovered. While she was convalescing, Mrs. Will Good helped her husband by copying out his long letters in her beautiful handwriting. He was in correspondence with the prime minister about Canada's naval program. As at the time of the Boer War, international politics were impinging on Canadian affairs, and by now, Mr. Good spoke with some authority as an acknowledged leader of the "farm movement."

Canada's great political debate of 1909 was caused by Britain's "naval scare." The torpedo had been developed, and it made old battleships obsolete. Britain needed more "Dreadnoughts," large, heavily gunned ships which could attack the enemy at long range; Germany was threatening to outdistance her in construction of these monsters. She was planning to build eighteen Dreadnoughts in three years, and many people felt that the cost should be shared by British dominions which were protected by the imperial navy. Prime Minister Sir Wilfrid Laurier was in a dilemma such as he had faced during the Boer War. He was a defender of Canadian autonomy, but he also thought that Canada should support Britain. He proposed a Canadian naval force which the government could place at the disposal of the British Admiralty in time of war. It was a typical Laurier compromise and it satisfied neither conservatives with a strong British attachment, French Canadians jealous of Canadian autonomy, nor "progressives" like W. C. Good, who were alarmed at the rise of militarism.

Sir Wilfrid wrote Mr. Good on October 29: "I can assure you that I am no more in sympathy than you are with militarism in any form, but the question of defence is one which cannot be altogether overlooked. It is the penalty of becoming a nation and which all nations have to bear and which, in course of time, I hope they may dispense with. Unfortunately our standard of civilization is not yet high enough for that ideal. I have no more intention today than I ever had of being drawn into what I once defined as 'the vortex of European militarism.' The nations of Europe are expending at least fifty per cent of their revenue on military armaments, both on land and sea; it would be a crime for us to attempt anything of the

kind, but if our revenue this year is ninety millions, and it will
be above that figure, an expenditure of two or three millions,
which would mean two or three per cent, seems to me a very
light burden." In his answer to the prime minister, Mr. Good
raised the question of the line between defensive and offen-
sive armaments.

"The smaller nations of Europe are, I believe, practically
unarmed and safer . . . for just that reason. . . . So far as I
can see the possession of armaments simply whets the appetite
for war, and is a temptation to make trouble where no trouble
is otherwise likely to occur, and, whatever the fancied necessi-
ties of the European powers, Canada's position is unique in-
sofar as she has lived for 100 years in peaceful relations with
the only country able to do her serious harm. . . . If we mind
our own business and deal fairly with our neighbors is it con-
ceivable that we shall be invaded by an armed force? . . . .

"If we are unarmed we cannot be dragged into quarrels not
of our own making, and are then much more likely to remain
on friendly terms with both Great Britain and other powers.
. . . I know you have no intention of being drawn into the
'vortex of European Militarism.' But you will not always occupy your present position of responsibility; and you may be
succeeded by one who has not your scruples and who sees less
clearly the dangers that you see. Once begun, the building of
armaments will be hard to check."

Many years and two world wars after the naval scare of
1909, we are still haunted by the escalation of armament. And
the geographical isolation of peaceful North America has for a
long time been little protection against attack. Will Good later
pinned his hopes on the League of Nations, and still later on
the United Nations. His theory that the small unguarded nation was relatively safe was sadly battered by the German invasion of Belgium less than five years after the correspondence quoted above.

Shortly after Mr. Good wrote the prime minister, several
members of western Canadian farm groups attended the annual meeting of the Grange and Farmers' Association in Ontario. The Canadian Council of Agriculture was formed, the
first national farmers' organization. E. A. Partridge of Saskatchewan, founder of the successful Cooperative Grain
Growers Company, Roderick McKenzie of Manitoba, and W.

C. Good of Ontario drafted the constitution of the new council. It was that same year of 1909 that the Cooperative Union
of Canada was organized. Mr. Good was not one of the original members, but soon became active, and eventually served as
its president for many years.

At the beginning of the new year, Ethel went to Paisley to
serve as bridesmaid when her cousin, Charlotte Ballachey,
married a young farmer from Burford, David Standing.
"George T." stopped off in Brantford on his way back to Buffalo, and told Mamie by phone (there was a phone at Myrtleville now, "in Willie's house") all about the wedding and how
pretty Lottie and Ethel looked.

Mamie's own wedding preparations kept being interrupted
by family crises. Jennie was strong again, but Aunt Bella, visiting her daughter, Fanny Ballachey, had to have major surgery
at the Brantford Hospital. While she was convalescing at Fanny's, her sister, Anne, now almost eighty, missed the bottom
step of the stairs there and broke her hip. There was no attempt at surgery, as there would be nowadays. Mrs. Tom
Good wrote: "Drs. Ashton & Palmer examined the injured
part & found that it had set itself, one end of the bone being
inserted in the other for an inch or more, so that leg will be
somewhat shorter than the other. The Drs. say that it was
broken in the best possible place & feared no ill results of a
serious nature."

Mamie stayed with Aunt Annie at the Panay Ballacheys' for
about two months, until the old lady was able to return to
Myrtleville late in April. No doubt Mamie was a great help,
not only in caring for her aunt, but also in the running of a
house where there were two toddlers and a new baby. Panayoti Allen Ballachey was born less than three weeks after his
great-aunt's accident. A "trained nurse" who had been with
Jennie Good, when she lost her baby, took care of mother and
infant at 64 Brant Avenue. When Will Doyle and the nurse
were both there, there must have been at least ten people in
the house. Myrtleville had dispatched two beds and their
bedding. It was all very well to have a hospital available for
surgery, but there was no question of either Anne Good or
Fanny Ballachey being hospitalized for broken hip or childbirth.

Mary Good described her sister-in-law's return to the farm:

"Aunt A. & Mamie came . . . in emergency ambulance, Willie bringing the luggage in his lumber waggon. . . . Aunt A. bore the journey very well. The springs were poor & so the vehicle jolted badly. Mamie & Aunt A. hope to subscribe & get others interested & purchase a modern & more comfortable one, or else get fresh springs for the present one. They pity the poor patients who may have to ride in it. . . . Mr. Doyle very kindly has offered to pay Aunt Annie's Drs. bill, which she has gratefully accepted, as he has plenty of means. . . . He is a generous-hearted man & Bella is equally kind."

The drawing room was converted into a bedroom for Aunt Annie, and in a few weeks she was outdoors in a wheelchair. She soon learned to get around quite well on crutches. Her long walks and her travels were over, but friends and family came to see her often, some from distant homes. And she was never idle; she read and wrote, sewed and knitted. By the summer a year after her accident, she was even gardening, a crutch in one hand and a hoe in the other!

On July 2, 1910, Mamie Good and Chris Lane were married at Myrtleville. It was a considerably larger and more formal wedding than Will's and Jennie's. The bride wore white, with veil and orange blossoms, and was attended by three little girls carrying baskets of flowers. The youngest of these was the Panay Ballacheys' daughter, Margaret, not yet two years old. She entertained many of the guests by showing them her "new shoes" (two words which she could already say clearly). Relatives were present from Buffalo, Paisley, and Maitland, and Arthur Qua (who seemed like a cousin) played the wedding music. Among the guests were Jennie Good's brother, Bert McCormick, and his bride, who had been Jean Carlyle.

After the great occasion was over, Aunt Annie wrote a description of it to her sister, Clara, and sent her some of the rich dark wedding cake. Clara Matthews was bitterly disappointed that she could not come, but her husband was in a period of financial difficulty.

With Mamie gone, it was logical for Louie to stay home and help care for Aunt Annie and the house. The family hoped housework would be easier for her than teaching; recently she had seemed very forgetful, and careless of her own well-being. Fanny, however, when she heard a sermon on Mary and

Martha, "thought about Louie very much, and thought we need not worry about her at all, but just be kind and let her look after her own affairs. She is more like Mary than Martha."

Physically, the work in Mrs. Tom Good's household was no longer heavy. Jennie fed the hired men; Charlie entered Agricultural College in Guelph that autumn; Ethel was in Cannington again, Fanny in Toronto. Psychologically, however, Louie's condition grew worse. Her mother wrote about it to Dr. Allen Jones in Buffalo: "I suppose it is a case of nervous depression. Sometimes she seems pretty well, & again lapses into sadness & makes one anxious. What makes it unusually hard to define in any way is a peculiar reserve or reticence which I think has always characterized her disposition to a degree, but seems to have increased in late years. She said the other day that 'There is a reason.' I have tried to think of any probable or possible reason. Not telling us clearly causes us to surmise reasons, which in nearly every case are not at all well founded. . . . She thinks pro and con, weighing small matters in her mind so long that she cannot distinguish which is the better path to follow."

Will Good was extremely worried about his sister and wrote to Allen Jones also. Years later, his most vivid recollection of Louie's illness was that she felt it was "a sin to be tired" and drove herself irrationally and unmercifully. The Gospel she claimed to believe in so fervently never seems to have brought her any conviction of forgiveness for human frailty. At Christmas, 1910, the family noticed that she was in a most disturbed and restless condition. She kept disappearing on long walks alone. Allen Jones suggested hospitalization. From January to April of 1911, Louie was in a small private hospital in Toronto. Fanny visited her often, and she seemed to improve.

From the Doyles' British Columbia fruit farm, one of Will's "retirement projects," Bella wrote Mary Good on January 29, 1911: "I am glad to hear dear Louie is improving. It is a sad thing that she ever got into such a condition. It is well to have a conscience, but foolish to allow it to run away with your health. . . . I have concluded that we owe something to ourselves as well as to those around us & it always ends up in our becoming a burden in some way when we neglect our health.

. . . I think [Louie] should go somewhere else beside home . . . when she comes out [of hospital] but you must all put your brains together & do the best. I believe in Allen's judgment very much. He has a level head."

Mamie wrote her mother at the beginning of April: "I would send Louie to Paisley [to Aunt Agnes', Mrs. Sam Ballachey's] as soon as possible and without any of the family. You know it is best for nervous patients to be with strangers. . . . If Aunt Agnes does not find she can manage, a nurse would be cheap, compared to present expense. . . . If only she had someone to love her hard and understand her, she would be all right, but of course she cannot marry, even if there was anyone who wanted her and she wanted, in her present health." When Louie came out of the hospital, she went with Charlotte Standing and her five-month-old son to visit at Uncle Sam's big new house in Paisley. She wrote her mother a pencilled letter on April 25.

"I began this with pen and ink, but am finishing it upstairs in bed as I cannot sleep very well. The baby has just been crying but is quiet again now. How is everything? You will wonder at not hearing from me all this time. . . . I've been starting letters, as usual, but couldn't get on with them. However, I mustn't begin and talk about myself. . . . [She then wrote several paragraphs about relatives and friends in Paisley.] I think I had better go home with Lottie (but am not sure) and then see what is next best. I have never before missed doing things as much as these last four months. . . .

"Uncle Sam has told me that the Hospital bills are paid. Did you pay them? I can find out later. It will be beginning to look lovely around home now. I ought to have quite a lot of news to tell you when I get home after such a long time. . . . You will be busy enough just now with housecleaning, and outdoors. I wonder if Charlie is home yet. . . . Please write when you can and ask Carol if she will, and, mother, I wish you would send some of Mamie's letters. How are you? It won't do me any harm to know."

A few days after Louie wrote home, Jennie Good was safely delivered of a brown-haired, blue-eyed baby girl, the writer of this book. I am sure my sex was a disappointment, but I never was aware of it when I was a child. I always felt that all the people at Myrtleville loved me.

Will Good was doing well on the farm, and was ready to start buying out his Aunt Annie. He contracted to pay her three thousand dollars for her share of Myrtleville, that is, the buildings, the fifty acres she had bought in 1864, and the eight acres she had inherited from her mother. Anne reserved for her use most of the main part of Myrtleville House and a "garden plot not to exceed one-quarter of an acre," also use of lawns and one-third of the cellar and "reasonable rights of ingress to and egress from said dwelling-house, garden and lawns." Upon her death, the rights reserved were to pass to Mary Good and her unmarried daughters "for and during their natural lives and the survivor of them."

During all of his hard farm work and the pains and pleasures of family life at Myrtleville, Will Good kept his eye on public affairs. Sir Wilfrid Laurier had been able to secure the Naval Service Act of 1910, without appealing to the electorate as Mr. Good had urged. In the summer of 1910 Laurier visited western Canada, and was met everywhere by deputations of farmers asking for tariff reduction. The following December, five hundred western and three hundred eastern farmers met in Ottawa and presented their case to the government. This was the biggest delegation which had ever descended on Canada's capital, and it has been recorded in history as "The Siege of Ottawa." Will Good's friend, Ernest Drury, was spokesman for the farmers of Ontario.

Canada was still predominantly rural and "the Siege" made a great impression on the government. For the first time since 1854, an agreement on reciprocal trade was negotiated with the government of the United States. Then came rebellion in the ranks of the Liberal party; a group of prominent Toronto Liberal businessmen issued a manifesto denouncing the agreement. Also Laurier's Conservative opposition began a filibuster against the treaty, and the prime minister dissolved Parliament and appealed to the country.

Antireciprocity campaigners whipped up the fear of American domination which has been built into Canada since 1783. Echoes of their arguments are in a letter Mamie wrote her mother in the spring of 1911: "I do not think the new Reciprocity Treaty will endanger Canada's loyalty. I say the two countries will have free trade some day, either by treaty or annexation, and better by treaty. Of course, I am so sure of

Canada's loyalty that it seems to me foolish to doubt it. Mrs. Lane [Chris's mother, an Englishwoman] and Aunt Jo [Ballachey] are disgusted with my ideas on the subject."

Will Good worked hard for Laurier in the election of 1911, though he had no enthusiasm for the prime minister's naval policy. But Laurier's naval compromise had angered many people, for very different reasons, and Canada's "infant industries" were strong enough to wield tremendous influence on their employees and clients. The government was defeated, and the farmers' movement had to regroup. (After sixty years, there is still the emotional question, "Free Trade: Would it drown Canada in U.S. Power?")

At the end of the summer there was also regrouping of the family at Myrtleville. Louie was home again, but far from well. Carol, who did not like teaching, lost her plea to take nurse's training at the Brantford General Hospital, and went to the Ontario College of Education in Toronto. (She lost her plea, not to the hospital, but to her mother and Aunt Annie, who felt that nursing the public was not a suitable occupation for a young lady.) In Toronto, Fanny and Carol lived together; Fanny was a senior at the university now. Ethel came back to teach in Brantford and live at home.

Louie was hospitalized again in the spring of 1912, this time in a "sanitarium" at Guelph. There are some pathetic letters from her there, written in pencil and with many erasures. She found it hard to do much reading or writing, and asked repeatedly for sewing or knitting to do. It is impossible to tell from the letters whether she could not settle at handwork, or whether the institution disapproved of it. There certainly does not seem to have been much attempt at "occupational therapy."

As the weeks went by, however, Louie began to feel much better. She wrote "Nana" (Aunt Annie) on May 23, "I really had terrible times when I was sick, but am glad those horrible feelings are gone." She wrote about pleasant walks and drives, and eventually of going downtown to do a little shopping. The last of the letters in the group, written June 9, is optimistic: "I have been hoping to go home soon. . . . I am really well now. I need no special attention, and I would like to prevent having to use up any more money. . . . My health is pretty well as-

sured now, and I feel that I know how to take care of myself
and I should very much like to teach again sometime soon.
. . . You know I never broke down when I was really
working."

These were brave words, but back in the tensions and fric-
tions of family life, Louie began to slip into depression again.
In the autumn, Fanny went to teach in a high school at Swan
River, Manitoba, and wrote Louie almost every day in a vain
effort to cheer her up. But Louie brooded on how far away
her little sister was, and she was deeply distressed by the death
of her kind Aunt Carrie Ballachey, after months of painful illness. Furthermore, many of the family thought that, with the
best of intentions, Louie's mother was very hard on her. She
fussed over her, and preached to her, and was constitutionally
unable to give her the peace she so badly needed.

There were plenty of cheerful activities at Myrtleville in
1912, though Louie was not able to enjoy them. There were
the usual summer guests, and this year the unusual joy of a
visit from the delightful Sioux City uncle, John Ballachey.
And Will was building a new house, across the lawn to the east
of his birthplace. Scorning "luxury," but admiring "convenience," he designed it himself, and, with the help of an Agricultural College student, laid all the bricks for a good-sized
two-story building. By autumn he had a temporary roof over
it.

That same autumn, Mamie gave birth to a daughter in
Sioux City, and the following spring, Myrtleville finally had a
male heir, a sturdy boy with red gold hair like his grandfather's. He was given two old family names, Allen Charles, and
he was the apple of Aunt Annie's eye.

During the summer the plastering, roof-slating, and plumbing for the new house were finished, and the Will Good family
moved into it in November. It was not really finished, but it already had "modern conveniences," a coal furnace and stationary washtubs in the cellar, a bathroom upstairs, hot and
cold water in kitchen, laundry, and bath. (The ladies of Myrtleville House still bathed in their bedrooms in a big, round,
portable tin tub, with water which they heated on the kitchen
stove.) The new house was wired for electricity, too, though
the power was not available yet. But, comfortable and well

built as it was, it lacked the aesthetic quality of the old house.

Will Good's move meant the end of an era for his birthplace. For three-quarters of a century, it had been the center of farm operations, as well as center for family living. Myrtleville House remained the symbol of the old homestead, but although for many years it housed a hired man's family in the north wing, it had retired from farming.

By the end of the year a painful decision had been made, and Louie, who had been so bright and beautiful, was committed to the Ontario Hospital at Hamilton. She lived for a long time yet, but was never thought well enough to come back to Myrtleville, except for occasional brief visits. My mother kept us children out of the way when Aunt Louie was at "Gramoozie's"; consequently I have only the haziest recollection of Louie as someone pretty and gentle who looked well enough, but was considered "sick in her mind." It is a sad story. Louie's brother seemed to have endless vigor. An editor friend wrote him, "I do not know of anyone who can get through so much work as you can with so little apparent expenditure of nervous energy. . . . Be careful of yourself, old man."

The election of 1911 had wiped out farmers' hopes of early tariff reduction, and their leaders turned to other avenues of economic assistance. Under the leadership of the Grange and Farmers' Association, of which W. C. Good was Master in 1913, a union was planned for Ontario which would take in not only the Grange, but the Farmers' Institutes, producer cooperatives, and local general-purpose cooperatives. This union took place in March 1914. One section of it, the United Farmers' Organization (later known as the United Farmers of Ontario, U.F.O.) was to look after education, propaganda, and organization; the other section, the United Farmers' Cooperative Company, was to do wholesale cooperative business. E. C. Drury was elected president of the U.F.O. and W. C. Good of the Cooperative.

Myrtleville, center of a big family, felt the winds of many changes that year of 1914. Charlie Good graduated from the Ontario Agricultural College, and went immediately to Nova Scotia, to work as assistant provincial entomologist. Charlotte Ballachey's husband, David Standing of Burford, died after more than a year of illness with tuberculosis. Lottie was left with two children under four years of age.

Her brother, Fred, a Buffalo dentist, became engaged to Leone Park, daughter of a well-known Brantford photographer. She was a neighbor of Fanny and Panay Ballachey, and a former classmate of Fanny Good. Of course, Fred took Leone to see his Aunt Annie, who received her graciously, although she was not entirely pleased with the young lady's Methodist background. Until he got to know her, Will Good was somewhat put off by Leone's modish appearance. She never wore extreme clothes, but "Louis heels" were much in vogue, and Will said privately to his cousin, "Fred, how could you have fallen in love with a girl who wears such high heels?" To which Fred replied, "When I asked her to marry me, I certainly wasn't looking at her feet!"

Romance was in the air at Myrtleville also. Fanny and Carol were engaged, both to former O.A.C. students who had worked on Will Good's farm. Fanny's fiancé was Arthur Hawtin, Will's helper just after his father died, and a good friend since. Arthur was now on his way to India as an agricultural missionary, and Fanny was to follow him there. He was a Methodist, too, going to work for a Presbyterian mission. And Willie had added to his distressing political and economic "radicalism" the error of leaving his ancestral church to join his wife's Presbyterian one. Aunt Annie's young relatives were a trial to her staunch Anglicanism and conservatism.

Ethel was not engaged yet, but she was the magnet which kept drawing Harry Sirett back to Myrtleville. He was the student who had helped build Will Good's revolutionary barn in 1907. He had graduated with honors in 1908, and gone to work for the Ontario Department of Agriculture. At intervals, he was able to get to Brantford. One time he wrote Ethel that he could be in town just between trains and asked her to meet him at the Kerby House for midday dinner. Ethel was not a young girl; she was twenty-five and an experienced schoolteacher when Harry first knew her, but Aunt Annie was horrified at the invitation. "What! Eat in a tavern with a man, alone! Someone must go with you." The result was that Carol unwillingly accompanied her sister, and three people regretted Aunt Annie's dictum, while they dutifully obeyed it.

In the summer of 1914, Canada watched with horrified fascination as what Laurier had called "the vortex of European militarism" sucked the great nations of Europe into war.

Harry Sirett and Ethel Good on their wedding day, June 1917

There had not been a major European upheaval since the time of Napoleon, a hundred years earlier. The century had been one of tremendous scientific and technological advances, and stirrings of international cooperation had brought about two multilateral peace conferences at The Hague, in 1899 and 1907. There was widespread belief in the inevitability of progress and many Canadians thought that Europe was too civilized for the eruption of war. But it came, and the mother-land was at war as of August 4. It was a shock, but there was very little realization of how long and horrible the conflict was to be.

This war affected Brant County very differently from the South African struggle. In almost three years of the Boer War, only about twenty men of Brant served. Less than two weeks after that fateful August fourth, more than that number of British reservists left Brantford, and during the four years of the war over five thousand Brant County men enlisted, roughly one for every eight inhabitants.

At first, soldiers left Brantford to the cheers of the local populace, but by the following summer enthusiasm had been replaced by the sense of a long hard job to be done. Mamie came to Ontario in June 1915 for her first visit since her marriage almost five years earlier. About a thousand service men had left Brantford by this time. Still, Mamie wrote Chris, "There does not seem to be any outward sign of war, except flags on almost every house. . . . [But] they talk of conscription . . . and feelings are deep underneath. . . . They say the last lot of men went in silence and sadness." She heard that four factories in town were making shells, and noticed that at teas she attended everyone was knitting for soldiers. Aunt Annie, almost eighty-four, turned out sock after sock.

What brought the war closest to Myrtleville at this time was the departure for camp of Maj. Panayoti Ballachey of the Dufferin Rifles, second in command of the Fifty-eighth Battalion, now in training for overseas duty. Before Panay left, Fred Ballachey and Leone Park were married. Mamie met her new cousin and thought Fred had chosen very well.

Other family weddings scheduled for 1915 did not come off. Carol's engagement was broken, and she was restless and unhappy. We can never know whether the romance might

have revived; the young man went overseas soon, and was
killed by a German he was taking prisoner. Fanny was still
preparing to go to India, and studying (too hard, they said) to
be a missionary herself. She visited Fred and Leone in Buffalo
that summer and Fred said privately to his bride, "Doesn't that
girl realize she's going to marry a man, not a missionary?"
Time went on and Fanny made no final plans for India. Harry
Sirett was still courting Ethel, but as yet there was no official
engagement. Mamie wrote Chris that there was "an air of nervous tension about the house most of the time." Aunt Annie
was well, but quite deaf, and unable to catch much of the conversation that swirled around her, which must have been a
trial to such a sociable person.

Perhaps the merry chase of child care was useful distraction
to Mamie at this time. Her little blonde daughter, Margaret,
was not yet three, but a very active and articulate child. Will's
children, Beth and Allen, were four and two years old. Allen
was an adventurous climber; his anxious father had already
brought him down from near the top of the windmill, and he
had spent even tenser moments while working on the roof of
the north wing of the old house, when he looked up at a
sound of scrambling to see Allen's red gold curls coming over
the ridgepole. But Beth's imagination was much better developed when it came to mischief. She was a "caution," her aunt
said, "bright and troublesome and certainly spoiled." One day
Mamie kept checking on the little girls while she wrote a letter
to her husband. First, she rescued the family's shoes from a
"train" constructed of them on the balcony railing. Finally,
Beth said, "Go downstairs, Aunt Mamie, before we do something we are going to do." This elicited various warnings,
which may have aborted the little girls' plans. At any rate,
there is no record of the dire mischief Mamie feared that
time.

Will's children spent even more time than usual at their
grandmother's that summer, not only because of Margaret's
presence but because early in July they had a new baby
brother, "little Willie." The newcomer was a good-looking
child with chestnut hair, unharmed by his mother's difficult
labor, but Jennie needed rest and quiet, and a nurse stayed
with her and the baby for weeks.

Mamie's adored young foster-brother, Charlie, came to Myrtleville for a vacation after his first year as an entomologist in Nova Scotia. She wrote Chris, "He is very striking-looking . . . and very nice." He brought pictures of "an exceedingly pretty girl," small and dark and jolly, to whom he had just become engaged. She was Helen Mary Woodroofe, librarian and demonstrator in bacteriology at the Nova Scotia Agricultural College, and the first Canadian woman to take a degree from such a school. In Aunt Annie's view, however, one of her best qualifications as a wife for Charlie was the fact that she was the daughter of an Anglican clergyman.

Mamie made one trip to Hamilton that summer to see Louie in the Ontario Hospital there. She found her sister looking well enough physically, but with a bewildered expression and rambling habit of speech. Louie's surroundings and nurses seemed pleasant, but the patient, as always, was pitifully anxious to go home. It was a painful visit.

Mamie and little Margaret spent about a week of July at Uncle Sam's big house in Paisley, and called on other relatives there. Lily Simons was cordial, but offended that the guests were not staying with her. Aunt Charlotte was delighted and "much better than [Mamie] expected to see her." Uncle Sam and Aunt Agnes gave a big benefit party for the Red Cross, and Margaret, overstimulated by all the attention, was unusually naughty.

Early in August, Ethel and Mamie left the three-year-old at Myrtleville, and visited the Buffalo relatives. George T., still a bachelor at forty, entertained them at an elegant hotel dinner, and Fred and Leone had them at their "lovely flat." The Allen Joneses were unfortunately out of town, but on the way home the sisters called on their cousin Panay at the Niagara military camp. There they saw hundreds of men practicing bayonet charges, signaling, and grenade-throwing. Mamie wrote Chris, "It was most interesting, but sad." She noticed that the powerhouses and bridges at Niagara were guarded by sentries with fixed bayonets, and the Welland Canal by an encampment of soldiers where the train crossed it. There had already been some frightening incidents of sabotage perpetrated by people slipping into Canada from the United States, which was to be officially neutral for almost two years more. Mamie went back to Sioux City, and Panay went overseas. There is a letter from him in the Myrtleville documents, dated April 18, the following year.

"I was very glad to get your letter, the day before yesterday, and I guess I had better answer it before I forget. We can't carry unanswered letters about with us, so if I don't answer mine at once, I find I forget which ones I have answered.

"This is rather a funny game we are playing out here. The artillery do nearly all the damage. Of course, snipers account for a few men, but by far the most damage is done by the artillery, and mighty nasty things the big shells are. In this trench fighting the Infantry are only for the purpose of preventing the enemy from getting up to the big guns; so it looks to us as though we were here principally to be killed and maimed and not for fighting. We have been lucky so far, have only had about 28 casualties. . . . After all, it is quite wonderful, when you see the immense amount of ammunition expended, to find it does so little damage. . . .

"The life in the trenches is a very miserable existence. The last place I was in I had a hole in the ground 6 ft. long by 4½ wide by about the same height. And I was lucky to have that. A great many of the men had no dugouts at all and had to sleep on the firing step. Yet they tell us they were good trenches. . . .

"This country anywhere near the firing line is the worst imaginable kind of a wreck. I spent about an hour last Friday . . . at daybreak, going through that famous city [Arras] of this region . . . [which] is so situated that the Huns can pour shells into it from every quarter. . . . In certain parts there is hardly a brick standing on another. They have been shelling it since we captured it a year ago. . . . Of course, all the civilian population has been removed, and there are only a few soldiers there now; they live in the cellars, which have been made shellproof. . . . Of course, back here in rest camp, we are quite comfortable. I have a very nice hut a bit larger than a bell tent and a good stove and bed. . . . The weather has been miserable this time out, raining nearly all the time. It makes the camp very sloppy and makes one feel very damp and cold."

Less than two months after he wrote this letter, Major Ballachey was killed by a shell while on reconnaissance. His widow brought up her children in Brantford, and the youngest, a lawyer, still lives there.

Meantime, Charlie Good had married his Helen and joined the Nova Scotia Highlanders. He spent a busy summer in the Maritimes as a physical training officer; he had been quite an athlete in his college days and was still only twenty-four. In October 1916, he went to England with his battalion, and a few weeks later his pregnant young wife followed him, being as miserably sick on shipboard as Eliza Good had been eighty years before. Fortunately the voyage was much shorter than Eliza's.

The C. A. Goods had sixteen months together in England, before Charlie left for the front in France, and the doting father was able to describe in his letters to the Myrtleville family the progress of his baby daughter. It was to his "old pal," Mamie, in Sioux City that he exploded at intervals about affairs at Myrtleville House. He was aware that there was "general protest at home" about Carol's plan to take nurse's training, and wrote Mamie: "Can't you persuade the others that it is the only step for Carol, for what she wants and needs is to get completely out among strangers? . . . Carol has waited long enough for Fanny's and Ethel's decisions."

He was disappointed that Carol entered nursing school in Brantford, rather than in Toronto or Montreal. (Of course, the fact that she went at all showed growing independence of spirit.) He wondered why Ethel and Harry delayed so long in making up their minds, "[They] . . . have been . . . losing some of the very best years of their life." As for Fanny, he wrote, "I suppose [she] is still wondering if she can be a missionary, and if she loves Arthur. . . . I wonder if she loves him at all? Don't you think that she . . . is considering the work out there far more than she is him? . . . Arthur must have the patience of a mountain of owls."

Charlie was perhaps too hard on Fanny. Always a worrier, she was torn by doubts about life in India, about the long voyage through submarine-infested waters, about leaving her mother and Aunt Annie, and even about her feeling for Arthur. She went through several unhappy years, but she was less high-strung and introspective than Louie, and seems, like her mother, to have been able to work off tension by "fussing." Eventually she learned to call herself "fussy Fanny" and laugh about it, but the habit of anxious activity clung.

Charlie and Helen spent months at Bramsholt Camp, where Charlie again instructed in physical training. They did not like it; it was muddy and isolated and they were prohibited from railroad traveling except on official business. At the time of one letter, March 18, 1917, Charlie wrote that no leaves were being granted. "They might as well call it a detention camp," he said. There was a welcome break of a month at Folkestone in the spring. He wrote: "The gymnasium is right on top of the cliff (for this one is just a continuation of those at Dover, and is about 200 feet high). . . . As we frequently have our drill outside, we have a fine view of the Channel. . . . It is a very busy place with the various destroyers, subs., transports, tramps, mosquitoes (sub. chasers) and mine sweepers. . . . Aeroplanes are always floating about with an occasional dirigible. . . . The other night we had a . . . Zepp raid. I woke up to hear the windows rattle. . . . Being ignorant of Zepps, we wondered whether the noise was a Zepp or a coast raid."

There was no lack of news from Myrtleville. By Christmas of 1916, Ethel and Harry were finally making plans for their marriage the following June: their decision and Carol's nursing career simplified Fanny's situation. She would stay at Myrtleville.

Will Good had been coping with help shortages, chicken thieves (all his chickens were stolen in the autumn of 1915), and a dangerously wet growing season in 1916. But he was still optimistic enough to buy fifty acres north of the farm for fifty-five dollars an acre. Perhaps he found some relief from agricultural worries by investigating Canadian taxation. He wrote a series of articles for the *Farmer's Advocate* based on his studies. He was enjoying his children, whom he described as "stirring." Little Willie was less adventurous than Allen, or perhaps just better watched; there was an English girl living with the Goods now, and she was an excellent mother's helper. Willie was smaller for his age than Allen, and learned to walk very early, emphasizing his smallness. His father called him "Midget," and after the noon meal every day, there was a ritual of the tiny boy walking round and round the dining-room table holding on to one of Papa's fingers.

The spring of 1917 was eventful at Myrtleville. Another little boy, Norman, was born in May, and late in June his Aunt Ethel married. It was a quiet wedding in the parlor (the old dining room) at Myrtleville. (For the past seven years the drawing room had been a downstairs bedroom for Aunt Annie.) Fred and Leone decorated the parlor with "orange blossoms" (sweet syringa) and pink carnations. Jennie's mother brought peonies, iris, and other flowers for the decoration of hall and dining room (the room which had been the old kitchen, and later the Will Goods' parlor). She took care of the new baby so that parents and older children and Carrie, the English girl, could attend the wedding. Carol wrote Mamie that Will escorted the bride with his six-year-old daughter holding his other hand. The child (myself) held Ethel's glove when she took it off during the ceremony, and was therefore said by her aunt to be "maid of honor." I remember little about the wedding except that I thought Ethel's blue silk suit was very pretty, and that I was embarrassed by my four-year-old brother Allen's taking refuge under our father's chair when refreshments were served.

The Siretts went to live in the village of Brighton on Lake Ontario, which was the center for Harry's work as a district representative for the provincial Department of Agriculture. The autumn after her marriage, Ethel had an operation, removal of an ovary, because of a Fallopian tube pregnancy. (I learned the nature of the operation after I was grown and married; it was not the kind of thing my Victorian elders told young girls about.) The Siretts remained childless people who loved children. I spent many happy holidays with them when I was young, and throughout their lives they took tremendous pleasure in their nieces and nephews, and the children of those nieces and nephews.

The year of Ethel's marriage was the year that electricity came to Myrtleville. The Hydro-Electric Power Commission of Ontario put a high tension line along the Second Concession Road to the north of Myrtleville Farm. (Since that time, it has acquired the name of Power Line Road.) Will Good was able to construct a line from it to his farm buildings—at his own expense—using secondhand poles from the Grand Valley electric railroad. It was wonderful having electricity. No more messy and risky coal-oil lamps to clean and watch; no more

Drawing room, Myrtleville House, showing Eliza Good's 1837 piano. Victorian chair and center table with kaleidoscope are Ballachey pieces

summer cooking on a hot stove in a hot kitchen, or on a dangerous kerosene stove in a "back kitchen"; no more heating of heavy irons on the kitchen stove.

Farm housekeeping at Myrtleville changed more in the first

seventeen years of the twentieth century than it had in almost seventy years before. When Will Good took over the farm, he gave up pig-killing and this spared his wife the laborious making of sausage and "head cheese." I do not remember any churning of butter, though I know that Aunt Mamie, like Aunt Annie, had been a great butter-maker. Will and Charlie as boys served their time with the churn; Will's sons never did. During much of my youth, a "cream separator" was used at the barn. The cream was then sold, and the skim milk used to feed stock. My mother had the job of taking the separator apart, cleaning and scalding it after each milking. Not only was butter purchased; most of the bread Mother served was bought from a baker who delivered it several times a week.

It was a blessing that commercial bread and butter were available, because domestic help became less and less available. Girls went to work in factories and shops, or, with more education, taught school or served as secretaries. There was no longer a pool of "maiden aunt" helpers, like Anne and Clara Good, Jo and Lizzie Ballachey, and Maggie Jones. However, there still was a tremendous amount of work for the farm housewife of 1917. There would be fifteen to twenty men to be fed two big meals a day at threshing and silo-filling times, and a number of extra men for apple-picking, also. Hundreds of quarts of fruits and vegetables were "put up" in glass jars for winter use, in place of the dried fruits and pickles Fanny Jones had written about.

The age of the automobile was about to engulf country as well as city. The province of Ontario took over the Paris Toll Road. The tollgates were removed and there were plans to pave the road—after the war was over. Meantime, one put up with dust or mud outside of town.

In that same eventful year of 1917, Myrtleville doubled its interest in faraway California. John Ballachey, now sixty-nine, retired from his position with the trust company in Sioux City and went to live in Long Beach, where the senior Doyles had been for several years. It was a small city of under fifty thousand population; there were no oil wells and no smog; the main industries were fish processing and ship building. John was delighted with his garden. He wrote his sister at Myrtleville on Bella Doyle's seventy-second birthday, November 1.

"Set out cauliflower last evening. Cabbage, Turnips, Beets, Parsley, Onions, Lettuce & Radishes are all up. Picked some beautiful Roses yesterday and Bella sent us over some Raspberries. . . . I sit in Sun Parlor or on Verandah reading every afternoon & Mother sews. . . . Well, Mary, what a place for us. All the whole six of us should settle here to end our days, if I could get children out I know there would be no question what I would do. No snow, no storm sash, no winds. Garden the year round, I think. . . . Nellie [his wife] and Mrs. Carpenter [guest] have gone to Bella's to wish her happy returns. . . . How she does work, & what she has passed thru with that cancer, now she says completely cured. . . . She spends 2 days weekly at Red Cross, besides sewing & working nights & today has gone to sweep up house for neighbor with Insane Daughter, who they bro't home yesterday, claimed was mistreated at sanitarium. . . . Have just run over to Bella's . . . took her Bouquet of white Roses & Scarlet Geraniums. . . .They have flowers, but it was all I had. The dear old girl appreciated the thought. . . . The streets here at first sight present a very novel appearance, no shade trees such as we have been accustomed to, all Palms . . . Roses grow over tops of Houses covered with Bloom, and all plants grow to such immense size, wagon loads of Geraniums trimmed off & Burned."

Will Doyle had made some unfortunate investments, John wrote, in mining, oil, and Vancouver real estate. But economy came easily to his wife, and he was helping his income by keeping chickens and selling eggs. The Goods chuckled over some of John's stories about the Doyles. He wrote on December 10, 1917: "He [Doyle] is a character, wonderful wide experience, and talkative, handles his chickens very scientifically. . . . [He] supposed a hen was laying in one of his trap nests & when he went to let her out discovered the old cat had gone in & had 4 Kittens. . . . Not wanting to keep the kittens, he killed them & as all offal & refuse goes to the chickens, he cut them up & fed them to the hens, & now the neighbors won't eat the eggs."

Across the Atlantic, the Charlie Goods were preparing for Christmas. They would have Helen's brother from Canada and Charlie's brother Morgan, on leave from France. They were now in comfortable quarters in Stafford, where Charlie was taking a general infantry course as a "refresher" after his long P.T. stint. They enjoyed views of the distant Welsh hills, and nearby Roman and Norman ruins, but could not find time to visit the famous potteries. When Christmas came they had a "bang-up" dinner with turkey, ordered weeks ahead, and a plum pudding which was "actually complete although the raisins were few and far between." They also "sported a whole pound of butter which had been carefully treasured for several weeks."

Early in the new year, Capt. Charles A. Good was sent to France. He wrote Mamie that when he left England everyone was eating blackish bread, but as soon as he landed on the continent he was "astounded to see the pure white bread of peace time with real butter. . . . Then we have eggs and bacon for breakfast (please note the plural), a fair amount of jam, plenty of meat, vegetables, etc., but abominable coffee!" He went on: "The States are doing wonders, I think. It's true they haven't got men into the line as quickly as little Canada did, but they are doing the right things first: building a solid foundation, hustling along the ocean tonnage, speeding up aeroplane manufacturers and adjusting legislation to suit the new requirements."

He wrote about conditions a few miles from the front, in the midst of the ruins left by earlier campaigns: "The Germans had not entrenched this far back but of course the French system of defense is very evident everywhere—trenches fallen into disrepair, and being rapidly filled in by the ancient but energetic French farmer and his equally aged and strenuous "femme"; gun-pits over-grown with grass and weeds; and long stretches of entanglements which shear through great fields of fallow or crops. . . . The other day, several of us meandered up towards the front, passed a famous spur which the French captured at a terrific loss of life, passed several things which used to be villages, but are now a heap of rubble under which our boys live like so many rabbits, passed a couple of monuments erected by the Canadians to the men who fell in capturing the Ridge."

Back in Canada, the older generation of the Goods was faltering. Charlotte Malloch's condition worried the family. On February 12, 1918, her sister Anne wrote her in a firm, clear

hand, telling her that she had four pairs of large socks ready
to give the ladies for the soldiers. She said she had been doing
a good deal of reading, and suggested that Charlotte have her
companion read the New Testament to her. The letter lay un-
sent at Myrtleville, because the next day news came of Mrs.
Malloch's death. Anne, the oldest of Allen Good's children,
was now one of three survivors, the others much younger than
she and living far away in California and Indiana.

Charlotte left a sizable estate, most of it in trust for her
daughter, Lily Simons. The trustees were Will Good, and a
doctor and lawyer in Paisley. Charlotte Malloch disapproved
of her nephew's radical tendencies, but she put great confidence in his ability and reliability. Perhaps she knew that he
was well suited to stand up to his cousin Lily's demands. Lily
wanted charge of *her* money.

About a month after Aunt Charlotte's death, W. C. Good
had a phone call from his old friend, T. A. Crerar of the western Cooperative, the United Grain Growers. Crerar had recently become Minister of Agriculture in the wartime Union
government of Sir Robert Borden, and he offered Mr. Good a
position under him. It is not clear what the position was, but
there is a copy of the letter Will Good wrote declining it, a
very revealing letter.

The objections which I feel may be put down as follows:

1. For the sake of the children and Mrs. Good, as well as on
account of my mother, aunt, and sister who live on the farm, I
cannot think of breaking up the home here—at least at present.
And I suppose the acceptance of the position you mention
would necessitate my more or less permanent residence in Ottawa.

2. The loss which my absence from the farm would involve
would be, under present conditions, very heavy, and could not
be made good by any reasonable salary.

3. My tenure of the office would be very uncertain, depending upon various contingencies.

4. So far as I understand the nature of the position in view, I
do not think I have any special qualifications for it. The work
will consist almost wholly of the execution of policy. . . . I do
not think I would find the work congenial, and I could not do

good work if I chafed under the harness. There are many respects in which, I think, I would find this kind of work very irksome—sedentary in character, loss of independence, restrictions upon freedom of discussion, etc., etc.

5. My acceptance of any permanent position of emolument in the civil service would, I fancy, largely destroy my influence for good with my fellow farmers, as well as change my whole outlook and plans for propaganda and literary work which I can work in with the farm.

Soon after Will Good decided against going to work in Ottawa, his Aunt Annie took a cold. She did not seem to be seriously ill, but she did lie abed for several days and left a soldier's sock half knitted. Finally, on the morning of April 3, she seemed very weak and did not eat her breakfast. On being asked about her condition, she said that she felt very sick. Soon thereafter, Fanny, working about the room, realized that the old lady had stopped breathing. She was almost eighty-seven years old. Her newspaper obituary has a ring of personal loss, beyond the routine reference to "one of the oldest and most respected citizens of the county of Brant."

"The late Miss Good as the eldest daughter of one of the county's most prominent citizens saw much of the social life of the day. . . . For just as long as she was able to do so she loved to keep up the amenities . . . by going frequently to call upon her friends. . . . [Lately] she was confined to the house on account of a broken hip that never perfectly mended. To the last, however, she maintained much of her great personal charm.

"A woman of wide reading, she kept herself interested in the affairs of the day. . . . One remarkable feature of her later years was the large correspondence she maintained with old friends, for of these she had a great many. As one who had known and loved her said, 'She was a comfortable person to be with.' And it was a great tribute."

Anne's estate was very small compared to her sister Charlotte's. Apart from some fine old furniture, books, and silver, there was under two thousand dollars. She left five hundred of that to Clara Matthews, and one hundred divided among three religious organizations. The rest was left for the use of her sister-in-law, Mary Good. On the latter's death, six hundred dollars was to be set aside toward the support of Louie, one hundred given to Charles A. Good, and the rest was to go to the children and grandchildren of Tom Good, Louie excepted. All of Anne's personal property was left for the use of Mary Good, and after her death it was to be divided among the surviving children of Tom Good. His unmarried daughters were to have the use of the front part of Myrtleville House. Carol never married and it was not until she was permanently hospitalized in 1964 that Will Good's family had full title to the old house. In a sense, Anne Good was mistress of Myrtleville for a hundred years.

The winter after Aunt Annie died, Mrs. Tom Good was at Mamie's in Sioux City, and her daughter Fanny went to visit the Doyles in California. For the first time in the eighty-one years of its existence, the main part of Myrtleville House was uninhabited.

16

Fifty Years On

W. C. Good was already owner of Myrtleville when his Aunt Annie died, but now, for the first time, he seemed head of the family, and he and his new house took on added significance. His farm remained the homestead for relatives far and near. They brought their children to see the old-fashioned house, now often empty, and to see the ever-changing operation of a fine modern farm. Will's house was the nerve center of Myrtleville, and its master continued to exert influence far beyond his own acres and community.

Soon after Anne Good's death in the last year of the war, the Union government in Ottawa canceled exemption of farmers' sons from conscription. This was just at the beginning of seeding, and it angered many farmers, who were already upset by the government's implacable hostility to tariff reform. About six thousand of them converged on Ottawa in May 1918. Prime Minister Borden was unsympathetic; a delegation went to the House of Commons and was denied admission. Resentment grew. Farmers all over Canada had already been organized for economic and educational reasons by men like W. C. Good and his father before him. Now they were organized for independent political action.

The war ended on November 11, 1918, and the following year an election in Ontario put into power a United Farmers' government under E. C. Drury. W. C. Good was one of those who drafted the U.F.O. platform. The same year Mr. Good, having revised and expanded his 1916 articles for the *Farmers' Advocate,* published them as a book, *Production and Taxation in Canada—from the Farmers' Standpoint.*

In the last autumn of the war, Lt. Fred Ballachey, dental officer, was sent to Fort Dix, New Jersey. Two weeks after his arrival there he developed pneumonia as a complication of the dreaded "Spanish Influenza" which was epidemic in the camp. About one hundred fifty men per day were dying of the flu at Fort Dix, and there were eight hundred to a thousand new cases per day in an encampment of seventy thousand men. Healthy men were being turned out of barracks, and the barracks used as hospitals. Fred's wife was telegraphed to come at once, and her brother-in-law, George T., went with her. They found her husband cheerful and optimistic, but the doctors held out no hope, and the following day he lapsed into unconsciousness and died. Following funeral services in St. Paul's, Buffalo, Fred was buried in Brantford. Will Good was one of the pallbearers; it must have been hard for him to realize that he was the only survivor of the three cousins who had been at the University of Toronto together just twenty years earlier.

There was more bad news to come. Over in England, Charlie's baby daughter had contracted abdominal tuberculosis from infected milk. Helen took care of the critically ill child while her husband and her brother were fighting near Cambrai in the great final push against the Germans' Hindenburg line. Jack Woodroofe was killed, but Charlie survived, and was able to be with his wife when their little girl died less than two weeks after the armistice of November 11. Charlie had already been offered a position at the Khaki University of Canada set up in London, and Helen was able to get work there, too. As Charlie wrote, she badly needed something to occupy her time and her mind. "She has been a perfect marvel to me," he said, "and I thank my lucky stars continually for giving me such a pal."

Before returning to Canada in the summer of 1919, Charlie visited his grandmother near Dublin. He thought the center of Ireland's capital resembled the town of Arras, France, in the character of its ruins. He carefully left the king's uniform behind in England; it might have been dangerous for his Irish relatives to entertain a British officer. Ireland's "troubles" had erupted into virtual civil war in Dublin in 1916, and guerrilla warfare continued. In 1921, the unhappy island split into the Irish Free State and Northern Ireland (Ulster), which remained British.

Carol Good was still in nurse's training at the Brantford General Hospital during the flu epidemic. It was a grueling experience, but she came through it safely. In 1919, she, who had studied nursing over the objections of her elders, graduated at the head of her class. She soon became a public health nurse, working mainly in the elementary schools, and making her rounds in a Model T Ford. Will Good had also taken to the automobile. His first car was a Willys-Overland touring model, with curtains to snap on if there was rain. At first the car was not used in the winters, but early in the twenties the Paris Road, by then part of Ontario Highway 2, was paved, and Myrtleville was motorized the year round.

In 1920, Bella and Will Doyle came east from California. Will was not well, and consulted his wife's nephew, Dr. Allen Jones. After some thirty years of practice in Buffalo, Allen was a highly respected physician, but he and his colleagues could not save Mr. Doyle, who died of cancer that autumn in Brantford, his great bulk pitifully wasted. His widow lived with her widowed daughter, Fanny Ballachey, for more than a decade. For several years, while I was a student at the Brantford Collegiate, "Cousin Fan" kindly gave me good hot lunches with her family. I sat across the table from Aunt Bella, who was a very alert and articulate old lady, but I am afraid I paid minimum attention to her reminiscences. How I have wished, during the writing of this book, that I could remember what she said, and that I had asked pertinent questions!

The Will Goods' fourth son, Harold, was born in 1920. He was a change in a blue-eyed, fair, or reddish brown-haired family; his hair and eyes were dark like his Grandfather McCormick's. It was soon after this that an early radio came to Myrtleville. It sat on the piano in Will Good's house, and was a local curiosity, but it could entertain only two people at a time, as it had no loudspeaker and listeners used earphones. There were also very few stations broadcasting at that time.

During these years, Mr. Good, as one of the founders of the United Farmers of Ontario, was in the councils of the U.F.O. government at Toronto. In fact, the first journey by train that I can remember was with my father to Toronto, where one small girl lunched with the Cabinet of Ontario in a room paneled in dark, shiny wood, and enjoyed a delicious peach dessert. When the next federal election came along, in 1921,

W. C. Good ran for office as an Independent Progressive and was elected to the Dominion Parliament, representing Brant County. There were 65 Progressive members, only 50 Conservatives, and 117 Liberals, whose leader, Mackenzie King, became prime minister.

Will Good was in Parliament for four years, renting the farm, except for the orchards, to a family who lived in the north wing of the old house. During this time, except for one winter, we continued to live in the new house at Myrtleville. Those of us children who were old enough attended the redbrick, one-room Moyle's School at the corner of the Paris Road and the Power Line Road. It was the third school at that corner, and we were the third generation of Goods to study there.

Will Good's family were with him in Ottawa the winter of 1922–23, because his wife was pregnant, and it seemed better for her not to be alone with five young children, although there were tenants across the lawn. Her youngest child, Robert, given a McCormick name, was born in June 1923. Like all of Jennie Good's babies, he came into the world at Myrtleville. All of her many grandchildren were born in hospitals, the first in 1940. It was not until the 1930s that medical supervision of pregnancy and hospital delivery of babies became commonplace, saving the lives of many mothers and infants.

W. C. Good's career in Parliament was busy, and frustrating. He argued hard and well for tariff reform, but the large Progressive minority beat in vain on the combined ranks of Liberal and Conservative protectionists. Some of Mr. Good's proposals were less well supported. Many of his colleagues were not really excited about his ideas on electoral reform and the suppression of racetrack gambling. He did, however, make a great contribution with his researches into financial controls. Much of his work in this field bore fruit in the 1930s when the central "Bank of Canada" became a reality. One historian, W. L. Morton of Trent University, says that W. C. Good queried financial orthodoxy by principles which in more sophisticated terms Keynes was to make respectable and effective a decade later.

In 1925, Mr. Good retired from politics. The family and the farm were calling loudly. His love of Myrtleville ran deep, and the farm was not being kept up to his standards by tenants.

Moreover, his wife found her few vacations, in Ottawa and in Nova Scotia with the Charlie Goods, a poor exchange for having a husband at home. She took a particularly jaundiced view of Will's two-month investigation of banking and credit systems in the summer of 1923, when he left her with a six-weeks-old baby and five other children. Will himself had reasons to be glad to leave political life. He was temperamentally more of a prophet than a politician, and the art of compromise was hard for him. Party discipline he thought extremely obnoxious; he insisted that every M.P. ought to study each question from all sides and vote with complete independence. And he was disappointed to find even among his Progressive colleagues those who put political power above principles. He had a great capacity, however, to surmount disillusionment and unpopularity without bitterness. He just kept on doing what he thought was right. On the surface, he did not have the serenity of his Aunt Annie, but he must have had the same kind of steady faith.

In 1923, Arthur Hawtin came to Canada on furlough. When he returned to India the following year, he took Fanny with him. (I remember that they were married the day that I began to attend the Brantford Collegiate.) Fanny blossomed in the East. Arthur, a man of God who was calmly efficient and gently humorous, was just right for her. She enjoyed traveling with him, playing tennis and climbing hills with him, helping him with his mission work.

When Fanny married, Carol left nursing to keep house for her mother, who was seventy-two. But she was never happy with domestic duties, and took up writing as a hobby, preserving many of Aunt Annie's reminiscences which have been used in this book. Eventually she hired a housekeeper and returned to her job. For years, her household lived in Brantford during winters and from spring to fall in the old house at Myrtleville.

Harry Sirett bought an apple farm a little west of Brighton, and soon left his government position to become a full-time farmer. His house was a pleasant white frame building, about the age of Myrtleville House; Ethel furnished it attractively with antiques, some of them from Myrtleville. She was a good cook, housekeeper, and flower gardener, as well as being active in the village book club and Anglican church. Every summer she entertained many friends and relatives, all of whom found her fun to be with. The family continued to tease her about her "Irishisms." Harry's favorite was her remark after a visit to a friend, "Bessie certainly is a talker. My jaws are aching!"

W. C. Good's return to the farm in 1925 did not end his public life. He had become president of the Cooperative Union of Canada in 1921, the year he was elected to Parliament, and he held that position for twenty-four years. He served on the board of the United Farmers' Cooperatives of Ontario (later known as the United Cooperatives of Ontario) for thirty-five years, and saw their business thrive after difficult early years. It was for his work in promoting cooperatives that he was honored with a Queen's Coronation medal in 1953.

When Will Good went back to farming, he began to build up a dairy herd of purebred Holstein-Friesians. They were expensive but seemed a worthwhile investment at a time of economic boom. Historians see the 1920s as strikingly similar to the 1850s in Canada. In both periods there was much foreign demand for export staples plus heavy domestic demand for the materials of a new technology. The 1850s ushered in the age of steel and steam; the 1920s brought the age of oil and electricity. With general prosperity, the "farm movement," so much of it a form of protest, lost momentum, especially in its political manifestations.

Myrtleville, with its capable, vigorous owner and his flock of healthy offspring, seemed to be heading into a period of expansion with the economy. The children had come unscathed through measles, mumps, and chickenpox. There had been one session of real worry when twelve-year-old Allen had a nasty case of pneumonia, but he soon was as strong as ever. Then active tuberculosis invaded the family again. Jennie Good had been carefully pasteurizing household milk for years (the government did not test herds yet), but somewhere her daughter had apparently been given infected milk. In 1927, a tuberculous gland was removed from my neck, and the following year I was taken out of school and given a prolonged "rest cure" because X-rays showed a small lung spot. I did not know at that time that my little cousin, Charlie's daughter, had died of "bovine tuberculosis"; my worried parents, of course, did.

My very mild illness cleared up slowly, and before I was back at school, thirteen-year-old Willie developed meningitis; after a short, severe illness, he died on February 27, 1929. His death was a double blow; he was a much-loved, promising child, and also a prime candidate for the farming of Myrtleville. His older brother, Allen, although an excellent worker, had already shown a marked talent for drawing and painting; there was doubt that he would make a career of farming.

On October 24, 1929, the New York stock market began a rapid and catastrophic decline, followed in a few days by the collapse of the Montreal and Toronto markets. Their troubles were spectacular symptoms of a diseased economy. The sickness soon became apparent all over Europe and North America. Canada suffered acutely, because over one-third of its national income had been coming from the sale of its products abroad. Agricultural prices fell farthest of all, thanks to a world surplus of wheat, and tariffs against farm produce in Europe and the United States. Prices of manufactured goods declined much less, but demand was, of course, greatly reduced, and hundreds of thousands of Canada's urban workers were laid off to cut back production.

Once more, as at the time of Allen Good's bankruptcy, and in the years of the long depression at the end of the last century, there was a painful shortage of money at Myrtleville. But because of his mixed farming and his closeness to urban markets, Will Good fared better than western farmers. At times he used a form of barter; he would take fruit and eggs to town and exchange them for groceries which could not be produced on the farm. He also took a good deal of the less salable fruit to Brantford's "social service centre" for distribution to the unemployed, of whom there were many in a manufacturing town like Brantford. At busy seasons, he employed as many men as he needed and could afford to pay; they were glad to work for fifty cents a day plus a hearty midday meal. He hired family men from town, but at intervals there were itinerants needing food and work. They usually left without work, but never hungry.

The mistress of Myrtleville rose to the occasion as her predecessors had. Like Eliza Good, she was "practical," and she was a better businessman than her scholarly husband. She kept a sharp eye on expenses; one of the few times I remember her being impatient with my father was when he spent some of the grocery money on a book. She had cousins who owned a silk mill in Galt; from them she obtained quantities of soft unbleached muslin bags in which unprocessed silk came from Japan. Out of these she made sheets and nightclothes and aprons, some of them attractively embroidered. She managed to send her children to school surprisingly well dressed considering her expenditures. And no matter how poor we were, she said, we must always be "clean and mended." She maintained the tradition of hospitality also, and with the prevalence of automobiles there were more frequent visits from Paisley and Buffalo Ballacheys, as well as nearby Good and McCormick relatives. Occasionally, the Joneses drove from distant Homewood, and Will Good's colleagues in the "farm movement" were often around at mealtimes. Besides the endless cooking and cleaning and laundry and sewing, Jennie Good for years prepared eggs for market. In this modern world, eggs were graded by being weighed and "candled" one by one before they were carefully packed in crates.

Fortunately, Will Good's family enjoyed good health most of the time in those difficult years, though little Robert had a very bad mastoid operation at the age of seven. Mastoiditis is another dread illness which today has almost disappeared with use of antibiotics. The family round of whooping cough in 1930 was greatly eased by the use of "shots," and most of the Goods' children were immunized against diphtheria in a public-school program.

After seven years in India, Fanny and Arthur Hawtin returned to Canada on furlough in 1931. While the Hawtins were still at home, Mamie and Chris Lane spent the summer of 1932 in Ontario, mostly in the old house at Myrtleville. Chris's childhood injuries in a schoolhouse fire had crippled him progressively and forced him into early retirement from his position with Armour and Company in Sioux City. He was a cheerful man, who loved the company of children, and Will Good's younger children had a wonderful time with him.

The year after the Lanes' visit to Canada, the last two of old
Allen Good's children died, Clara Matthews in Marion, Indiana, at the age of eighty-three, and Bella Doyle in Brantford, Ontario, at almost eighty-eight. Not long before her
death, Clara sent her mementoes of Myrtleville to Mamie in
Sioux City.

Occasionally, in the 1920s and 1930s, Charlie Good of Nova
Scotia came to Myrtleville. He was in government service for a
few years after the war with the Soldier Settlement Board.
Then until World War II he operated a farm in the Annapolis
Valley, and during this time was an officer of the Nova Scotia
Fruit Growers' Association and a marketing inspector for the
Canadian Department of Agriculture. We youngsters paid little attention to any business that might have brought Cousin
Charlie to Ontario; we just enjoyed his visits. He had a light-
hearted way with young people that Will Good never had. As
a teen-ager I found Charlie a dashing figure, tall, slender,
handsome, and charming, seeming more than sixteen years
younger than my father. Will loved to play with little children,
but as we became big children, he expected us to take life
seriously. He did not understand our harmless frivolities; I
remember his telling me when I was sixteen that I had "alarm-
ing yearnings after the fleshpots." Consciously, he did not
want to dominate us, but he caused his grown sons a good
deal of trouble by his fussy supervision of their farm work.

The Great Depression slowed the modernization of Myrtleville but did not stop it completely. Will Good was committed
to dairying and built a milk house containing electrical refrigeration. He bought a secondhand Willys-Knight sedan to replace the Overland touring car, and converted the old car into
a farm truck. Years before, in his first enthusiasm over having
electrical power, he had bought a fifteen-horsepower motor
and a threshing machine, but the combination had never been
satisfactory, and he sold both motor and thresher before
going to Ottawa. He was back to hiring the services of a
thresher, who now used tractor instead of steam engine.
The Goods wanted a tractor but could not afford it; however,
they worked out another kind of barter arrangement, trading
some of Myrtleville's ample "boy-power" for the occasional use
of a fortunate neighbor's tractor.

In 1932, I finally entered the University of Toronto, at the age of twenty-one. I went with some scholarship money, some part-time employment, help from hard-up Myrtleville, and above all, high hopes. My mother, who had not gone to college, was as determined as I was that I should go; my father protested mildly that I could educate myself at home. In fact, he used to argue that many of the best-educated people he knew were self-taught, and it is certainly true that his own reputation rests on his achievements as self-educated economist and social organizer rather than as a college-trained physical scientist. It is probable, however, that he discouraged advanced education for his children mainly because he feared, at least subconsciously, that they would be lost to farming, and he always had an almost mystical dedication to agriculture as a way of life, and an aversion to cities, at least in theory.

In spite of his father's attitude, Allen took off for Toronto in 1935, when he was twenty-two. He studied at the College of Art as well as at the university, and his mother borrowed some money on his behalf from Charlie McCormick, one of her silk-mill cousins. Myrtleville still carried some mortgage from its last expansion in 1916, and Will borrowed from his cousin, George T. Ballachey of Buffalo, to tide him over the lean years. It was certainly useful that not all of the family connections were as hard-hit by the depression as the farmer members.

It was also very useful for Will Good's public life that he had a capable wife and good help from his sons. Through the depression years, he went frequently to Toronto for United Farmers meetings, and annually to congresses of the Cooperative Union, often held in distant parts of Canada. He was interested in the revival of agrarian radicalism as hard times bore heavily on Canadian farmers. This radicalism combined with the philosophy of the British labor movement to produce the C.C.F. (Cooperative Commonwealth Federation). W. C. Good represented the United Farmers of Ontario at a Regina meeting of the C.C.F. in 1933, but he voted against the manifesto adopted there. It had too much "doctrinaire socialism" in it, he said. (Will Good had dabbled in socialism in his college days, but it never developed much hold on him. He once wrote to a journalist with whom he was discussing taxation, "I am as jealous of the rights of property as you are. I have no purpose other than to secure to each a just return for his labors.") He remained on very friendly terms with C.C.F. leaders, however, meanwhile rejoicing in the creation of the Central Bank of Canada in 1934, under the administration of R. B. Bennett, a Conservative for whose ideas in general he had scant respect. It did not upset him that Bennett would get credit for what W. C. Good had unsuccessfully urged on Parliament ten years before.

During the late 1930s the depression lifted slowly, but at the same time uneasiness about the Fascist threat in Europe grew. W. C. Good arranged for and prepared some weekly broadcasts on international affairs under the auspices of the local branch of the League of Nations Society. Early in 1939, he was also involved in plans for a conference of the five eastern provinces in Montreal on the marketing of agricultural products.

By the autumn of 1939, only the youngest of the Myrtleville children was still at school in Brantford, "last of a long and brilliant line," his yearbook said. The only daughter had married an American lawyer whom she had met while a graduate student in Cambridge, Massachusetts. The oldest son, Allen, was a high-school teacher, specializing in art. Norman had had one year at the University of Toronto, and Harold was just about to start, with several nice scholarships in pocket.

In September 1939, Canada declared war on Nazi Germany. She was militarily very unprepared, and at first the government indicated that her role would be chiefly that of training Commonwealth airmen and supplying material and funds to the United Kingdom. The Canadian economy went into high gear, and after a decade of depression the farms and factories of Brant County prospered again.

Fanny and Arthur Hawtin returned to Canada to live in 1939, shortly before Mrs. Tom Good died in January 1940. She was almost eighty-eight, and the family's last link with the old Myrtleville of the founders, Allen and Eliza. Following her death, Anne Good's small estate was finally distributed, though many of the furnishings of Myrtleville House were left there for the use of Carol, who had taken care of her mother for so long.

Hitler's "blitzkrieg" swept through Europe in the spring of

1940, and the pace of Canada's war effort quickened. By 1941 there was an army camp just outside Brantford (near Mohawk Park) and an air force camp a few miles away, near Burford. Farm labor was getting scarce, and W. C. Good, sixty-six years old, was lame from arthritis of the hip and lower spine. He had one hired man, who refused to "take orders from a boy of eighteen [Robert]"; so Norman stayed home from Toronto to keep the farm going. By the spring of 1942, the hired man had gone. Though it was difficult to get farm equipment as well as labor, the family luckily found it possible to buy a milking machine.

From the autumn of 1942 to the spring of 1943, Robert was able to leave Myrtleville and attend the Ontario Agricultural College, where he did excellent work. Then he too had to give up school. Harold sometimes left his studies in Toronto for a few days emergency help on the farm but suffered no serious interruption. (The military rejected him because of his poor eyesight.) Will Good, though partly crippled, remained healthy and vigorous. Relatively inactive, he finally put on weight, and for the first time began to look a little like the Ballacheys. (Except for his shorter, heavier build, he had always borne a strong resemblance to the men of his father's family, especially his handsome Uncle Charlie.)

Jennie Good, always physically and nervously less rugged than her husband, was showing the strain of years of heavy responsibility and hard work. Late in 1944, Mr. Good was away from home a great deal. As president of the Cooperative Union of Canada and a director of the United Farmers Cooperative Company of Ontario, he was busy preparing for the hearings of a Royal Commission on the Taxation of Cooperatives. His wife was left with the job of disposing of an enormous crop of apples. She sold them on the farm; she had no domestic help, and the housework piled up while she waited on customers. At this point, even the sugar shortage was helpful, because it prevented her from doing, though perhaps not from worrying about, her usual canning of hundreds of quarts of fruit. Still more useful was the assistance, off and on, of her oldest son, Allen, who had joined the air force in 1943. After serving in St. John, New Brunswick, and in Montreal, he was stationed for several months that autumn at Burtch, only six miles south of Brantford. He wrote his sister after Christmas.

"I found the station very small, the work negligible, and the freedom practically unlimited. I was able to stay at Myrtleville about three nights a week, and spend the week-ends in Toronto. [His wife and baby were living there.] Burtch Station, attached to Hagersville, provided a course in blind landing (radio beam approach) for Hagersville student pilots. As operator of the beam transmitters, my duties were not arduous; I turned the equipment on at 8 A.M. and off at 5 P.M.

"Then came the big snow storm of Dec. 12. Roads and airfields all over the province were blocked, and the priority of little Burtch was too low to rate a snow plow. So for a month we did nothing. At the end of the month it was decided to close the station and bring the ships back to Hagersville. December in Ontario was a month of record snow storms, and (strangely) most of the lads at Burtch were snowed out rather than in the station. The six miles from Burtch to Brantford was nothing, but the six-mile struggle from Brantford to Burtch was impossible. I managed to be away from the station 16 days in December.

"I've been back in Hagersville two weeks now, working on beam receivers and transmitters, and must admit this is a poor place compared to Burtch. There are only two 48 hour passes per month, and from these travelling time must be taken. There's a superabundance of parades and military baloney. Also, one has to line up for everything. I'm not alone in my dislike for the life. Every night at news time there's a prayer meeting around the radio. 'God give'em strength!' we cry as the Russians advance 40 miles and the British speed across the lowlands for another 200 yards!"

Will Good was still away from home a great deal as the Royal Commission did not finish its formal sessions until May 1945. His wife's fatigue continued, and her resistance to infection was low. She had many colds and sore throats, as well as attacks of digestive trouble and neuralgia, which were probably largely nervous in origin. Her happy disposition was very useful; a great deal of harassment could be overcome with laughter and jokes. She hated to have her husband absent so much, but she loved and admired and accepted him.

Work was simplified for Mrs. Good and her farmer sons by the sale of all the chickens the summer of 1945. She wrote: "We . . . have gone completely out of poultry. There is far more money in the cattle and not enough help on the farm to look after so many branches." By the end of the summer the great war was over. A deep sense of relief was mingled with qualms about atomic energy and fear of a postwar depression. But while devastated Europe began a long climb back to prosperity, the North American economy soared toward affluence. Myrtleville entered upon a period of mechanization, though equipment remained in short supply for several years. The makeshift truck was replaced by a surplus army truck, then by a regular pickup vehicle. A tractor came, then tractors. Eventually, Myrtleville had its own threshing machine again.

The sons of Myrtleville carried on their careers. Allen took a position as art teacher in the East York Collegiate, Toronto. Norman finished his course at the university, and proceeded to a Ph.D. in plant physiology at the California Institute of Technology. Harold took a Ph.D. in botany at the University of Toronto. Robert, however, did not go back to college; a stockman, he stayed with the fine herd he and Norman had helped to build up. In 1948, it won a Master Breeder's Shield for their father, who quite properly gave the credit to his sons.

For three years after the war, Will Good continued to spend much of his time and energy on work with cooperatives. At the end of 1945 he retired from his twenty-four-year presidency of the Cooperative Union, but the following year he began a long series of committee meetings on the reorganization of the United Farmers' Cooperative Company. Eventually the committee recommended that the company be incorporated in a new provincial organization to be called United Co-operatives of Ontario. This was set up by an act of the Ontario legislature early in 1948, and at the first general meeting of the U.C.O. Mr. Good announced that he was retiring after thirty-five years as a founding director of the old company. After all, he was seventy-two and lame.

It was in 1948 also that Carol Good gave up her summer use of old Myrtleville House and turned it over to her brother's children and the growing flock of grandchildren. There were seven of them by then, all city dwellers. Their use of the old house was an ideal arrangement; in July and August, Gram and Gramp enjoyed the company of the little boys and girls when they felt like it, and when they were too tired signaled the fact by hooking their screen doors. Will Good loved to watch the babies and toddlers, but as years went by met some resistance when he tried to organize the older boys to do useful farm chores. Children of the machine age, they were charmed only when they could use farm machines, and most of those were too big and dangerous for them. The little girls fitted easily into Gram's domestic life, and almost every day they had a "tea party" with her.

By the 1950s W. C. Good had officially retired from farming. He was hospitalized in the spring of 1951, for the first time in his seventy-five years. He was not ill, but he did need prostate gland surgery. There are echoes of the independent young man who found his work at the O.A.C. much like "slavery," in the words of the old man who said wryly to his wife and son when they left him at the hospital, "Well, I suppose I am virtually a prisoner for awhile!" His convalescence was slow, but complete. He was able to help occasionally with light farm work and he modernized the kitchen of his 1913 house. He continued to read widely and write for publication, and after he was eighty wrote a book, *Farmer Citizen,* a history of his fifty years in the "farmers' movement." He and his wife were living a more relaxed life at last. Jennie even persuaded him to watch television with her at times.

For most of the 1950s, Will's sisters were well and active, too. Ethel and Harry Sirett retired from their apple farm to the village of Brighton, where they kept a beautiful garden and, year after year, produced prizewinning flowers. Fanny and Arthur Hawtin sold vegetables and fruits from their large garden at Ayr, Ontario.

Mamie and Chris Lane lived together happily in Sioux City for many years after Chris's early retirement. Their only child presented them with three grandchildren, two of them teenagers when their Lane grandparents died, mercifully within a few weeks of each other, in the summer of 1957. Mamie was almost eighty.

Two years later, after more than fifty years of marriage, Jennie Good died suddenly following surgery. The loss of his devoted wife was very hard on Will, but at that time, and many times in the next eight years, he astonished the family with his recuperative powers. One of his daughters-in-law said, "He is a man with great inner resources."

The year after Jennie Good's death, Ethel went, also suddenly, with her intelligence and vivacity undimmed. Carol was not as fortunate; she developed hardening of the arteries, and spent her last few years in a nursing home, her memory gone.

Will Good made long winter visits at his daughter's home in St. Louis, Missouri, several times after his wife died. The rest of the year he lived at Myrtleville. The farm operation changed tremendously after the war. Robert bought two farms north of Myrtleville, and eventually rented the Carlyle place to the west, giving him almost as much acreage as his great-grandfather before the bankruptcy. Thanks to modern technology, he was able to farm it with no more help than his grandfather had needed for a quarter as much land. His father was pleased with his success, and Robert was certainly in the long family tradition of up-to-date farming, but the Myrtleville operation was now one which conflicted very obviously with Mr. Good's ideal of a society in which the majority of citizens were farmers. The houses on three of the four farms which Robert Good worked were lived in by people employed in Brantford, and this situation was typical of the whole area. The children of rural and urban workers alike went to large new schools, often by bus; one-room country schools were torn down or converted to other uses. It was well that Will Good did not believe in looking backward to plan the future. He once wrote his daughter, commenting on those who tried to turn the clock back to the simple life: "Nostalgic turning toward the past is natural enough, but essentially shortsighted."

Myrtleville in the 1960s was modern also in being a specialist's farm. The orchards Will Good had planted were abandoned, except for a few trees left for ornamental purposes. The last horse departed; there were now no animals on the farm except a few pets and a great number of dairy cattle. It was a very different kind of farming; it was a sort of mass production, big business; perhaps it even reconciled Mr. Good to the loss of three of his sons to the academic world he had rejected. Certainly he was proud of their success, as he was of his farmer son's.

Increasingly crippled with arthritis, he finally went to a small nursing home in Paris, where he spent his last four years. At first he responded well to the stimulus of companionship after his lonely days at Myrtleville, and he continued to read with great interest. In the summertime, he was taken to Myrtleville frequently, as long as he could be moved into a car. He had not been a patient man, and his children were surprised and touched by the good nature with which he bore his helplessness. Sometimes he would say, "I'll just have to make the best of a bad job."

In the last two years of his life he suffered a series of strokes. He made remarkable recoveries from several of them, but he grew thin again, and developed an almost uncanny resemblance to the picture of his grandfather, Allen Good, which hangs in the main hall of Myrtleville House. Gradually, his eyesight deteriorated, and he lost much of his ability to use words. Still, he seldom complained, and his beautiful smile was always ready. We knew his condition distressed him, because his mind often seemed to be working clearly behind his halting speech, and it was painful for us to watch the decline of a man of such physical and intellectual vigor. Finally, on November 16, 1967, he slept away. He was almost ninety-two.

The *Brantford Expositor* said of him in an editorial: "This many-sided man of science, agriculture, teaching, politics and authorship packed into [the] . . . years from 1914 to 1925 much more than most men do in a lifetime, and even when out of the spotlight he continued his endeavors, among them 25 years as president of the Cooperative Union of Canada. . . . If one can single out his most important and enduring work it might be his founding, with four farmer neighbors, of the United Farmers' Cooperative, now the United Cooperatives of Ontario, though also placing high was his liberal-spirited championship of the farmer-citizen resisting economic exploitation. One of a rare breed of men is no longer with us."

The farmers of Canada paid tribute to the memory of W. C. Good. In November of 1968 a portrait of him (painted by his artist son, Allen) was unveiled at the Canadian Agricultural

Will Good (1876–1967). Portrait painted by his son Allen about 1948

Hall of Fame in Toronto. The citation reads in part: "Few men in Canada did more to promote the welfare of farmers than W. C. Good. In 1909 he played a prominent role in drafting the constitution of the Canadian Council of Agriculture. Four years later he served as President of the Dominion Grange and Farmers' Association. He was one of the founders and the first president of the United Farmers' Co-operative Limited. . . . He was a prolific writer . . . and an outstanding farmer."

Before I attended the unveiling, I had been poring over the old letters on which this book is based, and searching my own memory. I thought of those strong old people of the family who lived at Myrtleville through the years and the world they lived in—and made. Surely they could say with Saint Paul, whose words they knew so well, "I have fought a good fight; I have finished my course; I have kept the faith." In spite of very different temperaments and widely changing circumstances, the people of Myrtleville were a race of believers and doers; they were people worth knowing.

Postscript, 1974

The history of Myrtleville as a farm is almost over. Brantford's city limits go through the field in front of the houses and urban buildings will soon be little more than a stone's throw away. Robert Good still lives in the house his father built; but, harassed by poor health and labor problems, he has retired from farming, and his sons are much too young to take over his work. So for the first time since the land was cleared more than one hundred and thirty years ago, none of Myrtleville is farmed by a Good. Moreover, the land is rented to an "agribusiness" which brings in its big machines at intervals, and the barns, built and rebuilt by four generations, are torn down. Standing deserted they would be an invitation to arson and vandalism. Now weathered boards have been carted away and the Highway Department will probably use foundation stones in road building. Only the concrete silos will remain, Tom Good's little hexagonal one and the two great cylinders erected by his grandson.

There is hope, however, that the two houses and a few acres around them will escape the inevitable "developer." Old Myrtleville House may eventually be some kind of historical museum; it has been lovingly and laboriously repaired and redecorated since 1966 and is full of antiques—Eliza Good's big fourposter bed, her Collard and Collard piano from England, the mahogany couch she and Allen bought in Montreal in 1837, the dollhouse they gave to little Anne. There are many interesting old books on the library shelves, and ancient pictures and embroideries upon the walls. Will Good used to say that Myrtleville would not be subdivided during his lifetime; his children are determined that Myrtleville House shall not be torn down during theirs, and their desire is to have it maintained as a place where mobile, rootless people of the twenty-first century may see how their ancestors lived when British North America was young.

Index